PERVASIVE PUNISHMENT

PERVASIVE PUNISHMENT

Making Sense of Mass Supervision

BY

FERGUS McNEILL
University of Glasgow, UK

United Kingdom — North America — Japan
India — Malaysia — China

Emerald Publishing Limited
Howard House, Wagon Lane, Bingley BD16 1WA, UK

First edition 2019

Cover image: Gabi Fröden
Cover Layout and Typography: Mike Hill

Reprints and permissions service
Contact: permissions@emeraldinsight.com

British Library Cataloguing in Publication Data
A catalogue record for this book is available from the British Library

ISBN: 978-1-78756-466-4 (Print)
ISBN: 978-1-78756-465-7 (Online)
ISBN: 978-1-78756-467-1 (Epub)

ISOQAR certified
Management System,
awarded to Emerald
for adherence to
Environmental
standard
ISO 14001:2004.

Certificate Number 1985
ISO 14001

INVESTOR IN PEOPLE

For Gordon and all the Paulines.

CONTENTS

List of Figures   ix

List of Tables   xi

About the Author   xiii

Acknowledgements   xv

1. Punishment Pervades   1

2. Punishment Changes   17

3. Counting Mass Supervision   41

4. Legitimating Mass Supervision   75

5. Experiencing Mass Supervision   105

6. Seeing Mass Supervision   135

7. Supervision: Unleashed or Restrained?   157

Postscript: Making Stories and Songs from Supervision
(by Jo Collinson Scott and Fergus McNeill)   179

Appendix: The Invisible Collar (A Story About Supervision)   195

Bibliography   211

Index   239

LIST OF FIGURES

Figure 1.   Untitled 1.   1

Figure 2.   Untitled 2.   5

Figure 3.   Dimensions of Mass Supervision.   11

Figure 4.   Untitled 3.   17

Figure 5.   Untitled 4.   41

Figure 6.   Total Prison and Probation Population Rates per 100,000
             in 2010.   47

Figure 7.   Probation and Prison Relative to Index Crime,
             1980–2010.   50

Figure 8.   Control Regimes Typology.   53

Figure 9.   Prison (sentenced), Probation and Parole Populations in the
             USA, by Ethnicity, 2015.   56

Figure 10.   Numbers of Community Payback Orders Commenced and
             of People Commencing CPOs per 10,000 in Scottish Local
             Authorities, 2015–2016.   62

Figure 11.   The Scottish Prison Population between 1980 and
             2013–2014.   65

Figure 12.   Community Sentences in Scotland since 1980.   66

Figure 13.   Number of Community Sentences, Average Daily Prison
             Population and Recorded Crime per 100,000 Population in
             Scotland, 1980–2016.   67

Figure 14.   Untitled 5.   75

Figure 15.   The Four Rs.   98

Figure 16.   Untitled 6.   105

Figure 17.   Untitled 7.   119

Figure 18.   The Long Walk by 'Messiah 10'.   120

Figure 19. Untitled 8 121

Figure 20. Untitled 9 125

Figure 21. Untitled 10 135

LIST OF TABLES

Table 1. Ethnicity, Age and Gender of Subjects of Community Payback
          Orders, by Percentage.   63

Table 2. Number of People Subject to Post-release Supervision (Statutory
          Throughcare) in Scotland, 2005–2016, by Type. 69

Table 3. Requirements of Community Payback Orders commenced in
          2015–2016..   83

ABOUT THE AUTHOR

Fergus McNeill is Professor of Criminology and Social Work at the University of Glasgow where he works in the Scottish Centre for Crime and Justice Research and in Sociology. Prior to becoming an academic in 1998, he worked for 10 years in residential drug rehabilitation and as a criminal justice social worker.

His many research projects and publications have examined institutions, cultures and practices of punishment and rehabilitation – particularly in the community – and questions about their reform. Between 2012 and 2016, he chaired an EU-funded research network on 'Offender Supervision in Europe' which involved about 70 researchers from across 23 jurisdictions. This book reflects upon and consolidates learning from that network.

Fergus has co-written or co-edited several previous books including *Offender Supervision: New Directions in Theory, Research and Practice, Offender Supervision in Europe, Reducing Reoffending: Social Work and Community Justice in Scotland, Understanding Penal Practice* and *Youth Offending and Youth Justice*. His most recent books include *Community Punishment: European Perspectives* (co-edited with Gwen Robinson); *Probation: 12 essential questions* (co-edited with Ioan Durnescu and Rene Butter); *Beyond the Risk Paradigm in Criminal Justice* (co-edited with Chris Trotter and Gill McIvor); and *Reimagining Rehabilitation: Beyond the Individual* (co-written with Lol Burke and Steve Collett and published by Routledge in 2018). *Pervasive Punishment* is his first sole-authored monograph.

Currently, Fergus is leading 'Distant Voices: Coming Home', a major 3-year Economic and Social Research Council/Arts and Humanities

Research Council project using creative practices to explore crime, punishment and reintegration. The project is a partnership between Vox Liminis (a third sector organization that Fergus helped establish), the University of Edinburgh, the University of Glasgow and the University of the West of Scotland.

ACKNOWLEDGEMENTS

This book has been a long time in the making, and I owe too many debts to acknowledge them all here … but I'm going to name a few.

Pervasive Punishment might never have been written but for the generosity of the British Academy in awarding me a Mid-Career Fellowship (Award No. MD160022). I'm especially grateful to David Garland for his support for my application. During session 2017–2018, the British Academy award paid for the wonderful Caitlin Gormley to cover much of my teaching (so well that I fear that colleagues and students won't want me back!).

The Fellowship also allowed me to travel to meet with some remarkable and generous scholars and friends so that I could road-test some of the ideas in this book. I had the great pleasure of visiting Reuben Miller (University of Chicago), Josh Page and Michelle Phelps (University of Minnesota), Jon Jacobs (John Jay College, City University of New York), Kristel Beyens (Free University of Brussels) and Miranda Boone (University of Leiden). I am also very grateful to colleagues and students who took time to attend seminars, offered insightful comments and showed me wonderful hospitality. As well as my 'official' hosts, particular thanks are due to Jess Bird, Jay Borchert, David Green, Lila Kazemian and Jennifer Peirce.

British Academy Mid-Career Fellowships also provide some funds for public engagement. I used these resources to establish the Pervasive Punishment blog (www.pervasivepunishment.com) and to support book-related events organized by the Howard League Scotland in Edinburgh and the Howard League for Penal Reform in Oxford. I'm very grateful to both organisations for these opportunities to share the work in progress. These events also included performances of songs related to punishment, reintegration and supervision written in workshops organized and run by Vox Liminis, a Scottish charity that brings creative practice to criminal justice and its reform (www.voxliminis.co.uk). Louis Abbott (in Edinburgh) and Donna Maciocia (in Oxford) provided these beautiful performances. It is a pleasure and a privilege to work with Louis and Donna and everyone else associated with Vox. I owe you all – and especially Alison Urie (that other Wayward Puritan) – a very great deal for teaching me so much about so many things; not least the importance and potency of creativity.

On the subject of creativity, I also want to thank Martin Cathcart Froden and Phil Thomas for some early advice in relation to the short story that is woven through this book's chapters, to Gabi Fröden for the cover art, and to Jo Collinson Scott for agreeing to write an EP of songs inspired by the story and the book. We say more about this process and about the relationships between the research, the story and the songs in the book's post-script. The cover art and EP were also funded by the British Academy Fellowship. It is a genuine delight to have been able to assemble all these different ways of seeing, hearing and sensing supervision with help from so many talented friends.

All but one of the photographs that illustrate this book were taken by supervisees and supervisors in the 'Supervisible' and 'Picturing Probation' projects (discussed in chapter 5). These projects were part of the COST Action IS1106 on Offender Supervision in Europe which I chaired between 2012 and 2016. Wendy Fitzgibbon inspired and led the Supervisible project, and Picturing Probation was led by Nicola Carr, Gwen Robinson and Anne Worrall. I am grateful for their permission to use some of these projects' photographs in the book, but my debt extends to all 70-odd active members of the Action. This book is, in large part, an attempt to consolidate what I learned from and with all of them. I want to pay special tribute to the Action's core leadership group – Miranda Boone, Niamh Maguire, Martine Herzog-Evans, Christine Morgenstern, Elena Larrauri, Ioan Durnescu, Christian Grafl, Gwen Robinson, Kerstin Svensson, Martin Lulei, Ineke Pruin and Sandra Scicluna and to pay special tribute to Kristel Beyens who, as Vice-Chair, offered me invaluable and unfailing support for those four years.

In places in this book, I have leant on and re-developed or re-purposed previous publications, some involving co-authors. Working with these scholars has been crucial to my development and, in some cases, I have to admit that I don't really know where their ideas end and my ideas begin. In particular, I've been co-writing with Gwen Robinson since we agonized over 23 drafts of our first co-authored conference paper in 2002–2003. Chapter 2 of this book draws on a more recent book chapter that we co-wrote (McNeill & Robinson, 2016); the section on Foucault leans very heavily on Gwen's contribution to that chapter. Chapter 4 redevelops elements of two earlier collaborations (Robinson & McNeill, 2015; Robinson, McNeill, & Maruna, 2013). It is typically generous of Gwen to let me use our previous work in this way, and I am also grateful to the editors at Palgrave, Sage and Routledge for giving their permission for me to use these earlier works here. Chapters 5 and 6 draw on my recent paper in *Punishment and Society* (McNeill, 2018); I am grateful to Kelly Hannah-Moffat and Sage for permission to do so. Thanks are also due to Wendy Fitzgibbon and Christine Graebsch for their permission to recycle the title of our co-authored chapter about the Supervisible project (Fitzgibbon, Graebsch, & McNeill, 2017) as the title of this book. Jo Collinson Scott and Oliver Escobar kindly allowed me to lean on their musicological (Jo) and political science (Oliver) expertise in writing Chapter 6, drawing on their contributions to our ongoing ESRC/AHRC funded Distant Voices project (www.distantvoices.org.uk).

While I have benefitted enormously from an extensive network of colleagues and friends, not just in the COST Action, but also in the American, British and European Societies of Criminology, I also owe a huge debt to all of my colleagues here at home – in the Scottish Centre for Crime and Justice Research. Since 2006, SCCJR has provided me not just with a great place to work among talented, critical scholars and students, but also with time and space and support. In particular, I want to thank the Centre's founding Directors – Michele Burman, Gill McIvor and Richard Sparks – and the current Director, Sarah Armstrong. Michele has been a hugely supportive, encouraging and effective supporter not just of me but much more importantly of the development of Scottish criminology. More than anyone else, I think, she has laid the foundations for and built the infrastructure to support a whole new generation of scholars who are doing remarkable and important work. My thinking has been continually challenged and enormously enriched by working with the constellation of stellar doctoral researchers clustered around the Scottish Centre for Crime and Justice Research. For example, I owe a debt to Maureen McBride for advice in relation to the brief discussion of sectarianism of sectarianism in Chapter 3, and to Javier Velasquez Valenzuela for comments on Chapters 5 and 7.

Several other people have also provided invaluable comments on drafts of parts of this book. Peter Conlong and Alan Fleming provided very useful feedback on my use of Scottish Government data in Chapter 3. Jo Collinson Scott sharpened up Chapters 5 and 6, and David Hayes did likewise for Chapters 6 and 7. However, I am most especially indebted to the two wise friends who, over the course of the last year, have provided me with critical but encouraging feedback chapter by chapter: Michelle Phelps and Gwen Robinson. Whatever its limitations, this book is much the better for your advice.

Looking much further back, my career began not in academia but with a decade in practice; first in drug rehabilitation and then in criminal justice social work. That experience still informs what I do even though I realise that it has lost its currency. Being a practitioner in both settings left me with respect and admiration for 'those who do'; especially those who persevere in pursuing justice and providing help despite the obstacles oftentimes placed in their way by society, by government, and by policies and systems. That's why this book is dedicated to Gordon McKean (a good friend and former colleague) and to 'all the Paulines' (if you read the short story, that dedication will start to make sense).

Finishing a book is often the hardest part. I want to thank Heather Irving lending me her lovely house in the beautiful Fife town of Anstruther in early June 2018 for the few days that I needed to piece together the fragments. Here's to the next Tall Ship Session.

Special thanks to my editor Jules Willan and to everyone at Emerald for supporting this project, for being interested in mass supervision and for accommodating my eccentricities. It's great to be part of something new and exciting. I hope this is the first book of many that Emerald will publish on this topic.

Finally, thank you Morag, Caitie and Calum. You keep my feet on the ground but let my head stay in the clouds – at least some of the time.

CHAPTER 1

PUNISHMENT PERVADES

THE WAITING ROOM

Joe sat on the bench in the waiting room. Looking down, he noticed that the bench was screwed to the floor. Not even the furniture here was free. Perspex screens and locked doors separated him and the others waiting

Figure 1. Untitled 1.

from those for whom they waited; the veils between the untrustworthy and those to whom they were entrusted. Joe absent-mindedly read the graffiti carved into the bench; testimonies of resistance that made the place feel even more desperate.

Joe scanned the postered walls, shouting their messages in pastel shades and bold print. Problems with drugs? Problems with alcohol? Problems with anger? Stay calm. Apparently, help was at hand – or at the end of a phone-line. But meanwhile remember that abusive language and aggressive behaviour will not be tolerated. Not in this room that itself felt like an installation of abuse and aggression. To Joe, it said 'You are pathetic, desperate or dangerous. You are not to be trusted. You must wait'.

He fidgeted and returned his eyes to the floor, downcast by the weight of the room's assault, avoiding contact, avoiding hassle, staying as unknown as possible in this shame pit. Better to be out of place here than to belong. This was no place to make connections.

Joe wondered what she would be like – Pauline – the unknown woman who now held the keys to his freedom. Her word had become his law: This was an 'order' after all. He was to be the rule-keeper, she the ruler – cruel, capricious or kind. She might hold the leash lightly or she might drag him to heel. Instinctively, he lifted his hand to his neck, but no one can loosen an invisible collar. At least it was not a noose. Joe swallowed uncomfortably, noticing the dryness of his mouth and the churning in his gut. He was not condemned to hang. He was condemned to be left hanging.

Joe wondered what Pauline would be like.

PERVASIVE PUNISHMENT?

Pervading, adj.: *That pervades; that passes or spreads through.*

Pervasive, adj.: *Having the quality or power of pervading; penetrative, permeative, ubiquitous. (Oxford English Dictionary)*

The opening episode printed *in italics* at the beginning of this chapter – like similar passages at the start of each chapter in this book – forms part of a short story. That story is a work of creative, imaginative writing but it is a fiction that, like the italic font in which it is presented, leans on research and practical experience of criminal justice supervision, both others' and my own – the same research and experience that forms the basis for the more conventional academic analyses that constitute each chapter of this book.

The purpose of the short story is to imaginatively bring to life the themes and content of this book. Ideally, I want you, the reader, to become curious about Joe and to care about what is happening to him and to the other characters we will meet in other episodes. I hope that by helping us to imagine how it feels to be supervised, and to be the supervisor, this fiction will help us to become curious and to care about the entirely real but largely hidden and neglected forms of suffering and support that this book aims to expose and explore. These are forms of suffering and support that affect millions of people around the world every day and that are imposed, at least in theory, on 'our' behalf, for the collective good. It follows that we all have a duty to imagine, examine and enquire about them carefully, and to consider whether we are content with these forms of pervasive punishment.

That title – *Pervasive Punishment* – perhaps already hints at the difficulty in delimiting such a project. This book concerns a diverse set of institutions and practices about which it is impossible to agree a common or settled language; institutions and practices that have evolved differently in different places. At least some of these definitional complexities will be unravelled later (mainly in Chapter 4). For now, the Anglophone terms 'probation' and 'parole' serve as useful starting points; suffice is to say that our focus here is on sanctions or measures imposed by criminal courts that involve some form of supervision in the community, whether instead of a custodial sentence (as in certain forms of suspended or conditional sentences), as a community-based sentence in its own right (like probation, in some jurisdictions), or as part of a sentence that begins with imprisonment but extends beyond it (as in parole). When US-based scholars write and talk about populations under 'correctional supervision', they sometimes mean *both* people in prison or jail *and* people on probation or parole. Here, I will use the term 'supervision' in the more limited European way, to refer *only* to those under some form of penal supervision in the community.

The title *Pervasive Punishment* is borrowed from a book chapter that I co-authored with Wendy Fitzgibbon and Christine Graebsch. That chapter explored how people chose to represent their experiences of supervision in and through photographs, as part of a project called 'Supervisible',[1] which will be discussed in more detail in Chapter 5 (Fitzgibbon, Graebsch, & McNeill, 2017). I will use images from that project and from its sister project 'Picturing Probation' (see Worrall, Carr, & Robinson, 2017) throughout the book to illustrate the short story; for example, the picture in **Figure 1** is taken from the Picturing Probation project.[2]

Fitzgibbon et al. (2017) concluded their chapter by arguing that:

> [...] *much of the Anglophone literature on probation practice (and on experiences of supervision) focuses on probation (or supervisory) meetings. The implicit assumption in these studies is that it is in these human encounters that supervision 'happens'. Our findings suggest that the experience of supervision is a much more diffuse and pervasive one; for our supervisees at least, it seems to extend in time and in impact across the life of the supervisee.*
>
> *Equally importantly, this pervasive impact of supervision is experienced as being painful. Looking across the common themes above, we might argue that this pain consists largely in the combination of being (continually) judged and constrained over time, and in the presence of a suspended threat. (Fitzgibbon et al., 2017, p. 318)*

In other words, we argued that the effects of supervision are often diffuse – they pervade the lives of supervisees – and that, even when experienced as helpful, they hurt. By way of illustration, one Scottish participant in the Supervisible project engaged the help of a friend in taking the picture shown in **Figure 2**. In it, cast as shadows, they dangle from a climbing frame in a children's play-park. Another Scottish participant, interpreting this picture, told me that it reminded him of a spider's web. He saw the two shadows as supervisor and supervised, one elevated and one degraded, both trapped in the justice system: 'the more you struggle, the more tightly it binds you'. However, unlike imprisonment (and here the spider's web metaphor breaks down), supervision seeks to bind not by confining the supervisee to a place, but rather by moving with him or her.

Figure 2. Untitled 2.

It is, in this sense, an ambulant or mobile punishment (Morgenstern, 2015).

The term 'pervasive' in the book's title also alludes to another sort of penal mobility. It is not just that supervision permeates the lives of individual supervisees; it has also spread through society itself – and even across societies. Indeed, as we will see in Chapter 3, in some places and for some segments of the population, supervision is becoming commonplace, if not quite ubiquitous.

As many readers will immediately recognise, this is far from being a novel observation. Several decades ago, Andrew Scull (1977, 1983), Thomas Mathieson (1983) Stanley Cohen (1983,1985) and others warned of the 'dispersal of discipline' beyond the prison. Cohen's (1985) highly influential book *Visions of Social Control* warned that a policy rhetoric of diversion and decarceration was cloaking the emergence of more expansive and penetrating forms of 'deviance control'. He argued that these new forms were serving to widen the penal net at the same time as thinning its mesh, dredging more people into rather than fishing more people out of the penal system. For both Cohen and Scull, the growth of 'community corrections' (meaning probation and parole systems and other forms of 'intermediate punishments') was an important part of this alarming picture.

Gwen Robinson (2016) has recently reminded us that these sorts of analyses had crystallised by the late 1980s to such an extent that Lowman, Menzies and Palys (1987) produced an edited collection on *Transcarceration*. Rather than accepting the logic of probation, parole and other measures as *alternatives* to imprisonment, the concept of transcarceration stressed the connections and conjunctions between different sorts of penal institutions and measures, suggesting a symbiotic rather than a substitutionary relationship between imprisonment and its supposed community-based 'alternatives'. As Robinson observes, the editors of the collection also stressed that transcarceration involves:

> *the marriage of exclusive and inclusive modes of social control, as evident in the emergence in some jurisdictions of home confinement schemes (Blomberg, 1987) and the expansion of parole and other mandatory forms of post-custodial supervision (Ratner, 1987). (Robinson, 2016, p. 100)*

However, Robinson (2016) goes on to argue that, during the 1990s and 2000s, rather than continuing to develop, test and refine these sorts of analyses, scholars became preoccupied instead with the advent of mass incarceration (Garland, 2001). In consequence, she suggests that what little sociological interest there has been in supervision has tended to focus on those forms of supervision that are most closely related to imprisonment, that is, parole and electronic monitoring. Other community-based sanctions and measures (like probation or community service) have been even more neglected. This leads Robinson to characterise community sanctions and measures as the 'Cinderella' of 'Punishment and Society' studies, leaving it as:

> *[…] a neglected and under-theorised zone – despite the fact that, as we have seen, several scholars in the 1980s foresaw the expansion and diversification of forms of non-carceral control in many Western jurisdictions, and the empirical reality that offenders subject to some sort of supervisory sanction in the community have, in many jurisdictions, come to substantially outnumber those subject to custodial confinement. (Robinson, 2016, p. 101)*

In writing *Pervasive Punishment*, one of my main hopes is to help Cinderella come to the 'Punishment and Society' Ball.

PERVASIVE *PUNISHMENT*

Robinson (2016) offers three reasons for the neglect of supervision since the 1980s: problems of definition, language and labelling; the relative (in)visibility of the field; and the debatable *penal* character of community sanctions – that is, 'the question of whether such sanctions are in fact instances of punishment at all' (p. 105).

In a formal or legal sense, this is a fair question – and one that, as we will see in Chapter 4, has different answers in different times and places. I have argued before (McNeill, 2013) that probation and parole emerged in many jurisdictions, particularly in Anglophone countries, as something to be done *instead* of punishment or, primarily in countries with Roman law traditions, as a form of *suspended* punishment or as something that follows on *after* punishment to mitigate its adverse consequences by promoting reintegration (Herzog-Evans, 2015; Morgenstern, 2015).

This peculiar status of supervisory sanctions and measures – as something defined by what they are not – may have suited penal reformers trying to divert people from the demoralising dangers of imprisonment and into nascent forms of social welfare (Garland, 1985). However, its current-day legacy is a profound problem of legitimacy for supervision. Rightly or wrongly, supervision has come to be seen, at least in some jurisdictions, as being a service rather than sanction, and one mainly concerned with the interests and needs of 'offenders'. The logic of diverting troubled people from punishment to help may have appealed to the sensibilities of some of our nineteenth- and twentieth-century forebears. However, as many have argued, in the last quarter of the twentieth century, 'welfarism' came to be displaced by 'populist punitiveness' (Bottoms, 1995). This shift in sensibilities conspired to produce a shrinking conceptual space for supervision as an *alternative* to punishment and demand its re-legitimation precisely as a *form of punishment* that also offers protection from certain risks and, crucially, does so at less cost than imprisonment (see Robinson, McNeill, & Maruna, 2013).

I will return to these legitimacy-related late-modern re-framings of supervision (and of punishment more generally) in Chapters 4 and 6. But there is a second problem posed by the origins of supervision as *diversion from* punishment (see McNeill, 2013; Sparks & McNeill, 2009); a problem that may partly explain the slower progress of human or civil rights discourses in relation to supervision rather than imprisonment. The difficulty rests in the historical roots of community sanctions in many jurisdictions as acts of clemency or mercy. Recipients of clemency or mercy are not diverted from or excused punishment because they *deserve* such treatment; rather, they are diverted because the state elects not to proceed with the measures of punishment to which it *is* nonetheless entitled. As philosophers of punishment have pointed out, part of the point of mercy is that it is undeserved (Murphy 1988; Smart 1969; Walker 1991). For that reason, mercy is not something to which someone can usually extend a rights-based claim.

Even though supervisory sanctions are now often located within a range of penalties with varying degrees of severity, and whether or not this 'tariff' is formalised in law, the public (and sometimes professional) perception remains that the ordering of such a sanction is an act of judicial or executive largesse rather than a determination of justice. When this perception is combined with the public suspicion that such largesse is tied to some aspect of the case that they deem to be of questionable relevance, public cynicism may be the result.

A recent example from England illustrates this point. It concerns the controversy around the sentencing of a 24-year-old woman named Lavinia Woodward, found guilty of 'unlawful wounding'. She had stabbed her then boyfriend in the leg while under the influence of drugs and alcohol. On 26 September 2017, the *Daily Telegraph* (a conservative newspaper, but not a tabloid) reported, on the sentence in the following terms:

> *An Oxford medical student 'too bright' to be given a prison*
> *sentence has been allowed to* walk free *from court – despite the*
> *judge acknowledging that she broke her bail conditions [...]*
> *Lavinia Woodward [...] was* spared jail *yesterday as she was*
> *commended for her 'strong and unwavering determination' to*
> *address her drug addiction [...] It comes four months after Judge*
> *Ian Pringle QC described Woodward, an aspiring heart surgeon,*
> *as an 'extraordinarily able young lady' whose talents meant that*
> *a prison sentence would be 'too severe' (emphases added).*

Despite the terms of the report, the Judge had in fact imposed a 10-month jail sentence, suspended for 18 months under a Suspended Sentence Order (SSO). The newspaper fails to report the conditions of the suspension; that is, what Woodward needs to do and not do for the next 18 months to avoid the implementation of a 10-month jail sentence.[3]

Setting aside important and reasonable questions about the fairness and appropriateness of this sentence – and the potential role of privilege in the process – for present purposes, the important point is this: in many of the press reports of this case, the sentence itself is misunderstood and misreported in such a way that its meaning and effects are misrepresented. Woodward was not 'spared jail' and she has certainly not 'walked free' from the court. She *was* spared immediate imprisonment, but for 18 months, a sword of Damocles hung above her head, and she was, at best, semi-free.

A wide range of other conditions can be added to an SSO (though I can find no media or legal reporting of the specific conditions in Woodward's case). Indeed, there are more than a dozen potential conditions in addition to the requirement that she must avoid further offending. Most commonly, a person might be required to submit to regular probation supervision, to undertake unpaid work, to complete an 'offending behaviour programme', or to submit to certain forms of addiction-related, medical or psychiatric treatment. Curfews, exclusion orders and restrictions on travel can also be imposed, with or without electronic monitoring ('tagging'). People subject to SSOs are therefore certainly not spared punishment; the law allows the court to use these conditions (and others, including fines) precisely to satisfy the demands of retribution and punishment. The further punishment of imprisonment continues to be held in reserve.

The misperception that subjects of supervision are recipients of mercy (and have been 'let off') is not a new problem; it has vexed reform-minded policy-makers and practitioners for decades (e.g. Morison Report, 1964; Casey Report, 2008). More broadly, public opinion research tends to show very little public understanding of the nature and requirements of contemporary supervision, although there is evidence of some support for the aims and methods of these forms of sanction when members of the public are given information about them (Allen & Hough, 2007; Maruna & King, 2008). This is an issue to which we will return in Chapter 6.

However, there is perhaps a still deeper problem occasioned by public misunderstanding of supervision and revealed by the Woodward case. Supervisory sanctions have failed to make significant inroads into almost all cultural representations of punishment (e.g. in film, theatre, television and books) and thereby into the public consciousness. Had she gone to prison, we might think we can imagine, whether accurately or not, some of what Woodward would have experienced. People know what prisons look like and, in broad terms, they may think they can imagine what it might be like to spend time inside one. Even if these imaginings are distortions of penal realities, they are at least within our grasp.

But most people would struggle even to begin to imagine what supervision *looks* and *feels* like. It has no obvious architecture and shape. There is no familiar setting and no predictable script to guide our imaginations. As I write, I find it easy to imagine Lavinia Woodward sitting in a prison cell, or working in the prison sheds or laundry, or sitting down to eat a meal in the dining hall, or taking exercise in the yard, or having a visit. It is very much harder to summon any visual imagination of what the SSO means for her and what it is doing to her right now. Is she waiting for an appointment impatiently and, if so, where and in what circumstances? Is she in a drug rehab undergoing some kind of therapy? Is she at home, desperate for a drink or something else to take the edge off the anxiety that the suspended sentence provokes? Or is she completely at ease, relaxed and confident that she can put her life back together, maybe even with the help of a sympathetic probation officer?

Not knowing the answers to these sorts of questions – not being able to visualise and imagine these situations and experiences – leaves us ill-placed even to formulate views about the justice or otherwise of her sentence. Because we cannot imagine what has happened to her, we assume that there is literally nothing to her punishment. That creates a legitimacy deficit. She stabbed a man. He bears a scar. But there is no mark and no measure of her 'punishment' so far as we can see in our imaginations. This is precisely why, in this book, I try to offer multiple forms of representation of supervision – through the creative writing in the short story woven in the text, through the use of photographs and songs (explained and elaborated in Chapter 5 and in the book's postscript) *and* through academic analysis.

MASS SUPERVISION

Our incapacity to engage in informed discussion of supervision matters profoundly, and the problem grows in proportion to the upscaling of supervision in many jurisdictions. The uneven and differently constituted surge in populations subject to some form of penal control in the community will be analysed in Chapter 3. Here, in briefly outlining the shape, structure and argument of this book, I draw out a preliminary map of some of the contours of what scholars have begun to call 'mass supervision' (McNeill, 2013; McNeill & Beyens, 2013; Robinson et al., 2013), 'mass probation' or 'mass penal control' (Phelps, 2013). Figure 3 (below) outlines some of the dimensions of mass supervision that need to be explored and charted.

Figure 3. Dimensions of Mass Supervision.

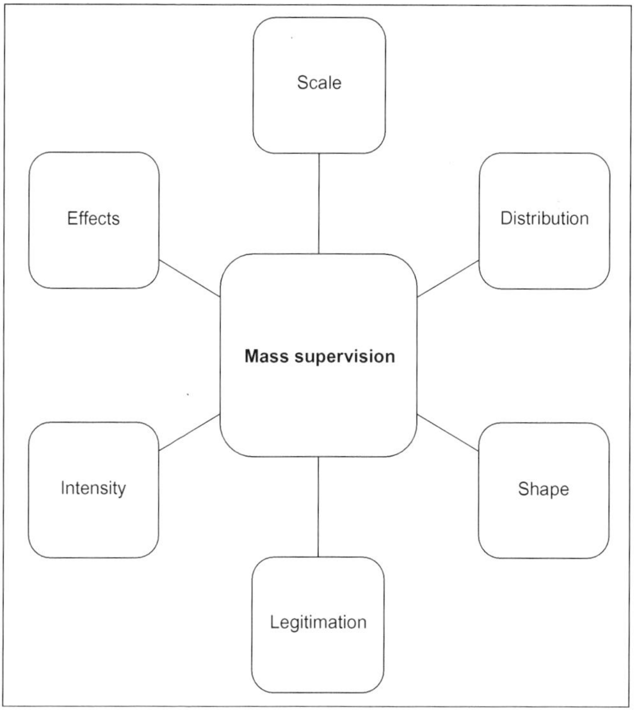

The 'mass' in these phrases is, of course, an allusion to the related and more familiar terms 'mass incarceration' and 'mass imprisonment': a penal phenomenon that, as I have already noted, has preoccupied scholars of punishment since the 1990s. More recently, mass incarceration, in the USA at least, has become a concern not just of a wider range of scholars but also of both social movements (Alexander, 2010) and policy-makers (Travis, Western, & Redburn, 2014).

Nonetheless, the meaning of 'mass' in these phrases has rarely been clearly articulated (though see Garland, 2001; Weisberg & Petersilia, 2010). Often, it is used simply to refer to the increasing number of people incarcerated, but to talk of the volume of supervision (and imprisonment) necessarily begs questions about the scale against which one is measuring and to which one is comparing. Is this a comparison of each jurisdiction's past and present, or a comparison between different places, or does it refer to the volume of supervision relative to the volume of imprisonment or financial penalties? Equally importantly, a more fine-grained analysis of scale requires an analysis of supervision's socio-spatial distribution. Where do we find it most concentrated in time and place and across social strata related, for example, to 'race', class and gender? Which social groups in which locations are most and least subject to supervision? These dynamics of volume, scale and distribution will be the focus of the analysis in Chapter 3.

The 'mass' in mass incarceration also invokes the notion of aggregation and the failure to differentiate, to distinguish, to recognise and to respond to difference. Here, the suggestion is that upscaling requires or is the corollary of a failure to individualise people subject to punishment. When the penal system processes 'masses', it processes them, at best, as 'types' and not as unique human subjects. To borrow Deleuze's (1990) term, the subjects of mass supervision are 'dividuals' rather than individuals, allocated to standardised responses on the basis of some kind of typification or classification, for example, through risk assessment.

In relation to mass incarceration, the most common visual representation of aggregation is the image of the 'warehouse prison', 'packing them in and stacking them high'. Although, as we will see, it does make sense to speak in some contexts of supervision as 'community warehousing' and to speak of 'probation overcrowding' (Solomon & Silverstri, 2008), in another sense, supervision itself is – or at least *can* be – highly variegated.

For example, we noted previously that, even within a single legal instrument like the Suspended Sentence Order in England, supervision can involve a very diverse range of conditions in an even more diverse array of combinations. This complexity will be discussed in Chapter 4, along with the policy discourses and associated organisational arrangements that seek to shape and legitimate supervision in a variety of different ways.

Of course, even if the official legal forms and penal functions of supervision have diversified, whether people *feel* that they are processed as mere dividuals or engaged with as individual human subjects is, of course, a different matter, to which we turn in Chapter 5. In that chapter, we will also explore another potential meaning of 'mass' related to weight. In Ben Crewe's (2009) important work on 'soft power' in an English prison, 'weight' refers to the psychological burdens of imprisonment, to how heavily it bears down upon prisoners. 'Depth' refers to the degree of physical security to which one is subject and to the distance from release and from the outside world that this implies, represents and constitutes. 'Tightness' is the dimension that Crewe adds to refer to the way in which soft power produces a kind of 'invisible harness on the self [which is] all-encompassing and invasive, in that it promotes the self-regulation of all aspects of conduct, addressing both the psyche and the body' (Crewe, 2011, p. 522).

Any analysis of mass supervision will similarly have to explore how, to what extent and with what consequences supervision burdens its subjects, distances them from liberty or autonomy and how it grips them. However, as I will argue in Chapter 5, we also need to explore whether, how and to what extent supervision degrades and misrecognises its subjects.

In the book's last two chapters, I move the discussion into somewhat different territory. Chapter 6 reviews the analysis of the preceding chapters. In sum, I argue that supervision has grown rapidly in scale and that it has spread within and across different societies and penal systems, that it has adapted to its changing environments, taking diverse forms which are differently legitimated and substantiated, but that, crucially, it imposes real suffering on the people who are subject to it, even if it can sometimes also be a helpful and supportive experience. For these reasons, I argue that we need to make supervision 'visible', bringing it out of the shadow of the prison so that we can study and debate it as an important social and penal phenomenon. We cannot develop a critical understanding of contemporary punishment without understanding 'mass supervision', and we cannot sensibly or wisely pursue penal reform (or abolition) without such an understanding. Chapter 6 then explores the challenges of making supervision more 'visible', exploring whether and how creative forms of 'public' and 'counter-visual' criminology might foster of a different and better political dialogue around crime, punishment and reintegration.

In closing, Chapter 7 offers us two visions of the future. The first, distinctly dystopian, ending imagines an unrestrained expansion of supervision that is more and more reliant on constraining or compelling compliance through technological control. Here, I engage with recent conceptual work exploring the relative penal severity and the 'pains and gains' of both electronic monitoring and 'human supervision'. I end the book by suggesting three principles by which we might avoid this future and restrain mass supervision, urging *parsimony* in its use, *proportionality* in its demands and *productiveness* in its design and delivery. I suggest that it is time to 'rehabilitate' supervision itself, partly through the application of these principles. Both the book and the story end by imagining such a future.

LOCATING THE ANALYSIS

In this short introduction, I have tried to outline the rationale for the book's title and subtitle and, more generally, to explain the scope and structure of the argument. Until now, however, I have avoided the question of where and when this analysis is to be located. The question of timing is easier to resolve than that of place. This is a book about contemporary punishment and about the ways in which, in recent decades, supervision has become more and more pervasive both in the lives of its subjects and in society. That said, understanding this present state of affairs necessarily entails some analysis of supervision's origins and development.

With respect to place, my answer is partly pragmatic. I focus mainly on those places I know best – the neighbouring but sometimes surprisingly different jurisdictions of England and Wales and Scotland. That said, I will also regularly look to the West – in particular to the work of Michelle Phelps and several others on contemporary probation, parole and community corrections in North America. I will also regularly look East, to the work of dozens of colleagues and friends with whom I collaborated in the recent COST Action (IS1106) on Offender Supervision in Europe. Between 2012 and 2016, that 23-country research network developed new approaches to studying and analysing the development of supervision in 23 European countries.[4] I want here at the outset to acknowledge my indebtedness to the many colleagues and friends who contributed to that network; they have contributed in countless ways to the thinking outlined in the chapters that follow.

This book does not aim to analyse supervision in Africa, Australasia or South America for two obvious reasons. Firstly, I know too little about these jurisdictions to do them any justice. Secondly, I suspect that the imposition upon them of Western, Eurocentric and/or Anglophone frameworks of analysis would be highly problematic and properly contentious.

The next chapter provides some of the resources that we will need to make sense of the emergence of pervasive punishment. To that end, it draws on the sociology of punishment to outline some of the key dimensions of penal change more generally. In my assessment, such an understanding is important not just for making sense of the past and understanding the present, but also for shaping the future.

NOTES

1. For more information on this project see: http://www.offendersupervision.eu/supervisible and http://howardleague.org/research/supervisibleproject/. Accessed on 4 October 2017.

2. The photographs used in this book come from the Supervisible or Picturing Probation projects, or were taken by me. The copyright in these images is held by their authors; their use here has been licensed by the copyright holders. The pictures should not be reproduced without permission.

3. A more thorough and scholarly discussion of this complex case can be found here: https://www.law.ox.ac.uk/centres-institutes/centre-criminology/blog/2017/09/were-discussing-lavinia-woodwards-sentence-wrong. Accessed on 4 October 2017.

4. See www.offendersupervision.eu. Accessed on October 4, 2017.

CHAPTER 2

PUNISHMENT CHANGES

SCREEN-WEARY EYES

Pauline put down the phone. The new guy, the 59th on her caseload, was 15 minutes early. A sign of eagerness maybe, but also an irritation. She

Figure 4. Untitled 3.

had too many other things to do and hadn't had time to prep yet. She took off her glasses, rubbed her screen-weary eyes and gulped another mouthful of her now-cold coffee (black, of course; no one in the office brought in milk anymore). Replacing her glasses in the twin dents on the bridge of her nose, she resumed her screen gaze, clicking the 'casefiles' icon and opening up no. 59 for the first time.

Joseph Earnshaw, aged 49 years, divorced and father of two. Two previous convictions for possession of cannabis and public affray ... but these dated from almost 30 years ago. The indiscretions of his youth perhaps? The standard format court report was light on detail and substance, but the account of his offence was interesting.

Having been made redundant two weeks before the incident, Earnshaw had returned to the offices of the accountancy firm where he had worked for 15 years. He was drunk and abusive, and proceeded to spray piss around the reception area before daubing the boss's office door with the one-word epithet: 'BLOODSUCKER'. The red paint had also found its way all over his former boss's designer suit in the scuffle that ensued.

The report said that Earnshaw scored 'low-risk' on the Offender Assessment Triage System (OATS). Pauline raised a single eyebrow; she was long enough in the tooth to be wary of that. She knew that these scores didn't save probation officers from shouldering the blame when things went wrong. Funny how the scoring system itself could never be at fault.

Joseph Earnshaw was either a bad case of an embarrassing and brief mid-life crisis or a man on the edge of a potentially violent meltdown who might lose Pauline her job. Maybe the court expected her to figure out which during the next 18 months.

Pauline sighed. When she had started out back in the 90s, she might have had the energy and enthusiasm – and the time – to suss him out and maybe even to help him get his head back together and his life on track. But caseloads back then were in the 20s or 30s not the 50s or 60s, and the bosses cared about and supported that sort of work. Now they cared only about targets.

She cast her eyes across to Norm's 'pod', wondering if her supervisor was even now watching her screen on his, or analysing the IT system's reports of the time she had spent in each of her casefiles in the last month. Glancing at her watch, she realised that she was probably already a

quarter way through the monthly time allowance for a 'low-risk' case.
She'd better go and see the guy before his time was up.

She just hoped he wasn't going to be a pain in the arse. She had enough
of those to deal with already, with Norm top of the list.

INTRODUCTION

Pauline's sigh expresses regret at the way that things have changed. She
began her probation career, like most others, wanting to work with people
in ways that could help them address their problems and benefit society at
the same time (Deering, 2011). Now, she feels increasingly frustrated by
the way that she has been compelled to become a 'pen-pusher' or, more to
the point, a 'screen-surfer', administering digital record-keeping about an
increasing number of cases; people that she has little time to get to know,
far less help, while she chases managerial targets. For her, the character,
potential and focus of supervision have changed. She is struggling in the
space between what her job has become and what she wanted and wants
it to be.

In and for the three legal jurisdictions of the United Kingdom (England
and Wales, Northern Ireland and Scotland), the role of the probation officer was defined in the Probation of Offenders Act 1907 (and for decades
thereafter) as being to 'advise, assist and befriend'. Yet by the start of the
twenty-first century, commentators were suggesting that the practice of
probation was being painted on a very different triptych: to 'control, confront and curfew' (Worrall & Hoy, 2005). In the USA, critics argued that
an even more harsh and cynical approach could be characterised by the
three-step injunction to 'tail 'em, nail 'em and jail 'em' (Skeem &
Manchak, 2010).

Although each of these phrases sums up something important about
the changing nature of supervision, they also risk grossly over-simplifying
both what supervision once was and what it has become. In reality, supervision has rarely (perhaps never) been in a settled or steady state. It has
always meant different things to different people. Its character has always
been contested. Supervision has typically been pursued and justified with
reference to multiple and sometimes competing purposes, even in one time
and place (as we will see in Chapter 4). Moreover, these discursive
struggles over how supervision should be understood, directed and

implemented are only contingently related to how it has been constructed *in practice* by people like Pauline, who play such a key role in determining how it is experienced by people like Joe (as we will see in Chapter 5). The purpose of this chapter is not to portray and analyse these complexities. Rather, the aim is to provide some of the conceptual resources for the analyses offered in the chapters that follow. Before we can start thinking about how, why and to what extent supervision has changed – and specifically about whether, how and why 'mass supervision' has emerged and what that might mean – we need to consider how penal change more generally has been understood. These wider questions have usually been answered via analyses of changing approaches to and levels of imprisonment rather than supervision (Robinson, 2016) and have often relied more on analysis of policy than practice (McNeill, Burns, Halliday, Hutton, & Tata, 2009). In this chapter, I explore the utility and limitations of these theories and models for building an analysis of the evolution of supervision.

I begin by briefly reviewing how the ideas of three particularly influential thinkers have been used to make sense of penal change in the 'modern' or 'industrial' period (broadly from eighteenth century onwards) and then explore how these ideas have informed explanations of rapid and unexpected penal changes since the 1970s, in the period sometimes referred to as 'late modernity'. I then go on to consider the limits of these kinds of explanations, reviewing contemporary debates about how to make sense of 'penal states', 'penal fields' and the contestation that seems to typify them.

Necessarily, this chapter is painted with a broad brush and on a large canvass. As such, it risks sacrificing depth and detail by trying to depict too much, perhaps leaving some readers dissatisfied and others overwhelmed. That said, its purpose is illustrative rather than encyclopaedic. The aim here is to draw attention to different ways of 'seeing' supervision's development and to different ways of seeing what lies *behind* supervision's continuing evolution.

MAKING SENSE OF PENAL CHANGE[1]

In this section, I focus on three key contributors to the sociology of punishment – Michel Foucault, Emile Durkheim and Karl Marx – reviewing how their ideas shed light on how and why punishment changes.

None of these thinkers wrote directly about penal supervision, and Marx himself had relatively little to say even about punishment, but other scholars have applied their ideas to varying degrees in making sense of the evolution of probation and parole. I have chosen to reverse the chronology of their three contributions, partly so that I can start our discussion with Foucault – the theorist whose work has undoubtedly been most influential amongst those seeking to explain and understand supervision as a social and a penal institution.

Foucault, Punishment and Probation

Foucault's notion of disciplinary power has been central to explaining the evolution both of punishment and of supervision (see Cohen, 1985; Garland, 1985; Simon, 1993). *Discipline*, in Foucault's work, is a rendering of the French *surveiller*, a verb which has no direct English translation but connotes surveillance, observation and supervision. It refers to a method of mastering or training the human body, not via the use of force or restraint but rather by exerting an influence on 'the soul', which, in turn, directs behaviour.

In Foucault's account, the prison constitutes the case study *par excellence* of discipline: it is conceived as epitomising the 'gentler forms of control', which came to replace the violent, repressive forms characteristic of the classical (or pre-modern, pre-industrial) age. At the core of disciplinary power are the principles of individualisation and constant visibility famously characterised by Bentham's eighteenth-century 'Panopticon' prison design. These twin aspects work in tandem to produce compliant subjects, who habitually behave in the required manner. Even in the realm of punishment, discipline is a mode of exercising control over individuals that is less punitive than it is corrective: its primary objective is 'normalisation' – that is, a re-adjustment of the individual towards the 'norm' of what Foucault terms 'docility-utility' (1977, p. 137). In the context of supervision and its practice, this is closely related to the imperative to secure 'compliance' both with supervision and with the law in general.

Foucault's analysis was centred on the development of *modern* industrialised societies from the eighteenth century onwards. As we will see in subsequent chapters, the way in which these disciplinary mechanisms have evolved or been supplanted in *late-modern* societies is, of course, a matter of much debate. Deleuze (1990), for example, has drawn attention to the shift from disciplinary societies to 'societies of control' in which:

> *the different control mechanisms are inseparable variations, forming a system of variable geometry the language of which is numerical [...] [Disciplinary] Enclosures are molds, distinct castings, but controls are a modulation, like a self-deforming cast that will continuously change from one moment to the other, or like a sieve whose mesh will transmute from point to point. (Deleuze, 1990, p.* 4, emphases in original)

Both Deleuze's (1990) invocation of these more flexible, fluid, shifting and interminable forms of control, and of how they operate on 'dividuals' (as units of a mass that is to be controlled, rather than as individualised subjects of discipline) seems consistent with some contemporary accounts of penal control and will be important in Chapter 5's analyses of how contemporary supervision is experienced.

Despite its historical focus, Foucault's *Discipline and Punish* (1977) and his wider social theory continue to have a profound impact on contemporary criminology and sociology. Importantly, *Discipline and Punish* provided a powerful illustration of the continuities between systems of regulation and control in the social and penal spheres. Foucault's analysis of 'the birth of the prison' aimed to address and expose not just changes in modern approaches to punishment, but also the spread of *disciplinary power* throughout the whole of society.

Both Garland's *Punishment and Welfare* (1985) and Jonathan Simon's *Poor Discipline* (1993) locate the formal, legal origins of (respectively) British probation and Californian parole in the context of the social, political and cultural shifts, which coalesced around the turn of the twentieth century to inaugurate a specifically *modern* penal system: one that brought the welfare and reform of the individual into the domain of state responsibility and, in that process, extended the reach of disciplinary power. Both also describe how the modernist quest for 'normalisation' was transformed in the early decades of the twentieth century as ideas about moral reformation gave way to a more 'scientific' discourse centred on diagnosis, treatment and 'rehabilitation'.

The collapse of confidence in rehabilitation in Britain and the USA in the 1970s necessarily ignited intense debate among scholars working within a primarily Foucauldian framework. The early 1980s saw some British scholars predicting the demise of disciplinary power, and with it traditional probation supervision, in favour of an expansion of 'non-disciplinary' disposals that did not aim to correct or transform their subjects, for example, the then relatively new sanction of community service (Bottoms, 1980; Pease, 1980). These analyses, however, went against the grain of other accounts, which were emphasising not the demise of discipline but its *extension* in the context of both formal and informal domains of social control.

As I noted in Chapter 1, the so-called dispersal of discipline thesis was the subject of three contributions to Garland and Young's (1983) classic collection *The Power to Punish* (Cohen, 1983; Mathiesen, 1983; Scull, 1983) and was further elaborated in Cohen's (1985) seminal book *Visions of Social Control*. In that crucial contribution, Cohen focused on the gap between, on the one hand, the rhetoric of decarceration and diversion and, on the other hand, the reality of the expanding 'deviance-control system', which he thought was emerging at that time. Cohen utilised a much-cited 'fishing net' analogy in which 'deviants are the fish' (p. 42) to describe the increasing extension, widening, dispersal and invisibility of the (non-carceral) social control apparatus as he observed it. It is from this source that penal scholars adopted the concepts of 'net-widening' and 'mesh-thinning' that have become staples in analyses of supervision – and penal trends more generally – over the last 30 years. Whereas the wider net catches more fish (or 'offenders'), the thinner mesh also catches smaller fish (or less serious 'offenders').

The naïve idea that the proliferation of 'alternatives' to prison should be seen as an inherently positive development was heavily criticised by Cohen, who was quick to point out that more and different forms of supervision (and other community-based measures) did not necessarily imply *less* (or less intensive) control, nor did they inevitably lead to a reduction in the use of imprisonment. This is a crucially important argument that I will develop in the next chapter.

The fate of disciplinary power in the wake of the collapse of the 'rehabilitative ideal' (Allen, 1981) was also the subject of the highly influential 'new penology' thesis, which has been much debated in the last two or three decades across a number of jurisdictions (Feeley & Simon, 1992, 1994; Simon, 1993). The new penology thesis essentially contends that late modern societies have moved on from the dominant disciplinary modes of control described by Foucault, in favour of managerial, risk-based strategies. For example, Jonathan Simon's (1993) research on the development of parole in California described a decisive shift, starting in the mid-1970s, from a 'clinical' model of practice (centred on the normalisation of ex-prisoners) to a 'managerial' model, characterised by significantly lowered expectations with parole functioning as a mechanism for securing the borders of communities by channelling their least stable members back to prison. The idea that penal (and indeed welfare) systems across a variety of jurisdictions have taken on a more 'managerial' character and become increasingly concerned with risk management is now part of criminological common sense, although whether this has been at the expense of more ambitious objectives of reform and rehabilitation continues to be the subject of debate (e.g. Garland, 2001; Hannah-Moffat, 1999; Phelps, 2017; Robinson, 2002, 2008; Robinson & McNeill, 2015).

Foucauldian concepts have also informed some recent studies of the rise and proliferation of surveillance technologies, including the electronic monitoring of offenders, which is an increasingly significant element of systems of supervision in the Western world (Nellis, Beyens, & Kaminski, 2012).

The rise of actuarialism, managerialisation and electronic monitoring all might be seen, in certain respects, as illustrative of a Deleuzian shift away from the use of corrective *disciplinary molds* that seek to shape us and towards *modulations of control* in and through which particular groups are sorted, processed, contained and constrained (cf. Rose, 2000). Such an interpretation might suggest that the mass of 'dividuals' subject to these forms of penal power are not passing through an institution that transforms them into docile subjects who comply normatively; rather, they are being held in a mobile, shape-shifting mesh that aims to constrain their ability to defy and disobey.

Durkheim, Punishment and Probation

Whereas Foucault's work drew attention to changes in the ways in which penal power was being deployed in modernity, highlighting shifting objectives, discourses and techniques, Durkheim's influential account of penal evolution placed its emphasis on the *cultural* contexts of penal change, or more accurately on the influence on punishment of the interplay between cultures, social solidarity and the nature of the state. Again, though writing decades before Foucault, at the turn of the twentieth century, Durkheim was seeking to make sense of *modern* societies.

Durkheim argued that social solidarity depends on the moral beliefs that unify social groups. Although solidarity's different forms reflect changes in its historical and national contexts, as well as the division of labour in any given society, punishment of crime is always a passionate collective reaction to violations of these unifying beliefs. Punishment's rituals are important as a means of allowing us to communicate, reaffirm and reinforce these values. As Garland (2013a, p. 25) puts it in his recent re-analysis of Durkheim, offending shocks 'healthy' (i.e. well-socialized) consciences into punishment as a reaction.

Two different sources of this shock – one founded in shared religious belief and one based upon respect for citizens as individuals – reflect the different forms of social solidarity that Durkheim distinguishes. *Mechanical solidarity* is characteristic of societies that are structured and dominated by the needs and interests of relatively small social groups whose unity of moral belief is religious in type. Law and sanctions here aim to repress rather than repair harms; their function is to express *and* to reinforce the *conscience collective* (Durkheim, 1984). In contrast, the division of labour in modern societies occasions the transition to more *organic* forms of social solidarity. Although repressive law and sanctions continue to exist, the development of increased social diversity and the necessity of complex inter-group cooperation require the moral code to be based on *moral individualism*. For this reason, forms of law and sanctions based on restitution (and repair) develop to regulate intra- and inter-group cooperation in ways, which rely less on repression and more on restoration to health of the social body (Durkheim, 1958, p. 48).

Garland (2013a, p. 36) insists on a reading of Durkheim that stresses that 'the social processes of punishment, insofar as they are social, *presuppose* solidarity as well as *reinforce* it'. In other words, punishment is *both* a project of building solidarity *and* a product of solidarity. But like any other social institution, the form of punishment in any society may be 'normal' or 'pathological'. For Durkheim, an institution is pathological if it does not correspond with or fit the prevailing conditions of social life. This kind of misfit often occurs because a social institution's form still reflects an earlier period characterised by different social conditions. Pathological institutions represent and cause both practical and moral problems. Indeed, Sirianni (1984) argues that the conception of organic solidarity in *The Division of Labour* is as much a normative as an empirical statement, with Durkheim often collapsing the two in his discussion. Putting this another way, organic solidarity is the *goal* of modern societies; it is a 'mission of justice' (Durkheim, 1984, p. 321) and not just a description of a modern social order. An out-moded, pathological penal system is therefore a failure to progress the mission of justice, hence the importance than Durkheim accords to analysing penal evolution.

Durkheim's famous essay *Two Laws of Penal Evolution* was first published in 1899–1900.[2] The first ('quantitative') law is that:

> *The intensity of punishment is the greater the more closely societies approximate to a less developed type – and the more the central power assumes an absolute character. (Durkheim, 1973, p. 285)*

The lack of complexity and the strength of the shared religious beliefs characteristic of mechanical solidarity beget severe punishments and repressive laws. However, Durkheim is careful to note a second influence – the absolute power of the sovereign – and, in this sense, he recognises the relationships between culture and political power.

Durkheim's second ('qualitative') law is stated thus:

> *Deprivations of liberty, and of liberty alone, varying in time according to the seriousness of the crime, tend to become more and more the normal means of social control. (Durkheim, 1973, p. 294)*

His explanation of this development in the *form or style* of punishment relies heavily on his account of the rise of moral individualism. To the extent that offending ceased to violate religious ideals and came to be seen as an offence of one citizen against another, forms of brutalising punishment were less likely to be invoked. Importantly, with the rise of individualism, collective sensibilities about punishment shifted. Moral individualism required that *both* the victim and offender be given appropriate consideration, undermining recourse to punishment for punishment's sake.

But this qualitative evolution in punishment and with it the rise of the prison are also accounted for in part by the prison's utility as a technological or architectural fix for a changing social problem:

> [...] at the very time when the establishment of a place of detention was becoming useful in consequence of the progressive disappearance of collective responsibility, buildings were arising which could be utilized for this purpose [...] In proportion as the penal law abandons the archaic forms of repression, new forms of punishment invade the free spaces which they then find before them. (Durkheim, 1973, p. 298)

Consequently, a new way had to be found of (literally) holding the *individual* to account. Durkheim recognises that this 'holding' originally developed as a place of pre-trial detention and thus as a prelude to punishment, rather than as a punishment *per se*. However, he argues that, in this case, the social function followed the new penal form; once the pains of imprisonment became apparent, its utility as a punishment became established. As imprisonment came progressively to be associated the deprivation of liberty its punitive character relied less and less on the particular conditions or peculiar hardships of confinement. It was not merely that the deprivation of liberty displaced the mortification of the body; it was also that the penal severity of imprisonment diminished over time.

However, Durkheim's diagnosis of punishment at the *fin de siècle* (at the end of the nineteenth century) was highly critical. He argued that, at the end of the nineteenth century, institutional forms of punishment appropriate to organic solidarity had failed to emerge, meaning that punishment was failing to fulfil its cultural functions in expressing and reinforcing shared beliefs. As we have already noted, for Durkheim this was not just an empirical sociological observation; it was a normative problem. The 'mission of justice' implied in organic solidarity was failing.

Given this historical context, it is tempting to read probation and parole – which emerged in many jurisdictions in the late nineteenth century – as precisely the new forms of punishment that Durkheim's 'mission of justice' required; both forms of supervision might be seen as restitutive; aiming at repair, return and restoration. We might therefore have expected scholars of supervision to look to Durkheim as providing ready-made resources for a *cultural* account of penal supervision's emergence and development. But no one has yet developed such an account. Seeking to begin to remedy this neglect, McNeill and Dawson (2014) have offered a sketch of how a Durkheimian account of probation in the UK might be developed and of how this might assist us in assessing probation's future prospects. They argue that a re-reading of Durkheim can serve to clarify how and why:

> *probation's future development – like punishment's – may depend less on evidence of its 'effectiveness' or 'quality' and more on shifting forms of social organization; on their expression in terms of changing moral sensibilities; and on the changing dynamics of political or governmental authority [...]*
>
> *The important practical question for those interested in probation is whether, how and under which social and political conditions probation might resist or moderate these forces. To begin to answer it, we need to examine much more closely, in a range of different contexts (historical and geographical), what it is that probation has communicated (or failed to communicate) about social solidarity, to whom and for whom, and under what forms of political authority? (McNeill & Dawson, 2014, p. 12)*

These are questions to which we will return in Chapter 4.

Marxism, Punishment and Probation

The development of critical perspectives on punishment and supervision owes much to the emergence in the 1970s of a series of revisionist histories of crime, punishment and social control. These works challenged the then prevailing narrative of gradual reform towards ever more effective penal solutions to the problems that crime presented, underpinned by the inexorable progress of positivist social science. Instead, historians like Ignatieff (1983) revealed the role played by penal power and its attendant technologies in the preservation of vested class interests. The challenge was that the penal system was rigged in favour of property owners and against the dispossessed.

This kind of Marxist critique – exposing the latent functions of punishment in defence of capital – was not merely historical. Sociologists of punishment inspired by Marx were also beginning to expose the role of penal systems in sustaining a capitalist system of economic production, based on the exploitation of wage labour (for a review of such scholarship, see Melossi, 1998). As De Giorgi suggests, such analyses:

> [...] contend that penal politics plays a very different role than defending society from crime: both the historical emergence of specific penal practices and their persistence in contemporary societies are structurally linked to the dominant relations of production and to the hegemonic forms of work organization. In a society divided into classes, criminal law cannot reflect any 'general interest.' (De Giorgi, 2013, p. 41)

The first serious attempt to apply Marxist ideas to understanding punishment was provided by Rusche and Kirchheimer (1939 [2003]) in *Punishment and Social Structure*. Although their arguments are more complex that the title of their book suggests, their analysis centres on the relationship between social and economic structures and penal systems and practices. The former exercise a determining influence on the latter. Thus, penal uses of slavery and servitude rely on and facilitate a slave economy; the development of fines requires a monetary economy; penal transportation both needs and feeds emerging colonial economies; and the emergence of the prison both requires and serves an industrial economy. More generally, fluctuations in 'demand' for punishment (and in support for certain forms of punishment) depend on the availability of material resources and on demand for labour.

However, as Cavadino, Dignan and Mair (2013) suggest, not all versions of Marxist analysis are equally economically deterministic in their accounts. For example, those influenced by the works of Antonio Gramsci place greater emphasis on the ideological domination through which certain regimes of power manufacture 'consent' to the existing social order; the idea of 'hegemony' and of 'hegemonic discourses' derive from Gramsci's work. That work leaves room for the exercise of human agency in resistance to domination. Such resistance might take the form of exposing and undermining hegemonic ideas, in this case about punishment and supervision.

Similarly, those influenced by Louis Althusser, whilst still advancing a structuralist and materialist perspective in which the economic arrangements in society are *ultimately* determining of its social order, nonetheless stress that the social 'superstructure' possesses 'relative autonomy'. In this context, the dominant ideology is reproduced both through the 'institutional state apparatus' (such as education and welfare systems governing the socialisation of children) and the 'repressive state apparatus' (including the policing and penal systems, as well as the military); the former is more covert in its coercion.

Perhaps one step further away from a materially deterministic form of Marxism, the historian E.P. Thompson (1924–1993) propounded a 'humanistic materialism'. This approach again recognises the determining force of economic arrangements and of the material distribution of resources, but left yet more room for agentic struggles against the social order – and specifically against the deployment of law and order by the ruling classes, even if the 'game' is rigged in their favour:

> *People are not as stupid as some structuralist philosophers*
> *suppose them to be, They will not be mystified by the first man*
> *who puts on a wig [...] If the law is evidently partial and unjust,*
> *then it will mask nothing, legitimize nothing, contribute nothing*
> *to any class's hegemony. (Thompson, 1977, pp. 262–263)*

Marxist perspectives have clearly influenced some important revisionist accounts of the histories of probation (and of social work more generally) although some of these emerging critiques were influenced by Foucault as well as Marx. Thus, for example, Donzelot's (1977) work on *The Policing of Families* charted the development of public intervention in the regulation of family affairs, illuminating the totalising power of the emergent social work profession. Similarly, Linda Mahood's (1981) *Policing Gender, Class and Family*, which includes significant discussion of the development of juvenile probation in the UK, challenged the traditional narrative of the evolution of a benign and caring welfare state by revealing how the 'child saving' movement served middle class interests rather than the interests of those whose lives it penetrated. Similarly, Garland's (1985) *Punishment and Welfare* took inspiration from both Marxist and Foucauldian perspectives (see Garland 1990, p. 132).

One or two similarly critical accounts have emerged of the history of probation in England and Wales. In particular, Maurice Vanstone, by building on the work of Bill McWilliams (1983, 1985, 1986, 1987) and focussing on practice-related discourses, significantly challenged and revised the traditional story of probation's origins as an essentially altruistic endeavour, characterised by humanitarian impulses linked to religious ideals. As Vanstone (2004) notes, Young's (1974) earlier account of the history of probation stressed the role of charity in maintaining the position of the middle classes by confirming that where 'unfortunates' failed to capitalise on the opportunities that charitable endeavours provided, they confirmed their own intractable individual degeneracy, deflecting attention from broader economic or political analyses of social problems. Amongst a broader range of philanthropic activities, probation emerges in this account as a class-based activity that justified the existing social order and defended it through its mechanisms of persuasion, supervision and control.

Young's (1974) account was arguably the first and only Marxist or Marxian reading of probation's development, but Walker and Beaumont's (1981) *Probation Work: Critical Theory and Socialist Practice* was more influential in offering a fairly downbeat Marxist assessment of the situation and prospects of probation in England and Wales at the start of 1980s, whilst also seeking to offer some sort of Marxist prescription for probation practice even under capitalism.

THE CHALLENGE OF LATE MODERN PENAL CHANGE

In seeking to differentiate and develop Foucauldian, Durkheimian and Marxist accounts of penal change and of supervision's development, it is all too easy to caricature the three perspectives. Hopefully, the brief summaries above avoid the risk of suggesting that Foucault explains punishment *only* in terms of relationships between power and knowledge, while Durkheim lays stress *only* on relationships between culture and morality, whereas Marxist perspectives stress *only* the ultimately determining influence of economic arrangements. All three thinkers explore all of these influences and the interactions between them. Of course, there are other social theorists who offer different explanatory resources. Perhaps most obviously Max Weber's ideas have much to offer an understanding of the professionalisation of supervision in the modern era, of the impact of managerialism in late modernity and of the ways in which supervision might (and might not) be legitimated (a question to which I will turn in Chapter 4).

Developing a convincing account of the development of punishment and supervision requires what Garland (2001) calls a 'conjunctural' approach. Indeed, his influential work '*The Culture of Control*' remains the best example of an attempt to combine structural, cultural and political analyses in an explanation of the rapid and (largely) unexpected penal transformations associated with late modernity. He summarises both his method and his conclusion thus:

> *I have tried to show how the field of crime control and criminal justice has been affected by changes in the social organization of the societies in which it functions, by the distinctive problems of social order characteristic of that form of social organization, and by the political, cultural and criminological adaptations that have emerged in response to these distinctive problems.*
> *(Garland, 2001, p. 193)*

Garland considers these contradictory (or in his term 'schizoid') responses to late modern crime problems; partly rational, managerial and utilitarian, representing some continuity from the 'modern' period, and partly expressive, emotive and symbolic, representing an apparent 'rupture' with or break from the modern. More specifically, his 12 indices of penal change – the late modern puzzle that *The Culture of Control* seeks to solve – include the following:

(1) The decline of the rehabilitative ideal.

(2) The re-emergence of punitive sanctions and expressive justice.

(3) A more emotional tone to crime policy.

(4) The rise of the victim in crime discourses.

(5) The emphasis on public protection.

(6) Politicisation and a new populism related to crime and punishment.

(7) The reinvention of the prison (and with it mass incarceration).

(8) A transformation in criminological thought.

(9) An expanded infrastructure of crime prevention and community safety.

(10) The development of the role of civil society in and the commercialisation of crime control.

(11) New approaches to management and practice in criminal justice.

(12) A perpetual sense of crisis.

Garland's 'conjunctural' explanation for these changes centres on the predicament of the late modern state — a 'crisis of sovereignty' linked to the state's impotence in the face not just of high crime rates but also of structural changes in the economy linked to globalisation. This impotence provokes the 'schizoid' reaction noted previously. On the one hand, the 'sovereign state strategy', characterised by 'hysterical denial', deploys a criminology 'of the alien other', different from 'us', to create a suitable enemy for the state to expressively and punitively attack (see also Pratt, Brown, Brown, Hallsworth, & Morrison, 2005). This stands in stark contrast to the 'criminology of the self', which underlies more pragmatic, 'adaptive strategies' typified in contemporary approaches to crime prevention and reduction.

Crucially, traditional rehabilitation (and penal welfarism in general) fits comfortably with neither of these criminologies nor with their related penal strategies. As Garland (1996) notes:

> the excluded middle ground here is precisely the once-dominant
> welfarist criminology which depicted the offender as
> disadvantaged or poorly socialized and made it a state
> responsibility [...] to take positive steps of a remedial
> kind. (pp. 461–462)

According to Garland, welfarist criminology came to be excluded partly because of its perceived failure, a perception which produced a profound loss of faith in the legitimacy of the traditional rehabilitative aims and purposes of probation — at least amongst policy-makers if not practitioners (cf. Vanstone, 2004; Zedner, 2002). This loss of faith resonated particularly powerfully in terms of public mentalities and sensibilities about crime and punishment. The eclipse of welfarism, Garland argues, owes much to declining support amongst the middle classes, now increasingly insecure as they navigate the risks and uncertainties of late modernity and increasingly distrustful of the expertise claimed by penal professionals (Garland, 2001). The resulting decline of collective social provision and the privatisation of risks mean that rehabilitation's traditional justification – as a means of reclaiming or helping disadvantaged people – has lost its cultural purchase (Bauman, 1997; McCulloch & McNeill, 2007). To the extent that rehabilitation endures at all, it survives only in a hollowed-out, managerialised form, not as an over-riding purpose but as a subordinate means. Garland (1997) argues that probation 'staff now emphasise that 'rehabilitation' is necessary for the protection of the public. It is future victims who are now 'rescued' by rehabilitative work, rather than the offenders themselves' (p6).

Loic Wacquant, in *Punishing the Poor* (2009), offers a somewhat different analysis. He argues that the punitive turn, in the United States at least, was a reaction not to rising *insecurity about crime* but rather to the *social insecurity* created by a broader reconstruction of the state. This reconstruction combines restrictive 'workfare' (meaning the restriction of welfare) and expansive 'prisonfare' (meaning the expansion of punishment) under a philosophy of moral behaviourism. Individual responsibility becomes a 'cultural trope' that blames poor people and 'people of colour' for their (structurally determined) fates and holds them to account both for their own problems and for their recovery. Wacquant argues that the fate of the 'precariat' (people stuck on the margins of society) is underwritten by economic and market deregulation but also that it produces:

> *a garish theater of civic morality on whose stage political elites*
> *can orchestrate the public vituperation of deviant figures – the*
> *teenage 'welfare mother', the ghetto 'street thug', and the*
> *roaming 'sex predator' – and close the legitimacy deficit they*
> *suffer when they discard the established government mission of*
> *social and economic protection. (from* Punishing the Poor'*s front*
> *matter)*

Wacquant argues (just as Garland [1985] did in *Punishment and Welfare*) that developments in welfare and criminal justice therefore must be combined into a single analytic framework that makes sense of both the instrumental and communicative aspects of penal and social policies. In this light, the prison is revealed not simply as a mechanism of delivering criminal justice but rather as a 'core political institution'. The emergence of what Wacquant terms 'the penal state' involves not a waning of the power of the state in a globalised world but rather the reverse: 'the building of an overgrown and intrusive penal state deeply injurious to the ideals of democratic citizenship'.

PENAL STATES AND PENAL FIELDS

Although these two accounts of late modern penal change differ in important ways, they also have much in common and, to some extent, may be susceptible to some similar criticisms. In contemporary 'Punishment and Society' scholarship, two main challenges have emerged. Firstly, some suggest that Garland's analysis over-states, over-generalises and sometimes under-evidences the changes he identifies within the USA and the UK. Others have suggested that globalisation and neoliberalism have occurred not just in the UK and the USA but also in many other jurisdictions where a culture of control has *not* emerged, or not to the same extent. Continental European jurisdictions and indeed, 'European values', are often mentioned in this regard (see Snacken, 2010). As a result, some contemporary scholars have stressed the importance of re-examining differences in political-institutional systems (see Gottschalk, 2013) and economic arrangements in order to explain differences between states subject to similar economic, social and cultural pressures (see also Lacey, 2008). These criticisms and Garland's own work on the persistence of the death penalty in the USA (Garland, 2010) have led him recently to reconsider the relationship between broader social and cultural changes and the different ways that penality evolves in different configured 'penal states' (Garland, 2013b; see also Rubin & Phelps, 2017).

Suggesting that Wacquant's critical and condemnatory use of the term 'penal state' is too loose and ill-defined for analytical or comparative purposes, Garland defines the penal state as that part of the state in which governmental authority is exercised to make penal rules and exercise penal governance and leadership. The term does not refer to the activities of the penal system itself in implementing punishment. Rather, it comprises elements of the Executive, the Parliament and the Judiciary, as well as the leadership of criminal justice agencies, but not their operatives or practitioners. Garland (2013) explains five key dimensions by which penal states might vary:

(1) *State autonomy* refers to the extent to which the state is independent of social forces refracted through the institutions of civil society or, conversely, to what extent social forces dictate state conduct.

(2) *Internal autonomy* refers to the relative independence of the penal state within the state itself and thus to its degree of independence from other state institutions. In other words, it concerns the extent to which penal officials themselves have the power to shape penal outcomes.

(3) *Control*: Different nations allocate the power to punish differently – at the national, regional or local level – and sometimes share this power in significant ways with others through transnational institutions. Thus, for example, in the case of the USA, federalism is critically important in shaping not one penal state but 50. Equally, in Europe, we must consider the influence of the European institutions like the European Union, the Council of Europe and the European Court for Human Rights. Control is also distributed differently amongst and contested between different actors and institutions in the penal process (prosecutors, judges, prison officials, probation services, public/private partnerships). These distributions of power change over time.

(4) *Modes of power*: It refers to quantitative and qualitative aspects of penal power; to how much power is exercised but also to the ways in which it is exercised. Inevitably this also involves modes of knowledge expressed in how penal actors think about penal objectives, techniques and practices. These modes of power have both negative and positive dimensions; they involve both incapacitating and capacity-building forms of penal power.

(5) *Power resources*: It refers to the extent to which a penal state has capacity to act in different ways. This is not just about the scale of the available infrastructure (i.e. numbers of prison places or probation officers) but all sorts of systems capacity – institutional, professional and academic. Power resources include not just economic or physical capital but also the cultural capital represented in knowledge, research and evidence. In this respect, Garland notes that negative, incapacitating penal power is easier to operationalise, not least because it can be exercised in relative isolation; by contrast, positive

(capacity-building) power requires coordination with social services and with economic forces outside penality.

Brangan (2013) has stressed the need to complement an analysis of these institutional dynamics of penal states and systems with an appreciation of the influences of culture and of human agency. She argues that once we have mapped out the institutions which inform penal practice,

> *the next comparative step we need to take is to fill these institutions with the dynamism of agency, examining the cultural currents that exist* inside *these criminal justice occupational sites. In attending to culture and agency we are comparatively assessing the embedded mores, values, beliefs, penal sensibilities and fears of penal actors – all of which form a sort of shared world view, or institutional ethos. (Brangan, 2013,[3] emphasis added)*

Crucially, Brangan also suggests the importance of an explanatory factor that we sometimes neglect: 'happenstance'. Both chance events and human agency may be vital sources of and resources for change in penality. She also adds to Garland's framework the importance of historical legacy and path dependency, suggesting that if we are to understand persistent differences between jurisdictions, we need to reflect upon their distinct histories.

Brangan's emphasis on culture, agency and history relates to the second major criticism of accounts of late-modern penal change like Garland's and Wacquant's. This concerns the relationships between the influences *upon* penal systems and institutions and processes of transformation *within* them. Drawing on the work of French social theorist Pierre Bourdieu, Page (2013, p. 157) has suggested that accounts of late-modern penal change have failed to 'investigate how contemporary crime control fields (or their sub-fields) affect agents' subjective orientation to penal practice. In other words, they do not concretely show if or how reconfigurations of crime control play out in practice'. The remedy for this neglect, he suggests, is to develop the concept of the 'penal field' to require us to take more seriously the positions, dispositions and relations of actors in that field and 'to examine how the structure and basic rules and assumptions of the penal game affect penal outcomes' (Page, 2013, p. 164; see also McNeill et al., 2009).[4]

CONCLUSION: CONTESTING PUNISHMENT
AND SUPERVISION

Page's ideas have recently been significantly developed in collaboration with Philip Goodman and Michelle Phelps (Goodman, Page, & Phelps, 2017). Their book, *Breaking the Pendulum*, argues that it is time to ditch the pendulum metaphor often deployed in accounts of penal change. Rather than seeing penal development as swinging between progressive and regressive, welfarist and punitive extremes, they propose a view of penal development that recognises and analyses the centrality of contestation within the penal field. 'Pendular logic' stresses (and tends to overstate) apparent 'ruptures' in the penal field; it treats criminal justice as a machine driven by wider social forces, and it homogenises and overgeneralises about penal change, usually at the national level. The logic of the 'agonistic' perspective, by contrast, stresses the centrality of struggles between actors with different types and amounts of power, endlessly contesting the nature of criminal justice. The outcomes of these struggles are profoundly influenced by macro-level social forces (structural, cultural and political), but they are not determined by them. In other words, to understand penal change we need to understand not just what forces press upon the penal field but also how the internal stresses that these forces create are manipulated and managed by the differently situated and resourced penal actors who struggle to construct or reconstruct criminal justice in law, policy and practice.

Goodman, Page and Phelps implore us to map out these struggles; showing how and why battles are (temporarily perhaps) won and lost and with what 'real' consequences. Following the authors' Bourdieusian inspiration, such mapping requires a complex analysis of the distribution of capital within the field, examining how its different forms (economic, symbolic, cultural and social) are distributed and redistributed and with what effects. For example, academics and professional educators may be endowed with the kinds of cultural and symbolic capital that help them to 'win' arguments about which models of practice shape reform programmes (and that allow them to write the official histories). However, the reserves of social capital in occupational groups and the economic resources available (or *not* available) in specific organisational settings may exercise a more powerful influence over whether, how and to what extent such models come to be implemented. We need to map out not just the rhetorical victories and defeats, but also the penal realities.

Equally – and again as Goodman, Page and Phelps conclude – penal fields must be understood in context; they are not independent of their situations – rather, their internal dynamics shape and are shaped by adjacent fields and by wider macro-social forces. The penal field cannot be understood in isolation from the welfare field, the juridical field, the legal field, the bureaucratic field and so on.

This chapter's brief review of a range of different attempts to make sense of penal change suggests that doing so requires us to analyse the penal impact of wider economic, social, cultural and political changes in the societies whose penal systems interest us. But, in addition to exploring these *distal influences* on penality, it seems clear that we need to examine the more *proximate influences* represented in more particular ways of ordering penal states and systems. This means attending carefully to variations between penal states (Garland, 2013b) in the ways in which penal power is generated and circumscribed, governed and deployed. It also necessitates close examination of state-level political and institutional dynamics, infrastructure and resources, law and policy, organisational structures and professional organisations and unions, and wider civil society engagement in the penal system. However, as we will see in the next chapter, even if we regard these characteristics of the penal state as important proximate influences on how penality develops in policy and practice, then to increase the granularity of our analysis, we will also need to zoom in on *local influences*. Here, the effects of distal and proximate influences are moderated by even more specific and peculiar characteristics, for example, by the acquired dispositions and habits of local actors (e.g. judges, prosecutors, probation and parole staff, and each of their professional associations) and by the distribution of capital within the (local) penal field (Page, 2013), whether in the form of material resources, cultural capital, social networks or the power that status, recognition or distinction confers. The potency of 'happenstance' of historical path dependencies and of human agency (Brangan, 2013) is also keenly felt at the local level where unforeseen events, problems and situations command a response from local actors.

To return, in closing, to our short story, Pauline's discomfort and dissonance reflect the increasing gulf between her disposition as a practitioner, forged in an earlier era, and the apparent realities of the system in which she is now compelled to operate. The field has changed in important ways; but she has not adapted to and internalised these changes. Somehow, the supervision 'game' has changed in ways that she neither desired nor anticipated, and faster than she could have adapted to (even if she had wanted to). As we will see in the chapters that follow, these changes reflect wider social, cultural and political pressures that have come to bear on the field, but those pressures do not determine precisely how it has changed, nor do they determine how she will construct supervision with Joe.

If the short story serves to offer a fine-grained, humanised illustration of how these dynamics might play out in just one imagined case, then the next chapter complements this by painting by numbers. Before we can begin to assess claims about 'mass supervision', we need to engage with the question of the scale and social distribution of the phenomenon that needs to be explained.

NOTES

1. This section draws on a previously published chapter co-authored with Gwen Robinson (McNeill & Robinson, 2016). I am grateful to Gwen, my co-editors and the publishers for permission to re-develop that material here.

2. Although Durkheim's two laws have often been disputed, his insistence on examining the relationships between social structures, culture and punishment endures.

3. See http://www.offendersupervision.eu/blog-post/a-framework-for-comparative-research-on-supervision. Accessed on December 30, 2014.

4. In this analysis Page echoes Garland's development of the concept of 'penality': 'It involves discursive frameworks of authority and condemnation, ritual procedures of imposing punishment, a repertoire of penal sanctions, institutions and agencies for the enforcement of sanctions and a rhetoric of symbols, figures, and images by means of which the penal process is represented to its various audiences' (Garland, 1990, p. 17).

CHAPTER 3

COUNTING MASS SUPERVISION

17 MINUTES AND 14 SECONDS WASTED

Norman stopped the video clip and lent back in his chair, stretching his back and trying to unfurrow his brow. He clicked open Pauline's quarterly appraisal form, took a deep breath and contemplated the section of the pro-forma entitled 'Video Practice Quality Audit'.

Figure 5. Untitled 4.

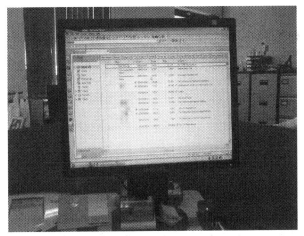

'1. **Relational skills** *(To what extent does the worker demonstrate an ability to develop a strong and appropriate professional working relationship with the offender?)[Rate on a 5-point scale, where 5 is 'fully demonstrated' and 1 is 'not demonstrated' at all].*

2. **Structuring skills** *(To what extent does the worker keep the interview focused on addressing needs and risks related to reducing reoffending, using appropriate techniques to motivate, rehearse and reinforce prosocial behaviours and to challenge antisocial behaviours?) [Rate on a 5-point scale, where 5 is 'fully focused' and 1 is 'not focused' at all].*

3. **Use of authority** *(To what extent does the worker maintain appropriate professional boundaries using their authority to promote and enforce compliance with supervision?). [Rate on a 5-point scale, where 5 is 'fully maintained' and 1 is 'not maintained' at all].*

4. **Brokerage** *(To what extent does the worker ensure that the offender is appropriately signposted to services relevant to addressing needs and risks?). [Rate on a 5-point scale, where 5 is 'fully ensured' and 1 is 'not ensured' at all].'*

Norman sighed. Pauline's performance in 59's induction interview was typical of the problems associated with 'lifers'[1] (as he liked to refer to his more 'experienced' staff). He admitted that she was a #4 for 'relational'. She put 59 at ease straight away— as simple as a warm smile, the offer of a hot drink and a firm but welcoming handshake (despite, he noted disapprovingly, the latest health and safety memo about avoiding the winter vomiting bug).

The issue was that, like most of her peers, her interviews often lacked appropriate focus and purpose. True to form, she had let 59 talk too much, wasting time, instead of cutting to the chase. Did she really need to know the ins and outs of his divorce or his worries about how the court case would affect his struggle to see his kids? Worse still, letting him bleat on about the injustices of his dismissal from his job just gave him time and space to repeat excuses for his offences instead of taking responsibility. If ever there was a moment for an 'appropriate challenge' of his 'cognitive distortions', that was it — and Pauline had either missed it or bottled it. At best a #2 for 'structuring'.

The lifers were stuck in their ways; ironic, he thought, since they considered themselves the experts at supporting change, always stressing their hard-earned experience at the frontline. But what good was decades of experience of doing things badly – or, at best, inefficiently? He had done the courses and read the correctional research. Most low-moderate risk offenders need, at most, brief, focused and structured interventions with prompt onward referral to interventions and services that addressed any 'criminogenic' factors. It wasn't rocket science... Nor was it social work, whatever the old-timers thought.

No, it was court-ordered supervision and its purpose was simple; reduced reoffending at reduced cost. 59 just needed to know what to do, what not to do, who to go and see, and who to keep away from. Cheerily telling 59 to keep out of trouble didn't cut it. It was a #1 for authority then. The risk assessment score justified only the most minimal intervention – and it was blindingly obvious that, if anything, he needed a few sessions of anger management. For now, the tag^2 could take care of keeping him away from his ex-boss, his ex-wife and his ex-life.

Norman re-opened the video file and checked the clock-counter. 37 minutes and 14 seconds. The contract allowed 1 hour of contact time per month for low-moderate cases. And, instead of referring him on, Pauline had promised to visit 59 at home in a few days. So, a #1 for 'brokerage' then. The home visit was another health and safety issue – and another waste of precious time.

Norman totted up Pauline's score. Nine out of a possible 20. He'd have to talk to her. This appraisal wasn't going to end well. Norman needed 75% of his staff scoring 15 or better in these audits to trigger the results-related bonus payment. For that he needed fresher, younger, hungrier staff. Pragmatists not puritans.

No wonder the furrow in his brow had become a trench.

INTRODUCTION

Despite her weariness, Pauline's old-fashioned pre-occupation is with individuals. She wants to *know* them and *help* them. Norman has quite different concerns. He is preoccupied with numbers and with the management of numbers; the numbers of supervisees and of hours and minutes spent with them; the numbers by which he assesses and constructs 'quality'; and – perhaps most of all – the numbers by which he is himself judged.

Critics of mass incarceration have also been preoccupied with numbers, though in a quite different way. The near-ubiquitous graphs depicting the dramatic upturn in US prison and jail populations after 1980, rising to a peak in 2009, provide a powerful visual statement of the phenomenon, even if they say nothing about its causes and consequences. The front cover of the influential National Academies of Sciences report (edited by Travis et al., 2014) on *The Growth of Incarceration in the United States* provides one such visual example.[3] Yet, until very recently, mass supervision has rarely been depicted in this or any other way. Perhaps this is one of the reasons it remains relatively invisible, as I noted in Chapter 1 (Robinson, 2016).

That said, in recent months, there have been some stirrings of public interest in mass supervision. For example, on 17 November 2017, the *New York Times*[4] carried an op-ed by Jay-Z (a prominent musician and philanthropist) entitled 'Jay-Z: The Criminal Justice System Stalks Black People Like Meek Mill'. Meek Mill is a 30-year-old rapper who, at the age of 19, received an 8-month sentence for convictions related to drugs and firearms. Since his release – 'for his entire adult life' – he has been on probation.

Meek Mill was arrested in March 2017 after an altercation at an airport. All charges were subsequently dropped. In August 2017, he was arrested for 'popping a wheelie' on a motorbike. Those charges, Jay-Z reported, would be dismissed if he stayed out of further trouble. But that didn't stop Meek Mill being sentenced to two to four years in prison for probation violation.

Meek Mill's case led Jay-Z to argue that more generally:

> [i]nstead of being a second chance, probation ends up being a landmine, with a random misstep bringing consequences greater than the crime. A person on probation can end up in jail over a technical violation like missing a curfew.

As well as focusing on the story of one famous probationer, Jay-Z paints this bigger picture with numbers:

> As of 2015, one-third of the 4.65 million Americans on some form of parole or probation were black. Black people are sent to prison for parole violations at much higher rates than white people.

In Pennsylvania, hundreds of thousands of people are on probation or parole. About half of the people in city jails in Philadelphia [Meek Mill's hometown] are there for probation or parole violations. We could literally shut down jails if we treated people on probation or parole more fairly.

And that's what we need to fight for in Philadelphia and across the country.

One month later, on 18 December 2017, the non-profit website Next City ran a more detailed story headlined 'Parole and Probation Reform is Bigger than Meek Mill', opening with the line that '[o]ne in every 52 American adults lives under court supervision, costing taxpayers and making it harder for families to move on post-incarceration.'[5]

These stories raise some crucial issues. Firstly, they speak of the scale of supervision and how we are to make sense of its growth. Secondly, they speak about who is subject to it and, more specifically, about its racialized and classed character. Thirdly, they speak of how supervision is constructed in practice – as a 'landmine' or as a 'second chance'. These two metaphors point to the crucial issue of how compliance with supervision is constructed and managed (Boone & Maguire, 2017).

In the next section, I briefly explore some data about the extent, reach and spread of mass supervision across Europe, before moving on to examine in much more depth the development of mass probation in the USA. The third section of the chapter analyses evidence from Scotland. The intention here is not to develop a systematic comparison but rather to present two quite different case studies, helping us to consider whether and to what extent the same term – 'mass supervision' – can be meaningfully applied to both countries and potentially to others. That said, in some respects, the most instructive comparisons may be *within* the two countries and *over time*, allowing more meaningful examinations of changing rates of supervision (in comparison with rates of imprisonment), of the populations subject to supervision (and imprisonment) and of breach or revocation rates.

Broadly, the intention of this chapter is to use the available statistical data to 'count' supervision, to show *that* it counts and to consider *what* counts as *mass* supervision.

THE SPREAD OF 'MASS SUPERVISION'?

I argued in the last chapter that to understand the dynamics of supervision's growth within and across different jurisdictions, we need to examine the ways in which social, cultural and political influences on the scale of punishment are channelled, exacerbated or moderated by legal, institutional and professional dynamics, at local, regional and national levels. However, another form of analysis also seems increasingly important. There is evidence that supervision's growth has also been affected by *transnational* developments and by the influence of international institutions and bodies.

In the European context, for example, many Post-Soviet Central and Eastern European countries have been required to embark on programmes of criminal justice reform as a pre-condition of accession to the European Union (see Durnescu, 2015). These reform programmes have included a focus on reducing prison populations by developing probation systems offering 'alternatives to custody'. The development, promulgation and revision of European Prison Rules and European Rules for Probation and for 'Community Sanctions and Measures' have played an important part in these processes (see Morgenstern & Larrauri, 2013; van Zyl Smit & Snacken, 2009). The Confederation of European Probation (CEP) – a member organisation of European probation services – has also played an important role, for example in sharing information and 'best practice', in building relationships and in helping to 'twin' established and emergent systems, to assist with the development of the latter. These kinds of 'twinning' arrangements represent important and rarely examined aspects of penal policy transfer (see, Canton, 2006, 2009; McFarlane & Canton, 2014).

However, analysis of European statistics on community sanctions and measures suggests that these sorts of initiatives have produced some intriguing and sometimes alarming effects.

Aebi et al.'s (2015) cross-sectional analysis of the evolution of prison and probation rates from 1990 to 2010 aimed to test whether European probation expansion had achieved the broadly diversionary aims of European institutions and of many national governments. The development of such an analysis is far from simple; community sanctions and measures take very different legal and institutional forms in different European countries and data about them are recorded in very different

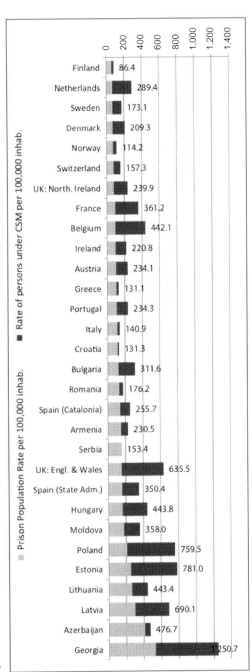

Figure 6. Total Prison and Probation Population Rates per 100,000 in 2010.

Prison Population Rate per 100,000 inhab.

Rate of persons under CSM per 100,000 inhab.

Country	Rate
Finland	86.4
Netherlands	289.4
Sweden	173.1
Denmark	209.3
Norway	114.2
Switzerland	157.3
UK: North. Ireland	239.9
France	361.2
Belgium	442.1
Ireland	220.8
Austria	234.1
Greece	131.1
Portugal	234.3
Italy	140.9
Croatia	131.3
Bulgaria	311.6
Romania	176.2
Spain (Catalonia)	255.7
Armenia	230.5
Serbia	153.4
UK: Engl. & Wales	635.5
Spain (State Adm.)	350.4
Hungary	443.8
Moldova	358.0
Poland	759.5
Estonia	781.0
Lithuania	443.4
Latvia	690.1
Azerbaijan	476.7
Georgia	1250.7

Source: From Aebi, Delgrande, & Marguet, 2015.

ways. Nonetheless, Aebi et al.'s, (2015, p. 589) painstaking work enabled them to conclude that:

> The data analysed in this article show that the number of persons serving CSM [community sanctions and measures] has rapidly increased in Europe during the 1990s and 2000s. Prison populations have also increased during the same period. Crime trends cannot explain such trends. As a consequence, it is possible to conclude that the increased use of community sanctions and measures did not lead to a decrease of prison populations across Europe [...] In sum, instead of being alternatives to imprisonment, community sanctions and measures have contributed to widening the net of the European criminal justice systems [...] These results suggest that CSM have become one of the instruments of an increasingly punitive approach to crime control.

In this context, Figure 6 (above) is notable not just for the scale of the correctional populations that it reveals, but also for the very high probation rates apparent in some Post-Soviet states, including Georgia, Latvia, Estonia and Poland; these rates clearly merit further examination, including in relation to any role that 'Europeanisation' may have played in generating them (see Durnescu, 2015). Within and between other regions of the world, the ways in which transnational institutions and bodies have (wittingly or unwittingly) encouraged or restrained the development of 'mass supervision' require much closer study.

However, the case study, *par excellence*, of both mass incarceration and mass probation is a country which, in some respects, seems to be relatively immune to the influence of transnational institutions: the USA.

MASS SUPERVISION IN THE USA

Mass Probation, Parole and Mass Incarceration[6]

According to the latest available statistics from the US Department of Justice (Kaeble & Glaze, 2016[7]), at yearend 2015, there were an estimated 6,741,400 people within US adult correctional systems (including prisons, jails, parole and probation). That amounts to 1 in 37 adults.[8] The population on probation or parole stood at 4,650,900, meaning that about 7 in 10 of those under penal control were under supervision in the community.

Huge as these numbers are, the total correctional population (of people incarcerated, on probation and on parole) in the USA has, in fact, been declining since its peak in 2007 when it stood at 7,339,600 (as noted previously, the sub-population of people incarcerated peaked a little later in 2009). Looking across the different forms of community-based supervision, the numbers of people on probation have *declined* from 4,293,000 to 3,789,800 – a drop of 503,200 – accounting for 84 per cent of the total drop in the correctional population. By contrast, between 2007 and 2015, the numbers of people on parole *increased* by 44,400, from 826,100 to 870,500.

The University of Minnesota-based sociologist Michelle Phelps has examined these sorts of statistics more closely than anyone else, applying a longer historical lens to try to make sense of mass supervision in the USA. More specifically, her initial research (Phelps, 2013a) examined the relationships between mass incarceration and what she terms 'mass probation' across all 50 states and over the period of 1980–2010, a period during which the prison population (excluding jail) rose from 0.3 million to 1.5 million and the probation population (excluding parole) increased from 1.1 million to 4.1 million. By exploring ratios between the number of index crimes and both supervision and imprisonment rates, Phelps (2013b) was able to show that this dramatic increase in probation could *not* be accounted for by changes in the crime rate (Figure 7).

Crucially, Phelps has sought to understand whether, under different conditions in different US states, probation's growth exacerbated or moderated mass incarceration. More generally, Phelps' work – like mine and that of several European colleagues (McNeill, 2013; McNeill & Beyens, 2013; Robinson, 2016; Robinson & McNeill, 2015) – has sought to renew scholarly and public interest in supervisory sanctions.

Phelps (2013b) notes a key contrast between the ways that policy reformers and critical academics discuss probation. The former have tended to see probation as a progressive strategy for diverting people from imprisonment. The latter (as already noted in chapter 1) draw attention to the risks of 'net-widening' and 'mesh-thinning' – drawing minor cases 'up' into the penal net and then applying processes of breach or revocation that can

Figure 7. Probation and Prison Relative to Index Crime, 1980–2010.

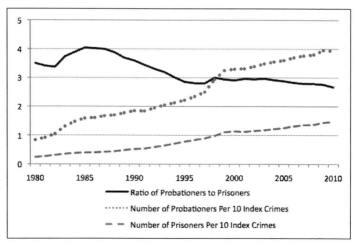

Ratio of Probationers to Prisoners

•••••• Number of Probationers Per 10 Index Crimes

━ ━ Number of Prisoners Per 10 Index Crimes

Source: From Phelps, 2013b.

produce more severe custodial sentences than might have been imposed in the first place (see, e.g. Caplow & Simon, 1999; Lucken, 1997). Klingele (2013, p. 1015) goes so far as to suggest that, with an estimated half of all people admitted to US jails and more than one-third of those admitted to prison arriving as a result of revocation, 'community supervision is not an alternative to imprisonment but only a delayed form of it'.

Indeed, looking at national-level data, Phelps (2013b) finds very limited evidence to support the policy reformers' confidence in probation's diversionary effects. In only one period in the early 1980s is she able to find evidence of probation being used as an alternative to prison. Thereafter, probation appears to have acted as a net-widener. Even when correctional populations began to decline, as noted previously, it seems that probation and imprisonment rates have declined *together* (with probation declining faster than imprisonment between 2007 and 2015; see Kaeble & Glaze, 2016), rather than probation substituting for imprisonment.

However, Phelps' (2013b) sophisticated methodological approach also allows her to identify important differences between states that are obscured when looking only at national trends. Grouping states into those with high, medium and low rates of probation growth, Phelps shows *both* that, overall, states with larger increases in probation rates also had larger increases in imprisonment rates *and* that there is considerable state-level heterogeneity within each of the three clusters. In other words, probation growth *tends* to be positively associated with imprisonment growth but the dynamics of this relationship vary state by state. By using regression modelling to produce a yet more fine-grained analysis, Phelps (2013b) shows a wide range of different relationships; in some states probation had a strong net-widening effect, in others it had a strong diversionary effect, and in others its effect was neutral.

To make more sense of these findings, Phelps (2013b) offers brief examinations of examples of sentencing and probation reform efforts in different states. In Kansas, for example, it seems that a 2003 legislative reform aiming to divert low-level drug offenders, in fact, produced net-widening effects (Rengifo & Stemen, 2010). By contrast, in Michigan, fiscal incentives have been in place since 1988 that aim to keep people supervised at county level, encouraging Community Corrections Advisory Boards to develop plans to decrease the numbers sent to state prisons and to improve probation. The rate of commitments to prison for felony offences in Michigan has steadily declined between 1989 and 2010, from 35 to 21 per cent (Michigan Department of Corrections, 2011), despite national increases. Michigan has also reformed probation supervision, introducing new approaches to risk assessment and to staff-probationer interactions, as well as using gradated sanctions to manage compliance. Since 2000, the annual number of people imprisoned for probation violations has dropped by 16 per cent (for a more detailed account of Michigan's story, see Phelps, 2017a).

By combining her statistical analyses with exploration of reform strategies, Phelps (2013b) produces a compelling reading of state-level variations in the relationships between prison and probation populations, arguing that two factors shape these relationships: (1) the extent to which probation diverts from or feeds into imprisonment and (2) the extent to which probation supports people (through processes and practices of rehabilitation) away from future prison admission or pushes them more deeply into these institutionalised forms of penal control. She concludes that factors such as sentencing laws, election processes for judges and prosecutors and fiscal incentives shape the institutionalised practice of sentencing, producing diversionary or expansionary effects. Similarly, state-level structures of probation (both organisational and fiscal) shape the effectiveness of its practices in pursuit of rehabilitation and its approach to violation and revocation. These two sets of probation practices — supporting rehabilitation and managing compliance — produce increases or decreases in rates of future prison admissions.

In sum, the lesson from Phelps' (2013a, 2013b) initial work was that if we are seeking to avoid mass supervision and mass incarceration, then probation must be carefully targeted and constructively administered and practiced.

Explaining Probation Expansion and Exploring 'Regimes of Control'

More recently, Phelps (2017b) has taken her analysis further, seeking to understand the causes of probation's huge expansion in the USA. She finds that between 1981 and 2007, the average time spent on probation nationally fluctuated only between 1.7 and 1.9 years, but that the number of entries to probation increased by 214 per cent, accounting for most of the 250 per cent increase in the probation population. Since this increase cannot be explained by changes in crime rates, Phelps suggests that the causes lie in increasing *criminalization* through changes in policing, prosecutorial and sentencing practices (Pfaff, 2014; Stuntz, 2011). These changes affected processing both of more serious 'felony' cases and of less serious 'misdemeanour' cases.

However, by analysing state-level variations, Phelps (2017b) again complicates conventional readings of which US states are more and less progressive in penal terms. She proposes an approach to conceptualising the 'scale of punishment' that, rather than focusing only on imprisonment rates, examines *multiple* forms of criminal justice control and theorises 'both *how* and *how much* states punish'. She therefore divides the prison––probation space into four 'control regimes', by separating US states into those above or below the median rate for each form of criminal justice control (prison or probation) (see **Figure 8** below).

Thus, a regime of 'incapacitative control' has a higher imprisonment rate and a lower probation rate; a regime of 'sparing control' has both lower imprisonment and lower probation rates; a regime of 'punitive

Figure 8. Control Regimes Typology.

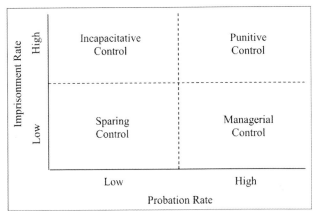

Source: From Phelps, 2017b.

control' has higher imprisonment and higher probation rates; and a regime of 'managerial control' has higher probation rates and lower imprisonment rates.

Phelps (2017b, p. 61) finds that after three decades of growth following 1980, the expansions of probation and imprisonment have been progressively 'decoupled'. Whereas, in 1980, the two rates tended to rise together across the country, by 2010, the picture was more complex and variable. Moreover, by ranking each state in terms of its relative rates of imprisonment and probation in 1980 and 2010, Phelps finds that whereas there is stability in imprisonment rankings (meaning that high imprisonment states in 1980 tend to remain high imprisonment states in 2010 and vice versa), there is much more change in state level probation-rate rankings; indeed, '[s]ome states nearly flipped in the probation rankings from low to high or vice versa' (Phelps, 2017b, p. 61). Phelps (2017b, p. 66) suggests that 'this decoupling is due in part to the massive increase in probation admissions in some low imprisonment states and in part by the tendency of some high imprisonment rate states to underreport misdemeanour probationers'.

Perhaps most importantly, at least for those seeking to explain penal change, Phelps (2017b, p. 66) demonstrates that comparative research reliant on imprisonment rates,

fundamentally misconstrues state variation [...] Rather than a
monolithic expansion, states followed diverse trajectories, likely
driven by local, social, political and economic conditions,
producing a multi-faceted array of control strategies.

Thus a full account of the carceral state requires us to
understand each of the various mass *punishments. (emphasis in*
original)

Phelps (2017b) does not go on to offer such an account, but she does suggest that what we might term the 'usual suspects' for explaining penal change – social, economic and political forces – don't seem able to adequately differentiate, for example, between different kinds of low imprisonment states; that is, between those with lower and higher probation rates, and thus between regimes of sparing or managerial control. For example, relatively 'progressive' Midwestern and Northeastern states that do not share the South's legacy of slavery fall into *both* categories; some have higher and some have lower probation rates. Consequently, Phelps argues that probation rates may be shaped not so much by these broader historical and sociological influences as by state-level institutional variations in judicial and correctional structures (as discussed previously). In some states, the drift into mass probation, she suggests, may have been occasioned by myopic efforts to tackle prison growth that failed to see the risks inherent in probation growth.

The puzzles that Phelps does so much to unpick represent both a set of complex analytical challenges and a source of hope. If states with similar social, economic and political structures can have vastly different rates of probation, then mass probation *must* be amenable to reform, and indeed, some states already demonstrate parts of the answer to arresting mass supervision.

The Socio-economic Distribution of Supervision

The racialised character of mass incarceration in the USA is widely acknowledged and much debated (Alexander, 2010; Wacquant, 2009). Indeed, as Bruce Western (2006) shows in *Punishment and Inequality in America*, the US criminal justice system's effects are heavily concentrated amongst the most marginalised and excluded, meaning that punishment plays a central role in constructing and reinforcing social inequalities. Young men of colour without high school diplomas are its primary targets; 3 in 10 such men were in jail or prison on any given day in the year 2000. Moreover, by the age of 34, nearly 6 in 10 men of colour who came to adulthood during the prison boom of the early 1980s had experienced incarceration, compared to 1 in 10 White men without high school diplomas.

Going to prison reinforces existing social inequalities by damaging work prospects, health, family stability and educational attainment (see Wakefield & Uggen, 2010). Indeed, drawing on but extending Western's (2006) analysis, Miller and Stuart (2017) argue that US carceral expansion does more than condemn its largely poor and black targets to second class citizenship; criminalisation and penalisation constructs a new kind of 'carceral citizenship', which renders certain subjects suitable for governance through institutions of both control and care. Carceral citizens live in a kind of 'alternate legal reality' (Miller & Stuart, 2017, p. 534). Conviction 'translates' them into carceral subjects, changing their relations with state agencies and civil society associations, drawing them into supervision and empowering other public and private actors to 'manage, correct, sanction and care for them' (Miller & Stuart, 2017, p. 536).

Probation is one such institution of control and, sometimes, care. As Phelps (2017b, p. 60) shows, and as Jay-Z suggested in the New York Times story, probation supervision is also disproportionately concentrated among men of colour. Phelps estimates that, in 2007 (at its peak), one in 12 men of colour was subject to probation supervision, compared to one in 41 White men. But as Figure 9 (below) suggests, even this level of disproportionality was much *less* extreme than for imprisonment:

As Phelps (2017b, p. 60) notes, even given the significant over-representation of people of colour in probation populations, 'the massive scale of probation [...] means that there are more White probationers under supervision today than prisoners of any [other] racial/ethnic background'.

Phelps (2018) suggests that this difference in the ethnic composition of the population subject to mass probation most likely reflects those markers of social privilege that are correlated with more lenient sentencing (e.g. see Kim, Spohn, & Hedberg, 2015) and with having the resources required to comply with supervisory sanctions (for example, see Doherty, 2016). In

Figure 9. Prison (sentenced), Probation and Parole Populations in the USA, by Ethnicity, 2015.[9]

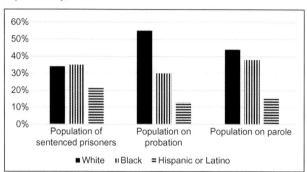

consequence, probation may divert those who are relatively *less* socially disadvantaged (compared to those imprisoned) while acting as a net-widener for those who are *more* socially disadvantaged. Indeed, by analysing a national household survey, Bureau of Justice surveys of correctional populations and data on probationers in custody as a result of revocation, Phelps (2018, p. 56) is able to show that:

> *disparities in probation supervision rates across race, gender, age, and educational attainment are substantially less pronounced than those for imprisonment rates. Yet when we examine probationers behind bars, they are once again the 'usual suspects' – disproportionately young, non-white men with low levels of formal schooling. This supports the hypothesis that probation provides a bifurcated pathway, diverting relatively more privileged defendants toward community supervision (which they can more easily complete) while their less advantaged counterparts are funnelled deeper into the criminal justice system.*

Thus, 'probation plays a crucial role in stratifying outcomes in the criminal justice system, providing an off-ramp for some and conveyer belt towards prison for others' (Phelps, 2018, p. 44); or as Jay-Z put it, a second chance for some and a landmine for others.

Of course, parolees, unlike most other subjects of mass supervision, are completing sentences of imprisonment in the community and, as such, one might expect their socio-economic status and disadvantaged social position to closely mirror that of the wider prison population. But the data in Figure 9 suggest that White former prisoners make up a higher proportion of the parole population, and Black, Hispanic or Latino people make up a lower proportion of the parole population than one might expect. Again, this may reflect similar dynamics of relative disadvantage and privilege to those at play in shaping probation populations, though a much more careful analysis, for example considering crime types and criminal records, would be required to demonstrate this.

Nonetheless, the fact that the US probation population is falling while the parole population is rising and that the latter is, in its ethnic composition, somewhat closer to the prison population, suggests that the familiar racialized concentration of penal power demonstrated by Western (2006) will likely be exacerbated (at least in relative terms) if these trends continue.

MASS SUPERVISION IN SCOTLAND?

In this section, I reverse the order of the previous one. I begin by briefly introducing some salient features of the Scottish context and go on to provide an examination of available evidence about the socio-economic distribution of imprisonment and supervision in Scotland. Then, I explore imprisonment and supervision rates in Scotland and what can be inferred about the relationships between them.

The Socio-economic Distribution of Punishment in Scotland

Scotland and the USA are, of course, very different countries. Indeed, with a population of about 5.3 million (according to the 2011 Census), Scotland is smaller by population size than the largest 20 of the 50 United States of America. Its population size is closest to that of Minnesota and its land mass (30,000 square miles) to that of South Carolina.[10] Despite sharing a common language, and despite the role that Scots have played (for better and worse) in the settlement and development of the USA, the two countries have very different histories (not least of emigration and immigration), cultures, economies, political systems and population demographics.

Given the focus above on the differently racialized characters of mass incarceration and mass supervision in the USA, it is important to note that the Scottish population is considerably less ethnically diverse than that of the USA. In the 2011 Census,[11] the percentage of people in Scotland from minority ethnic groups had risen significantly, but only to 4 per cent of the total population, with the Asian population accounting for about 3 per cent and African, Caribbean or Black groups making up about 1 per cent of the total. Scotland's minority ethnic populations are geographically concentrated in Scotland's larger cities but even in the largest, Glasgow, that population stands at only 12 per cent.

According to the latest publically available statistics[12] that provide an ethnic breakdown, on 30 June 2013, only 1.7 per cent of the Scottish prison population identified as Asian (meaning Asian people are underrepresented in prison), and only 1.4 per cent of the Scottish prison population identified as Black (an over-representation). The Scottish prison population therefore seems to be even more ethnically homogeneous than the Scottish population in general, although the paucity of publicly available data should caution us about reading too much into these snapshot figures.

This is certainly not to say that Scottish society and its justice system do not have problems with racism (see Davidson, Linnpaa, McBride, & Virdee, 2018). However, particularly in Glasgow and in the West of Scotland more generally, it is another form of discrimination that tends to provoke debate: religious sectarianism. About 16 per cent of the Scottish population identify as Roman Catholic, a cultural and religious identity historically linked (for many but by no means all) with inward migration from Ireland, particularly in the nineteenth century. This population in Scotland has undoubtedly suffered significant and enduring prejudice and discrimination, with some of it having been formally enshrined in law. Even if the law has changed, in a recent Scottish Social Attitudes Survey (Scottish Government, 2014), 14 per cent of Scottish Catholics self-reported experiences of employment discrimination (compared to 1–5 per cent for other groups) and 15 per cent reported experiences of harassment or threats related to their religious beliefs (compared to 2–10 per cent for other groups). The Scottish Crime and Justice Surveys tend to report low levels of sectarian crime. In the 2016–2017 survey, 5 per cent of those reporting experiences of harassment thought the harassment may have been motivated by sectarianism.[13]

The Scottish Government's (2015) *Examination of the Evidence on Sectarianism in Scotland: 2015 Update*[14] found that, with respect to indicators of (relative) structural disadvantage, Scottish Catholics are younger than the larger Protestant population (which stands at 32 per cent of the general population), they are more ethnically diverse (partly because of recent immigration), they are more likely to have dependent children and they are more likely to be lone parents. There appears to be little difference between the two groups in terms of income, occupational class or educational attainment, and a historical gap in health outcomes seems to be disappearing (although, as McBride [2017] argues, this may be as much about the adverse impact of deindustrialisation on working class Scottish Protestants as it is about improvements in the position of Scottish Catholics).

That said, rates of unemployment remain slightly higher in the Catholic population (although they are in line with the overall national average), who are also more likely to rent their homes and to be victims of crime. Whether these adverse indicators reflect discrimination linked to ethnic and religious identity or the higher proportions of Catholics living in more deprived areas is less clear. On this question, the report notes that 'evidence suggests that 'individual' factors […] have a greater effect than religion in shaping economic outcomes, with no evidence found to suggest persistent anti-Catholic discrimination' (Scottish Government, 2015, p. 8).

However, one area where significant differences persist is in relation to imprisonment. The same report notes that 'some commentators have argued that the Scottish criminal justice system discriminates against people of Irish origin and that Catholics are disproportionately represented among the prison population' (Scottish Government, 2015, p. 62). In 2015, while Catholics represented around 16 per cent of the Scottish population they made up 22 per cent of the prison population.[15] Fourteen years earlier, in 2001, these differences had been even more pronounced, standing at 16 per cent and 28 per cent, respectively. As with other adverse outcomes, it has been argued that the difference is most likely a direct result of the fact that people in prison are more likely to come from the most socially deprived areas. Indeed, Wiltshire (2010)[16] suggests:

> *The question [...] should shift from asking why Catholics are disproportionately represented in Scottish jails to why so many Catholics continue to live in areas of deprivation in Scotland, particularly the West, and why they score worse on a range of social indicators. It seems clear that Catholics are disproportionately represented in Scottish jails because of the compelling relationship between deprivation and imprisonment.*

The work of a former Governor of Barlinnie prison in Glasgow, Roger Houchin (2005), has been particularly instructive in exploring links between place, deprivation and imprisonment. Houchin used prison records and the Scottish Index of Multiple Deprivation to show that half of the population in Scottish prisons on the night of 30th June 2003 came from home addresses in just 155 of the 1222 local government wards in Scotland. Although the overall imprisonment rate for men in Scotland at that time was 237 per 100,000, for men from the 27 most deprived wards in the country, the imprisonment rate was 953 per 100,000. Perhaps most strikingly of all, he found that about one in 9 young men from these neighbourhoods would spend time in prison before they were 23. More recent Scottish Government analysis suggests that 43 per cent of prisoners come from the 15 per cent most deprived data zones, and the incarceration rate per 100,000 of the working population in these areas is 660 compared to 150 per 100,000 for the other 85 per cent of Scotland. In other words, the incarceration rate in the 15 per cent most deprived data zones is 4.5 times higher than in the rest of the country. The concentration of incarceration is even more marked for the 5 per cent most deprived areas, which account for 19 per cent of prisoners and have an incarceration rate 4.9 times higher, than the rest of the country[17].

These patterns – linking experiences of profound socio-economic disadvantage and imprisonment – echo some aspects of the situation in the USA, even if there is much less evidence of a clearly racialized dimension. Broadly speaking, it may be that just as the US prison system exists in a deadly symbiosis with the 'hyper-ghetto' (Wacquant, 2001), so the Scottish system feeds on Scotland's most disadvantaged communities.

More generally, in relation to prisoners in the three UK jurisdictions (England and Wales, Northern Ireland and Scotland), there is a wealth of research into their backgrounds, characteristics and needs, which demonstrate their serious and chronic social exclusion and, in turn, its association with the cycle of re-conviction and re-processing in the penal system. It is not just that the most deprived *communities* are over-represented in the prison population; it is highly likely that the most disadvantaged *people* (even where they live in less deprived communities) are over-represented in that population.

Perhaps most influentially, the then UK Government's Social Exclusion Unit (2002) report *Reducing re-offending by ex-prisoners* revealed that, compared to the general population, people in prison were 13 times more likely to have been in care as a child, 10 times more likely to have been a regular truant from school, 13 times more likely to be unemployed, 2.5 times more likely to have a family member who had been convicted of a criminal offence, 6 times more likely to have been a young father and 15 times more likely to be HIV positive. In respect of their basic skills, 80 per cent had the writing skills of an 11-year-old child , 65 per cent had the numeracy skills of an 11-year-old child, 50 per cent had the reading skills of an 11-year-old child, 70 per cent had used drugs before coming to prison, 70 per cent suffered from at least two mental disorders, 20 per cent of men in prison had previously attempted suicide, and 37 per cent of women in prison had attempted suicide. For younger people in prison (aged 18–20 years), these problems were even more intense; their basic skills, rates of unemployment and previous levels of school exclusion were a third worse even than those of older prisoners (Social Exclusion Unit, 2002, p. 6).

In comparison with those in prison, we know much less about the social circumstances of people under supervision in the UK and in Scotland. To date, there has been no study of the geographical distribution of supervision that might allow us to make direct comparisons with Houchin's (2005) neighbourhood level results. However, Figure 10 (below) shows the geographic distribution Community Payback Orders (CPOs) in Scotland in 2015–2016. In this figure, the Scottish local authorities are ranked left to right according to the local share of 'Deprivation Zones' that are found in the 20 per cent most deprived zones in Scotland;[18] by this measure, the most deprived local authority is Glasgow and the least is the Shetland Islands. The Community Payback Order

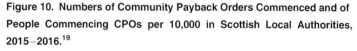

Figure 10. Numbers of Community Payback Orders Commenced and of People Commencing CPOs per 10,000 in Scottish Local Authorities, 2015–2016.[19]

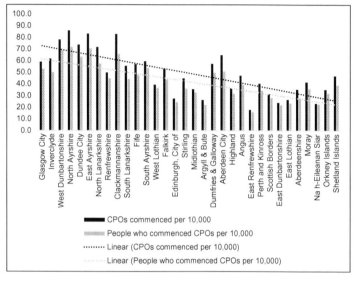

(CPO) is a generic community sentence with a range of possible conditions, but which usually involves unpaid work and often includes something akin to what was formerly probation supervision. As such, the Scottish CPO population is our closest comparator to the US probation population.

Broadly speaking, as shown in **Figure 10**, there does appear to be some association between the social concentration of deprivation and supervision, but the fit is far from perfect. Part of the reason may be that as we move to smaller and smaller units of analysis, the influence of particular local dynamics comes more clearly into play. Firstly, in an area as large as some local authorities, looking only at the overall share of the most deprived data zones may mask pockets of more localised deprivation that impact on supervision rates. Secondly, differences in the criminal business of different courts, the idiosyncrasies of their cultures, the nature and quality of relationships between judges and social workers and the availability of services and resources locally, will all affect sentencing in general and the use of supervisory sanctions, even within one small jurisdiction.

Thinking back to Phelps' (2013b, 2017b) analyses of variations between the US states, this Scottish data would approximate not to state but to county-level variations, driven less by differences in a jurisdiction's laws, institutional structures and policies, and more by how these are mediated and moderated by local demographics, problems, actors and elationships.

Returning to the national picture, Criminal Justice Social Work Statistics[20] (for 2015–2016) profile the ethnicity, age and gender of subject of CPOs in 2011–2012 and in 2015–2016. I have added 2011 census data for comparison:

Table 1. Ethnicity, Age and Gender of Subjects of Community Payback Orders, by Percentage.

	Scottish Population 2011	CPO Population 2011–2012	CPO Population 2015–2016
Ethnicity			
White	96.0	97.5	97.1
Asian	2.7	1.0	1.1
African, Caribbean or Black	0.7	–	0.5
Mixed	0.4	–	–
Other	0.3	0.9	1.0
Age[a]			
16–17	[Age 15–19 = 6.3]	5.7	3.1
18–20		15.7	11.7
21–25	[Age 20–24 = 6.9]	21.7	19.7
26–30	[Age 25–29 = 6.5]	16.3	18.0
31–40	[Age 30–39 = 12.5]	22.8	26.1
Over 40	[Age 40 and above = 51.8]	17.8	21.5
Gender			
Male	48	86.3	84.8
Female	52	13.7	15.2

[a]Note: The age bands differ for the census and the CPO statistics.

As with imprisonment in Scotland, ethnic minorities appear to be *under-represented* in the CPO population, with the exception of the 'other' group (which is mostly made up of people identifying as Arab, Arab Scottish or Arab British). As might be expected, the CPO population is much younger than the general population. Intriguingly, however, it does appear that the population of CPO subjects is becoming older, with declines in the overall share in all age bands below 25 years and increases in all those older than 25 years. There is also a slight increase in the share of CPOs made in respect of women, although the CPO population remains overwhelmingly male. Over the past 10 years or so, somewhat similar age and gender trends are apparent among 'direct sentenced receptions' to Scottish prisons[21]. Men over 30 accounted for 37.6 per cent of all receptions in 2004–2005 and 52.0 per cent of all receptions in 2013–2014. Women accounted for 6.8 per cent of direct sentenced receptions in 2004–2005 and 7.5 per cent in 2013–2014. Unfortunately, no data are available concerning the religious identity or affiliation of CPO subjects. The only available data that hint at their socio-economic situation show that only about a quarter were in employment or full-time education.

In Scotland, people subject to compulsory supervision after release from prison – the nearest equivalent of the US parole population – are described as being on 'statutory throughcare'. This term encompasses people granted discretionary early release on 'life licence' (after having served the 'punishment part' of a life sentence and having been assessed as suitable for release), people granted discretionary early release on 'parole licence' (between one half and two-thirds of the way through a determinate custodial sentence of four years or more), people automatically released early on 'non-parole licence' (at the two-thirds point of a sentence of four years or more) and people on whom judges have imposed various forms of post-release supervision at the point of sentence.

The total population of 'currently supervised' statutory throughcare cases in 2015–2016 stood at 2,436, with 428 on life licence, 445 on parole licence, 339 on non-parole licence, 423 on (judicially imposed) extended sentences, 255 on (judicially imposed) supervised release orders, 86 being supervised as short-term sentence sex offenders and 387 being prisoners recalled to custody for non-compliance. Women made up only 3.8 per cent of this total population and no further data are available about age, religion or employment status.

The Scale of Supervision and Imprisonment in Scotland

In Scotland, as in the USA and many other Western countries, reasons for and consequences of the growth in the prison population have been much debated (Scottish Prisons Commission, 2008). Figure 11 (below) shows the extent of that growth between 1980 and 2014, during which time the prison population rose from under 5,000 to around 8,000. The prison population in Scotland on 12 January 2018 stood at 7,436[22] or about 140 per 100,000 of the population; it remains amongst the highest rates of imprisonment in Western Europe.[23]

Clearly, both the Scottish prison population and imprisonment rate are low in comparison with the USA's prison population in 2015 of 2,173,800 (Kaeble & Glaze, 2016) and rate of 677 per 100,000. Dramatic though it seems to Scottish eyes, the rate of growth of the Scottish prison population after 1980 also pales in comparison with the USA's. Scotland's prison population today is about 1.6 times that of 1980; the USA's prison and jail population is at least 4 times larger.[25]

However, these comparisons are reversed in the case of supervision. Drawing on Phelps' (2013a) analysis, I noted previously that the US probation population increased from 1.1 million to 4.1 million between 1980 and 2010, indicating an increase of about 4 times. Over the same period,

Figure 11. The Scottish Prison Population between 1980 and 2013–2014.[24]

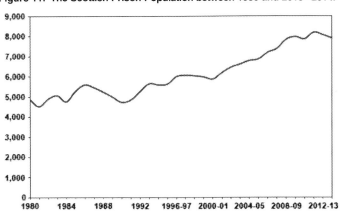

the US parole population increased from around 220,400 to 875,500[26] –
again, an increase of about 4 times. Figure 12 (below) shows the growth
in community sentences in Scotland since 1980. The annual number of
community sentences in Scotland increased from 2,739 (before the introduction of community service) to 15,616 in 2010–2011 (an increase of
almost 6 times) and peaked in 2015–2016 at 18,949 (about 7 times the
number in 1980).

The Scottish numbers quoted previously refer to the number of new
orders, rather than the total caseload of supervisees. Unfortunately, no
criminal justice social work caseload data are collated in Scotland.
However, criminal justice social work statistics show that the *average
length* of a community payback order was 15.6 months in 2015–2016.
On the other hand, since the same person can be subject to more than one
order, there are more orders than separate individuals subject to them; in
2015–2016, there were 19,410 new orders passed on 16,491 separate
individuals. Considering the countervailing effects of these two factors, it
seems that the total number of new orders is a reasonable proxy for the
population on community sentences. On that basis, we can estimate the
community sentence supervision rate in Scotland in 2015–2016 stood at
about 378 per 100,000 population. The total population on probation in

Figure 12. Community Sentences in Scotland since 1980.[27]

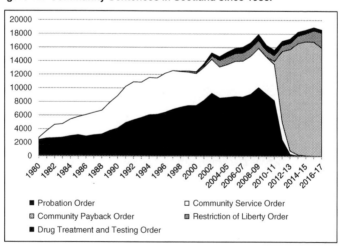

the USA in 2015 stood at 3,789,400, equating to a probation rate of 1,181 per 100,000[28]. Whereas the USA's imprisonment rate is almost 5 times that of Scotland, its probation rate is just over 3 times higher.

In Scotland, as in the USA, changes in the level of recorded crime cannot account for the growth in the size of the populations supervised or imprisoned. Figure 13 (below) plots the growth in the number of community sentences against growth in the average daily prison population and in the number of recorded crimes per 10,000 population. The data suggest that whereas the numbers of community sentences grew with (but faster than) recorded crime until the early 1990s (with crime peaking in 1991), they continued to grow long after crime rates began to decline. In 2015–2016, the ratio of recorded crimes to community sentences was 24:1. In 1980, that ratio had stood at 256:1. Putting this another way, there were more than ten times as many community sentences per crime in 2015–2016 as there had been in 1980.

Historical comparisons of rates of post-release supervision are difficult, both because of a lack of available data and because of significant changes in legislation in the early 1990s (see McNeill & Whyte, 2007), but it is likely that the numbers subject to post release supervision in 1980 would

Figure 13. Number of Community Sentences, Average Daily Prison Population and Recorded Crime per 100,000 Population in Scotland, 1980–2016.[29]

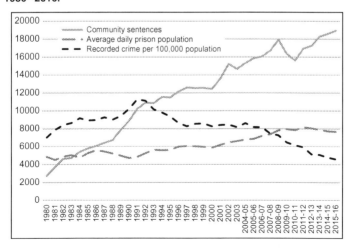

have been very low; by 2015–2016, the population supervised post-release stood at around 2,500.

Table 2 (below) provides data on trends in the post-release supervision population since 2005. The slight increase in the overall numbers conceals a sharp decline in the numbers on (discretionary) parole licence from 876 to 445, and very significant rises in the numbers of recalled prisoners (i.e those who have been returned to custody, their release licences having been revoked), from 85 to 387[30], and in the number of people subject to forms of post-release supervision imposed by judges at the point of sentence, from 334 to 764.

Recalling Phelps' (2013b, 2017b) analysis of the complex and diverse relationships between mass incarceration and mass probation in different US states, the Scottish case presents its own conundrums. Here, both imprisonment and supervision have grown but, unlike in the USA, the growth in supervision far outstrips the growth of imprisonment. One important consideration in the Scottish context is the sustained decline in the use of monetary penalties, which, historically, had been a much more commonly used sanction in the UK jurisdictions than in the USA (see O'Malley, 2009). Munro and McNeill (2010), for example, report that by the 1980s, the use of monetary penalties (mostly fines, but also a much smaller number of compensation orders paid to victims of crime) had declined from a peak of about 80 per cent of all court sentences to 59 per cent by 2008–2009. By 2015–2016, that proportion had dropped even further, to just under 50 per cent[31]. This decline, combined with the lack of any evidence of significant increases in the seriousness of the criminal records of those receiving community sentences, leads to the conclusion that the expansion of supervision in Scotland, as in the USA, has not led to a reduction in the use of custody; rather, as in many European jurisdictions and most states in the USA, it has expanded the extent of penal control (Scottish Prisons Commission, 2008). While the overall rates of imprisonment and supervision in the USA are very much higher, the *rate of growth* in the use of supervisory sanctions is higher in Scotland than in the USA. At the national level in both countries, there is little evidence that these expansions in the populations subject to supervision have reduced the prison population, although there may be quite different reasons for this similar outcome. The reasons for the super-charged growth in supervision in Scotland (and for changes in the forms of supervision to which

Table 2. Number of People Subject to Post-release Supervision (Statutory Throughcare) in Scotland, 2005–2016, by Type.

	Total	Life Licences	Parole Licences	Non-Parole Licences	Judicially imposed post-release Supervision	Recalled Prisoners	Other
2005–2006	2,293	449	876	455	334	85	94
2006–2007	2,314	447	745	483	430	142	67
2007–2008	2,306	417	686	433	449	219	102
2008–2009	2,349	387	667	479	464	206	146
2009–2010	2,365	421	563	466	609	240	66
2010–2011	2,285	435	473	379	599	326	73
2011–2012	2,372	438	479	424	610	368	53
2012–2013	2,431	445	476	403	662	359	86
2013–2014	2,685	467	482	438	889	341	68
2014–2015	2,524	464	457	425	743	364	71
2015–2016	2,436	428	445	339	764	387	73

people are subject) are complex and will be discussed further in the next chapter.

However considerable their differences, in both Scotland and the USA relationships between imprisonment, supervision and inequality clearly exist, even if the forms and extents of inequality in question may differ both between the two countries and between populations in custody or supervised in the community.

CONCLUSION: A 'SUITABLE AMOUNT' OF SUPERVISION?

In this chapter, I have tried to explore and make sense of the scale and social distribution of supervision. Although the analyses offered (particularly of Scotland) raise as many questions as they answer, the two case studies and my brief discussion of supervision's spread across Europe illustrate the need to think carefully and creatively about these questions.

Ultimately, however, there is no fixed standard against which to make a judgment about what counts as 'mass supervision'. For example, Scotland's current supervision rates look massive compared to its past or to most of its Western European neighbours, but they look paltry in comparison with the USA. We have also seen great state-level variations *within* the USA and very different effects of probation growth in different states.

Even setting these problematic comparisons aside, a normative question remains that no statistic can settle: *What is a suitable amount of supervision?* That question, of course, invokes Nils Christie's (2004) discussion of what constitutes *A suitable amount of crime* or of punishment. Christie's (2004) answer remains instructive and pertinent. He suggested, firstly, that if we believe in kindness and forgiveness as values, then we ought to keep 'the institution of penal law' a small one; secondly, that if we believe in keeping civil societies civil, then we should keep the institution of penal law small; and thirdly, that if we value living in cohesive, integrated societies, then we must restrain the growth of that institution.

On the evidence presented in this chapter, it seems obvious that in allowing the rapid expansion of supervision – even when intended to shrink the penal system – we have failed Christie's (2004) test and confirmed Cohen's (1985) fears, at least in Scotland and the USA. This expansion has tended to draw more people into the penal net; and the people caught up have been predominantly marginalised and excluded people living in the most deprived parts of both countries. The greater the extent of their marginalisation and exclusion, the more deeply they have been drawn into the penal net.

That said, we have also uncovered some important clues (primarily from Michelle Phelps' important work) about what it might take to pursue Christie's vision. As well as targeting supervision more carefully, it matters how supervision is constructed and experienced in policy and practice. To borrow Jay-Z's analogies quoted in this chapter's introduction, we can construct supervision as a landmine (or perhaps even a minefield) or as a second chance.

In the next two chapters, we turn to more qualitative examinations of these issues. First, in Chapter 4, we explore how supervision has been justified and legitimated in policy and practice discourses and how it has adapted to changing social conditions. Then, in Chapter 5, we explore how supervision has been experienced by those subject to it.

NOTES

1. See Mawby and Worrall (2014).

2. 'Tag' is the colloquial term in the UK for an anklet worn to allow electronic monitoring of people subject to certain kinds of 'curfew' or 'home detention' or other movement restriction.

3. See https://www.nap.edu/catalog/18613/the-growth-of-incarceration-in-the-united-states-exploring-causes. Accessed on 17 January 2018. An open access summary of the research is available here: https://www.nap.edu/resource/18613/dbasse_087837.pdf. Accessed on 17 January 2018.

4. https://www.nytimes.com/2017/11/17/opinion/jay-z-meek-mill-probation.html. Accessed on 15 January 2018.

5. https://nextcity.org/features/view/parole-and-probation-reform-is-bigger-than-meek-mill. Accessed on 15 January 2018.

6. In the USA and for US writers like Michelle Phelps (see below), the term correctional supervision is often used to refer *both* to prison and/or jail *and* to community-based forms of supervision like probation and

parole. In the UK and Europe (and therefore in my usage), supervision usually refers *only* to supervision in the community.

7. https://www.bjs.gov/content/pub/pdf/cpus15.pdf. Accessed on 15 January 2018.

8. In the USA, a distinction is made between jails and prisons. Jails tend to be county-level facilities holding people awaiting sentence or serving short sentences, usually for misdemeanour offences (up to 2 years). Prisons are state or federal government facilities holding people serving longer sentences arising from felony convictions.

9. Sentenced prison population data from Table 3 in Carson and Anderson (2016) (Retrieved from https://www.bjs.gov/content/pub/pdf/p15.pdf. Accessed on 16 January 2018). Probation and parole population data from Tables 4 and 6 in Kaeble and Bonczar (2016) (Retrieved from https://www.bjs.gov/content/pub/pdf/ppus15.pdf. Accessed on 16 January 2018).

10. The total population of the 50 states of the USA in the 2010 census stood at about 310 million and its land mass was over 3.7M square miles.

11. See http://www.scotlandscensus.gov.uk/ethnicity-identity-language-and-religion. Accessed on 17 January 2018.

12. See http://www.gov.scot/Publications/2015/12/5123/0. Accessed on 17 January 2018. An unpublished internal briefing produced and presented in 2016 (on the prison population at 1st December 2016) suggested that 98.4 per cent of the total prison population was classified as 'White', compared to 96 per cent of the general population.

13. See http://www.gov.scot/Resource/0053/00533870.pdf. Accessed on 21 May 2018, Figure 8.1.

14. See https://www.voluntaryactionfund.org.uk/files/9614/3393/3877/2015-05-29_Evidence_review_update.pdf. Accessed on 17 January 2018.

15. The same unpublished briefing (discussed in footnote 9 above) suggests that amongst the prison population on 1 December 2016, 19.7 per cent identified as Catholic, suggesting a continued narrowing of this gap.

16. See http://www.brin.ac.uk/2011/catholics-in-scottish-prisons/. Accessed on 17 January 2018.

17. I'm grateful to Peter Conlong of the Scottish Government's Justice Analytical Services for providing this information.

18. See http://www.gov.scot/Resource/0051/00510709.pdf, page 4. Accessed on 18 January 2018.

19. The data are derived from http://www.gov.scot/Topics/Statistics/ Browse/Crime-Justice/Datasets/SocialWork/CPOs. Accessed on 18 January 2018.

20. See http://www.gov.scot/Resource/0051/00514220.pdf, accessed 17th January 2018.

21. See http://www.gov.scot/Publications/2015/12/5123/3#ch31, accessed on 17 January 2018.

22. See http://www.sps.gov.uk/Corporate/Information/SPSPopulation. aspx, accessed on 19 January 2018.

23. For comparisons of imprisonment rates, see: http://www.prisonstu- dies.org/world-prison-brief-data accessed 19th January 2018.

24. Reproduced from http://www.gov.scot/Publications/2015/12/5123/ 3#ch31, accessed on 17 January 2018.

25. See https://sentencingproject.org/wp-content/uploads/2016/01/Trends- in-US-Corrections.pdf, accessed on 19 January 2018.

26. See https://felonvoting.procon.org/view.resource.php?resourceID= 004353, accessed on 19 January 2018.

27. The figures for 'probation' here include small numbers of more rarely used community disposals including Supervised Attendance Orders, Anti- Social Behaviour Orders and Community Reparation Orders. Figures for 1980-1982 are taken from http://www.gov.scot/Resource/Doc/933/ 0113714.pdf; 1983-1987 taken from http://www.gov.scot/Resource/Doc/ 933/0113781.pdf; 1988-1994 taken from http://www.gov.scot/Resource/ Doc/933/0122171.PDF; 1994-2003 taken from http://www.gov.scot/ Publications/2005/03/30152104/21260; 2004-2011 taken from http:// www.gov.scot/Publications/2012/11/5336/13; 2011-2017 taken from

http://www.gov.scot/Publications/2018/02/7427/31; all accessed on 1 June 2018.

28. See https://www.bjs.gov/content/pub/pdf/cpus15.pdf, Table 1, accessed on 19 January 2018. The probation rate was calculated based on an estimate of the total US population in 2015 of 320.9M.

29. These data on community sentences were gathered from the sources noted in fn. 28 above. The partial data on the average daily prison population were taken from http://www.gov.scot/Publications/2015/12/5123/6, accessed on 1 June 2018. The data on recorded crime are taken from http://www.gov.scot/Publications/2016/09/2960/332798, accessed on 1 June, 2018. The prison population data were supplied directly by Justice Analytical Services.

30. This is accounted for (at least in part) by rising (and accumulating) numbers of people subject to post-release supervision under the Prisoners and Criminal Proceedings (Scotland) Act 1993. It does not show that the *rate* of recall is increasing that would require a different kind of analysis.

31. See http://www.gov.scot/Topics/Statistics/Browse/Crime-Justice/ Datasets/DatasetsCrimProc/CPtab16, accessed on 19 January 2018. The decline in financial penalties may be related to increased use of 'direct measures' by the Police and fines issued in lieu of prosecution by the Procurators Fiscal.

CHAPTER 4

LEGITIMATING MASS SUPERVISION

WE'RE NOT HERE TO BUILD THE COMMUNITY,
WE'RE HERE TO PROTECT IT

Pauline noticed too late that Norm had directed her to the seat furthest from the door of the meeting room, placing himself between her and the

Figure 14. Untitled 5.

exit. A familiar ploy. There was going to be no escape until he was finished, unless she went over or through him ....

'Pauline', he began, 'you know how much I respect your skills and experience, right?'

She waited for the inevitable 'But'.

'But things have changed and you need to change with them', he continued, passing her the print-out of her appraisal score.

'This sort of performance just won't do'.

She sighed.

'Norm, tell me this: How am I supposed to help the guy if I don't get to know him and what makes him tick. That takes time.'

'That's the problem right there, Pauline'.

Norm lent back in his seat and smiled his patronising, faux-patient smile, pausing for dramatic effect.

*'You're still labouring under the illusion that your job is to **help** these people. It's not. Let me put this in the simplest possible terms: Your job is to stop them from reoffending – at least until their good behaviour triggers our results-related payment. I know what you're thinking but it's not about profit for profit's sake; I want to invest that revenue in getting better and better at protecting communities'.*

She couldn't resist: 'What? You mean communities where people don't have time for each other, don't know each other and don't help each other?'

Norm's face coloured a little, his fixed smile starting to look like a rictus grin, but he retained his composure:

*'Pauline, please. You know me better than that. I value community as much as the next individual, but we are not here to **build** the community, we are here to **protect** it.'*

The slow-spoken bold-print was starting to make Pauline's eyeballs itch.

'And we need to do that as time-efficiently as possible. We need to reduce costs and maximise returns. We owe it to the taxpayers. They don't want their money wasted on tea and sympathy. We're here to control and challenge behaviour that threatens communities. And we're here to make offenders pay back for their crimes. Yes, it's great if we can also improve and develop them as people, but the thing is Pauline, there's really no convincing evidence that 'help' is all that helpful... at least not in reducing offending.'

Pauline couldn't believe that Norm was putting air-quotes around 'help'.

Trying not to rise to the bait, she settled in for the duration. She determined to apply her apparently outmoded appreciative perspective to the significant challenge of understanding the genesis of Norm's distorted worldview. The sad thing – the dangerous thing – was that he genuinely seemed to believe this shit.

INTRODUCTION

Pauline and Norm see supervision somewhat differently. Although both claim to want to make communities safer, Pauline believes that the best route to that outcome is through engaging Joe and helping him address whatever issues and problems lie behind his predicament. For her, reducing the likelihood of him reoffending is a by-product of helping him rebuild a good life within the community. Norm's vision is somewhat narrower; first, Joe's behaviour needs to be controlled, then it needs to be challenged. He should also payback for his crime. But the main goal is that he shouldn't reoffend – especially during the contracted period that matters most to the supervising agency. Public accountability matters to Norm; not just in protecting the community but also in using its limited resources efficiently.

These different visions – and the simple exchange above – might be analysed philosophically in the sense that the two visions rely upon somewhat different justifications of the harms and threats that community-based supervision imposes on Joe. Although the justification of punishment has been a source of much debate for philosophers of punishment (Canton, 2017), there has been surprisingly little work until recently on the normative justification of *supervision* (but see Hayes, 2015; van Zyl Smit, Snacken, & Hayes, 2015). As I noted in Chapter 1, this neglect may arise in part from assuming that subjects of supervision have been dealt with leniently or mercifully or even that they have avoided punishment altogether. The next chapter, which explores the lived experience of supervision, aims in part to remedy these misunderstandings.

This chapter, however, is *not* concerned with justifying supervision philosophically; rather, it concerns the legitimation of supervision. Though legitimacy is a normative concept, I use the term *legitimation* to direct our analysis towards social and political processes in which certain discourses and narratives are used to generate, sustain or extend support for criminal justice institutions and practices. As I argued towards the end of Chapter 2 (following Goodman et al., 2017 and Page, 2013), the penal field is a site of contestation in which different institutions and actors struggle for and employ material resources (finance, infrastructure, capacity), symbolic resources (status and prestige), social resources (connections and alliances) and cultural resources (knowledge and skills). These struggles are contested on many fronts – in the crucible of public debate, in newspaper columns and other media, in Parliaments and Committees, in management meetings, in professional associations and trade unions, even in conversations among colleagues like the one between Pauline and Norm. One of the painful lessons learned by advocates of supervision is that, to come out on top in these contests, it helps to have a compelling narrative or set of narratives; narratives that, recalling Durkheim, appeal to prevailing public and political sensibilities; that, recalling Foucault, secure power through the ways that they construct and use knowledge; and that, recalling Marx, reflect or serve economic imperatives or, more narrowly, the interests of the ruling class.

Both in laying out some of the theoretical or conceptual resources for making sense of supervision in Chapter 2, and in analysing its scale and social distribution in Chapter 3, I have already argued that the influence on the penal field of broader cultural, political and social developments is contingent; these forces shape possibilities and probabilities, but the closer we look – the more fine-grained our examination of penalty – the more we see evidence of different dynamics producing different effects. In this chapter, I focus on just one extended case study of the struggle to legitimate supervision. Partly to provide some continuity but also to analyse the case that I know best, the focus is on Scotland. The Scottish case, however, should be of wider interest, not least because the Scottish penal system is sometimes characterised as being unusual in the persistence of a welfarist ethos, even in the late-modern era (see, e.g. McAra, 1999). If it is true that penal welfarism has survived late modernity in Scotland, then understanding why and how this happened is of obvious importance (McAra, 2005).

Before focusing on the Scottish case, however, and to provide some conceptual resources for that case study, I return briefly to some earlier work with my colleagues Shadd Maruna and Gwen Robinson (Robinson,

Maruna and McNeill, 2013; Robinson & McNeill, 2015), work that explored how probation in the UK and the USA has somehow not just survived but thrived in recent decades, despite its apparently perennial struggle for legitimacy.

THE PROBATION LEGITIMACY PARADOX: THRIVING IN ADVERSITY

At the start of our 2013 chapter, we set out the terms of the paradox we were trying to unpick in the following terms:

> *Things were looking awfully bleak for probation at the turn of the last century. Despite being around for nearly 100 years, probation in the United Kingdom, for instance, was said to be 'uncomfortable, threatened, unsure of its role, and not at all confident of its social or political credibility' [...] (Garland, 1997, p. 3). Similar perceptions led to a series of high-profile conferences and reports on the state of probation in the United States [...]. (Robinson et al., 2013, p. 321)*

Although readers of Chapter 2 will understand why a quintessentially penal – welfarist institution (Garland, 1985) might feel the chill of the late-modern *Culture of Control* (Garland, 2001) or the *New Punitiveness* (Pratt et al., 2005), those readers who persisted through Chapter 3 might well be puzzled. How could it be that this apparently 'failing' penal institution, at the same time, was expanding rapidly in both the USA and the UK jurisdictions and extending its reach into new countries?

Robinson et al. (2013) sought to solve this puzzle by exploring how those institutions through which 'community sanctions and measures'[1] are delivered had evolved in late modernity, to adapt and survive in a climate that seemed profoundly hostile. Drawing on analyses like those of Hannah-Moffat (2005) and Hutchinson's (2006), we argued that developments in the penal field have often been characterised by the braiding of 'old' and 'new' forms and functions. Rather than displacing it, the new tends to grow *through* and become entwined with the old, sometimes feeding on it. Our analysis identified four, sometimes inter-connected, adaptations through which, probation had more or less successfully adapted to new social conditions, labelling these 'managerial', 'punitive', 'rehabilitative' and 'reparative'.

The *managerial adaptation* of supervision reflects broader processes of managerialisation and systemisation within criminal justice (and across the public sector). Hence, the systemic role of probation services came to the fore, most clearly in terms of their assumed potential to offer progressive 'alternatives to custody', aiming to reduce imprisonment or at least moderate its growth. This diversionary systemic goal was linked to an associated shift in emphasis from the pursuit of *outcomes* (like reduced crime or rehabilitated 'offenders') to *outputs* (like achieving 'key performance indicators'). Probation and parole agencies also embarked on inter-agency partnerships with others in the system in pursuit of 'risk management' or 'offender management' or 'public protection'.

If the managerial adaptation was instrumental, the *punitive adaptation* had a more expressive or symbolic quality. Turning away from their previous identity as an expression of welfarism, late-modern supervisory sanctions adapted to become *and to be seen to be* punitive (at least in some jurisdictions). Allied to the need to deliver 'alternatives to custody' referred to above, agencies of supervision aimed to enhance their credibility with judges and with the wider public. For some policymakers and professional leaders, that seemed to require the sharpening of supervision's punitive 'bite'.

The *rehabilitative adaption* treaded a well-established path in seeking to reframe supervision's traditional rehabilitative raison d'être, encouraged by some promising new research findings and by re-assessments of existing evidence about rehabilitation. Responding to the new penal climate, advocates back-pedalled on aspirations to restore 'offenders' to full citizenship and promoted instead rehabilitation's capacity to manage and reduce risks and thus to protect the apparently more nervous, fearful and perhaps vindictive 'law-abiding' public of late modernity. Rehabilitation now had both managerial aspects (in the use or risk assessment tools) and expressive qualities; the new 'offending behaviour programmes' were consistent with a wider project of 'responsibilisation' (holding individuals to account); and their common pursuit of 'victim empathy' or 'values enhancement' suggested some moralising aspects.

Finally, Robinson et al. (2013) discussed concerned the *reparative adaption* of supervisory sanctions. Indeed, the development of 'community service' or 'unpaid work' might lay claim to being perhaps the most common and most successful innovation in supervisory sanctions since the 1970s (perhaps since the establishment of probation). However, the goals of community service – and its practices – have rarely been defined solely in reparative or restitutive terms. Robinson et al. (2013) suggest that community service has been 'all things to all people' – sometimes advocated for its punitive bite, sometimes for its rehabilitative effects, sometimes for its re-integrative potential.

Contestation, Adaptation and Legitimation

Each of these four adaptations offered (and continues to offer) certain kinds of resources to supervision's advocates. These include, for example, claims about and uses of the cultural capital represented in particular forms of knowledge (like knowledge about 'what works' and its associated tools and technologies), the symbolic capital founded in associating supervision with expressive punishment or with 'protection', the social capital secured by linking agencies of supervision with other justice agencies in pursuit of common managerial goals and the economic capital promised by the efficient and effective use of public funds.

In assessing the outcome of these struggles for legitimation, Robinson et al. (2013) drew on Wodahl et al.'s (2011) distinction between *pragmatic legitimacy*, which rests in the ability to meet the needs of stakeholders; *moral legitimacy*, which relates to the pursuit of goals that conform to societal values; and *cognitive legitimacy*, which arises only when an institution's actions and functions are so woven into the social fabric that they 'simply make sense' in such a way that 'alternatives become unthinkable' (Suchman, 1995, p. 583). In sum, we argued that, while each of the adaptations could be understood as efforts to maximise supervision's pragmatic or moral appeal, none had delivered *cognitive legitimacy* or taken-for-grantedness. Certainly, in comparison with the prison, supervision continued to seem insecure.

Even so, we moderated our somewhat pessimistic conclusion in the following terms:

> *In a very important sense, for all their travails, the position of*
> *CSM [community sanctions and measures] may be symbolically*

fragile but materially secure, expressively insufficient but instrumentally necessary. CSM will survive because they must; we could not afford to do (punishment) without them'. (Robinson et al., 2013, pp. 335–336)

In other words, even in the absence of cognitive legitimacy, supervision had become too big to fail. Penal expansion itself had pragmatically secured supervision as a socio-penal institution, even if it left the form and content of supervision vulnerable to continuous reformation in the image of changing penal sensibilities.

To delve more deeply into these processes of continuous reformation in pursuit of legitimacy, and to better equip us to think about how supervision's forms and functions have evolved (and may evolve in future), I turn now to the Scottish case.

SUPERVISION IN SCOTLAND: WHERE REDUCTIONISM PRODUCED EXPANSION

Introduction

Scotland has a relatively long history of provision of prisoner aftercare and of probation services, dating back to the nineteenth century. But before exploring this history, it makes sense to begin with a brief account of these two forms of penal supervision[2] as they exist in Scotland today, and with some information about their uses.

After a successful prosecution, Scottish judges (called 'sheriffs' in our intermediate Sheriff Courts) can impose a limited number of different community sanctions, but these nonetheless permit and provide for a wide range of different forms of intervention. Since the passage of the Criminal Justice and Licensing Act 2010, the main community sanction is the community payback order (CPO). Despite its name (which might imply a central focus on unpaid work or community service), the CPO replaced not just community service orders but also probation orders and supervised attendance orders (an alternative to fines). The CPO, like the community order in England and Wales, is a generic community sentence, in as much as there are many possible conditions that a judge can attach to it. These include conditions requiring people to submit to supervision, to undertake unpaid work (or other activities) and/or to participate in offending behaviour programmes, mental health treatment and alcohol or drug treatment. Requirements related to residence, conduct or compensation may also be imposed. The only other community sanctions currently available are drug treatment and testing orders (DTTOs) and restriction of liberty orders (RLOs) (which impose electronically monitored curfews).

Table 3 (below) outlines the numbers of requirements imposed in CPOs that commenced in 2015–2016, and the percentage of new orders containing each kind of requirement. By far, the most prevalent requirements are those related to unpaid work (77.8 per cent) and supervision (51.0 per cent). The proportions of orders with explicitly rehabilitative elements, for example, related to offending behaviour programmes or treatment for mental health or substance use issues, are perhaps surprisingly low. That said, 'offender supervision' requirements do entail the one-to-one casework that is the traditional locus of rehabilitative work in Scotland (more of which below).

People leaving Scottish prisons can be released under a range of different forms of release licence. Since the passage of the Prisoners and

Table 3. Requirements of Community Payback Orders commenced in 2015–2016.[3]

Type of Requirement	Number	Percentage of All New Orders With This Requirement
Offender supervision	9,912	51.0
Compensation	591	3.0
Unpaid work or other activity	15,102	77.8
Programme	1,031	5.3
Residence	30	0.2
Mental health treatment	43	0.2
Drug treatment	166	0.9
Alcohol treatment	264	1.4
Conduct	1,090	5.6
Total number of requirements	28,229	100.0
Total number of orders	19,410	–

Criminal Proceeding Act 1993, all those who have served sentences of over four years are released on parole licence (if they succeed in gaining early release between the halfway and two-thirds points in their sentences) or on non-parole licence (if they are released automatically at the two-thirds point). More recently, the Prisoners (Control of Release) Act 2015 removed automatic release on non-parole licence at the two-thirds point, extending the maximum period that can be served in custody up to six months before the expiry of the sentence.

The standard terms of parole and non-parole licences are similar, requiring licensees to 'be of good behaviour' (that is, not to offend) and to submit to social work supervision for the remainder of their sentence, as well as limiting their mobility in various ways. As I noted in Chapter 3, other forms of post-release supervision can also be imposed by judges at the point of sentence – including on people subject to shorter prison terms – usually where there are significant concerns about public safety. Those who have served life sentences are subject to parole licence conditions for life (although the conditions related to social work supervision can be lifted after 10 years).

Of course, while the legal scaffold around supervision and the extent of its use are important, neither tells us much about the *character* of these sanctions as experienced by those subject to them. That character and those experiences are also influenced by the institutional and organisational contexts in which the practice of supervision is located. Importantly for present purposes, these institutions both reflect and are influenced by the ways in which they seek legitimation.

In Scotland, community sanctions are implemented almost exclusively by professionally qualified *social workers* working within and for *local* authorities (although a wider network of practitioners in state, private and third sector organisations also plays important roles). The twin commitments to social work and to localism have been and remain important in shaping debates about supervision in Scotland, even if, as we will see in the following section, both have been regularly contested. Certainly, Scottish criminal justice social workers have tended to disavow any expressly punitive intentions; as we will see in the following section , their central preoccupation has been rehabilitation (see McGuinness, 2014). Whether and to what extent their dispositions and intentions moderate or influence the penal bite of supervision is, however, a question to which I will return in the next chapter (see also McNeill, 2009).

Foundations and Early Development of Scottish Probation

Although voluntary societies created to provide aid to 'discharged prisoners' have a slightly longer history,[4] the limited available sources for probation history in Scotland suggest that probation emerged in the context of Victorian and Edwardian concerns about the 'demoralising' effects of imprisonment and in particular its adverse effects on *civic* well-being (McNeill, 2005). Unusually perhaps, the origins of Glasgow's local probation service do not appear to have been directly associated with religious ideals or church organisations. Rather, they were linked to public concern about the excessive use of custody. This narrative – about the utility of probation as a means of *penal reductionism* – as we will see, is perhaps the central recurring theme in the history of supervision in Scotland.

At the turn of the twentieth century, Glasgow (then known as the 'second city of the [British] Empire') faced very high rates of imprisonment for fine default. A brief history of the local probation service initiated to address this problem was published in 1955 by the Glasgow Probation Area Committee (City of Glasgow, 1955). It suggests that probation emerged largely because of the efforts of a local councillor (Bailie John Bruce Murray) who had visited the USA to explore the operations of various probation and parole services there. On 14 December 1905, a special committee of the Glasgow Corporation recommended that the Chief Constable select police officers for each District Police Court to act, in plain clothes, as probation officers of the court. By 1919, there were 11 (male) police officers working as probation officers and five women probation officers.

The Glasgow service's 1955 history presents a narrative of inevitable progress through social work professionalisation towards a new consensus about 'modern' probation approaches. But recent work by Christine Kelly (2017) paints a somewhat different picture. Through a careful analysis of evidence submitted to a committee of inquiry appointed in 1925, chaired by Sir George Morton, K.C. and reporting in 1928, Kelly has revealed the existence of very lively debate at that time about 'the treatment and training of young people and young offenders requiring care and protection'

(such was the inquiry's remit). It was the Morton Report (1928) that proposed the national organisation of Scottish probation, clearing the way for
the 1931 Probation Act.

For the first time, Kelly (2017) provides a comprehensive picture of the
various arrangements for probation services across Scotland at that time.
The police-probation arrangement in the Glasgow service was replicated
only in one or two other towns. Others used a hybrid arrangement, combining police probation officers and volunteers and some (like Edinburgh)
relied mostly on volunteers supported by a small number of paid staff of
philanthropic societies. In some areas, only one or two part-time officers
were drawn from religious or philanthropic groups. Other local areas
('burghs') had no probation officers at all.

Most importantly for present purposes, the evidence presented to the
Morton Committee suggests very lively contestation of the best model for
probation and, relatedly, of the sorts of people and skills required to do
the work well. Some strongly advocated the use of volunteers who, they
argued, were better placed to offer the 'human touch' or a 'bond of friend-
ship'. By way of illustration, Kelly (2017) discusses the evidence of
Mr Stevenson (a businessman and an Edinburgh-based volunteer probation officer). Though his submission sometimes implies a degree of condes-
cension towards his charges, it is also refreshingly irreverent in places and
is underpinned by what Kelly (2017, p. 178) describes as:

> carefree enthusiasm [...] His ideal method in helping a young
> offender is to 'jolly him along until he begins to take a pride in
> himself', appealing to his 'sporting side' to encourage him to
> 'play the game'.

Stevenson's approach was not just generous and kind-hearted; it was
practical too – for example, in using his business contacts to find employment for his charges.

Illustrating the opposing view, Kelly (2017) cites evidence from John
Bruce Murray (Glasgow's probation pioneer) in which he argued that
police probation officers could combine discipline, care and professionalism more readily than volunteers, and, importantly, that the Glasgow
police probation scheme offered a more secure financial and organisational
model for probation's development. Murray's view did not ultimately hold
sway. In the Morton Report (1928), the committee argued that the

position of police officers as authoritarian agents of the criminal justice system undermined their capacity to win the trust and confidence of probationers.

Though trust and confidence were seen as critical to the success of probation, Kelly (2017) argues that this may have been less to do with ideals of treatment or social casework and more to do with a certain view of the qualities of moral (and sometimes spiritual) character and social conscience that marked out a good officer (on which see Buchanan [1934, 1936] for the views of Glasgow's then Chief Probation Officer). Kelly's (2017) careful archival work suggests that my own previous characterisation of the 1931 Act as marking a shift 'from supervision to treatment' (McNeill, 2005) may have been unduly influenced by the version of probation development that suited the writers of the Glasgow history (City of Glasgow, 1955).

Indeed, an oral history study of Scottish probation in the 1960s undertaken in 2008–2009, confirms that social work or treatment ideals had taken only a tenuous hold on probation practice even by that time (McNeill, 2009, 2011). That British Academy-funded study was inspired by an initial meeting with Vera Hiddleston, who had established professional probation training in Scotland in the 1960s. On the advice of a colleague, I had sent her a copy of my 2005 article in draft form, and she invited me to her home to share what remained of her archive of probation training material and to talk about my article. She consented to the audio-recording of our discussion which took place in September 2004.

Regarding the debate over practice approaches, and with typical acuity, Ms Hiddleston remarked:

> I was wondering [...] who actually wrote this thing that you had based, you know, most of your research on because that interests me. I thought 'Who actually wrote that?' because it was, as you say in your paper, sort of pushing the idea of treatment which was by no means fully accepted by the Probation Service at the time. But the person who wrote it clearly was saying this is the [...] 'in-thing' or believed in it.

In other words, the Glasgow history was itself a case-study of how certain kinds of legitimating narratives come to be written and disseminated. She went on to discuss the two camps that existed in the 1960s. The advocates of social casework or treatment approaches were, broadly speaking, more academic in their backgrounds and interests, and were influenced by a small number of dynamic and influential women in the social work field (like Ms Hiddleston herself), some of whom had training and experience in psychiatric social work. Ms Hiddleston described the opposing camp thus:

> It was almost like, you know, the Boys' Brigade[5] kind of approach to things. Going on to the history [...] I think it was very significant that it was the Glasgow police that started it off and that is really, you know, that was the background to it all. And there was still this sense of how the police would see things, you know, doing the right thing and obeying what you had to obey.

These exchanges encouraged me, with the help Beth Weaver, to develop an oral history of Scottish probation in the 1960s; we interviewed 12 former probationers and 13 probation staff or educators.

The accounts provided by officers and educators tended to confirm the existence of the two camps that Vera Hiddleston had discussed. However, most of the former officers reported that, most of the time, their approach was neither disciplinarian nor 'treatment' focused. Rather, it was intensely practical. Indeed, although they were salaried professionals, their approach very much echoed that which Mr Stevenson had reported to the Morton Committee in the 1920s; they tried to get to know, get alongside and encourage their young charges, and they tried to work in their neighbourhood 'patch' with and through parents, beat police officers, local churches and local businesses to develop networks of both supervision and practical support. Some used former probationers to informally mentor their current charges. Although the diagnostic model informed their approaches to assessment, treatment – in the psychological or psychodynamic sense – was generally reserved for a small proportion of the caseload comprised of adults with mental health problems. As one remarked, 'you never saw yourself as a person with a magic wand but you saw yourself as the shepherd, you know?'.

Although there may be a rosy glow of self-justification in these former officers' accounts of their work, several of the probationers to whom we spoke credited their officers with providing life-changing support at key moments in their lives. Some recognised the benefits of the constraints that supervision imposed, hard though they were to accept at the time. But a few others related painful experiences of what they perceived as an illegitimate exercise of authority; two of the 12 reported verbal, physical or sexual abuse at the hands of probation officers (see McNeill, 2009).

In her efforts to steer the development of Scottish probation towards a more professionalised and scientific approach, Vera Hiddleston travelled to California, visiting the probation service in Los Angeles and also meeting with Elliot Studt, the pioneering social worker and first women governor of a men's prison in the USA. However, despite her travels, her energies and her best efforts, she recognised that probation education alone could not change probation culture; and that recognition made her a supporter of the move to disband Scottish probation services, integrating them with generic social work departments under the provisions of the Social Work (Scotland) Act 1968.

THE INSTITUTIONALISATION OF 'SOCIAL WORK WITH OFFENDERS'

The drive to reform the organisation of probation in Scotland, which eventually led to the Social Work (Scotland) Act 1968 can be traced through the decades following the Second World War. The Criminal Justice (Scotland) Act 1949 created new duties for probation services and their officers, including the provision of 'social reports' on those aged 17–21 years and pre-trial reports on children (previously provided by education authorities). Indeed, a Scottish Office promotional booklet, *The Probation Service in Scotland: Its Objects and its Organisation* (1947) shows that, by then, the courts used probation orders predominantly for children rather than adults. By 1945, the use of probation with juveniles had risen to 2,557 of 18,983 court disposals (13.5 per cent) but the use of probation for adults had fallen to just 513 of 58,764 disposals (0.9 per cent). No adult probation orders at all were made in 1945 in 19 of the 51 probation areas.

It is not clear precisely how or why probation had become, in effect, a measure for juveniles, but it seems plausible that it was partly accounted for by the increasing 'feminisation' of the service, particularly during the war years (when many male officers were engaged in war service). More

generally, Scottish judges may have seen supposedly caring or rehabilitative responses to offending (however 'scientific') as more fitting for children than adults.

Nonetheless, and evidencing the durability of reductionist aspirations
for probation, later versions of *The Probation Service in Scotland* (revised
and re-issued in 1955 and in 1961) attempted to promote the use of probation, especially with adults. These later documents offered guidance on
the kinds of cases for which probation might be appropriate, that is in the
middle ground between 'minor offences committed by those with clean
records and good home backgrounds, and grave offences where there
would be an undue risk in allowing the offender to remain at liberty'
(Scottish Office, 1955, 1961, p. 6).

These booklets also reveal an increasingly modern and recognisable
pre-occupation with performance (perhaps even a proto-managerialism),
albeit expressed in terms of the numbers of probation disposals rather
than the outcomes of supervision. Although the absolute numbers of
orders rose unevenly from 3,666 in 1951 to 4,558 in 1959, probation's
share of the increasing number of disposals in the same period declined
from 3.8 per cent to 2.9 per cent. Probation continued to be a much more
popular disposal option for juveniles than adults; the proportion of juvenile cases involving crimes (as opposed to less serious offences) leading to
probation orders fluctuated between 26.7 per cent and 34.5 per cent
during 1951–1959, and the corresponding figures for adults varied
between 4.3 per cent and 8.0 per cent.

The publication of the Kilbrandon Report (1964) revolutionised juvenile justice in Scotland by arguing that courts were not the best places to
deal children in trouble. Kilbrandon's most significant and enduring legacy
is the Scottish Children's Hearings system, a system that firmly established
the pre-eminence of a welfare-based approach to children in trouble predi-
cated on social education principles (Moore & Whyte, 1998). More significantly in the context of this discussion, the report also led, through the
Social Work (Scotland) Act 1968, to the integration of probation services
within the new generic social work departments. Although this could be
read as a logical extension to *adults* in trouble of Kilbrandon's welfarist,
social educational approach, some of the respondents in my oral history
study suggested that the disbandment of the probation service was (also) a
pragmatic manoeuvre occasioned both by the low numbers of adult

probation cases and by the need for the comparatively well-trained probation staff to join and shape the new social work departments.

With respect to the legitimation of social work supervision, the Kilbrandon reforms, in fact, provided *both* continuity and change. The continuity resided in the retention of both an essentially reductionist approach (e.g. with respect to children and young people, the 1968 Act enshrined a 'no unnecessary order' principle of minimum necessary intervention) and a refreshed commitment to rehabilitation. This refreshment of rehabilitation was perhaps subtle: Kilbrandon's philosophy argued for *social* education rather than a treatment model that understood the causes of offending mainly in terms of individual or familial pathologies (cf. Johnstone, 1996; McNeill, 2014). Even if the evidence of the oral history is that the treatment model had never been fully embraced in practice, the Glasgow history (City of Glasgow, 1955) suggests that it was being used to legitimate probation's claims to professional status and public support. The continuity here lies in the attempt to generate professional status and recognition (and thus symbolic capital) by commandeering and deploying evolving forms of social scientific knowledge (and the cultural capital it represented).

Nonetheless, the dissolution of Scottish probation services represented a major organisational rupture and proved to be traumatic. By the late 1970s, academics, judges and professionals were expressing concerns about the viability of criminal justice services within generic social work departments (Marsland, 1977, Moore, 1978, Nelson, 1977). For a variety of reasons, the social work profession and the new social work organisations had become preoccupied with and defined by the challenges of tackling child abuse and promoting children's welfare.

In the 1980s, crime was continuing to rise and Scottish prisons were in crisis. Prison overcrowding, riots and suicides in the 1980s compelled political and professional leaders to take action. Unlike in some other Anglophone jurisdictions, the problem in Scotland was not cast around *ideas and practices* of rehabilitation and their apparent ineffectiveness (see Allen, 1981; Martinson, 1974); rather, it concerned the near complete failure to *implement* these ideas and practices in the penal system.

In 1989, in response to this crisis of penal legitimacy, the Scottish Office introduced ring-fenced central government funding for most social work services in the criminal justice system. This was interpreted by some as recognition that services had fallen into a state of comparative neglect, despite the successful piloting and then rolling out of community service by 1979 (see McIvor, 2010).

In this context, it is not surprising to detect the emergence of a new *managerial* narrative. However, as I have noted previously, in Scotland (and perhaps elsewhere), managerialism's preoccupation with systems, efficiency, outputs and outcomes has a much longer history than we tend to assume. From its inception, supervision was intended to produce both *systems effects* (on sentencing and imprisonment) and *individual effects* (on those subject to it) – and both policymakers and practitioners have always been concerned to gather evidence about and to analyse these effects.

In the late 1980s and early 1990s (just as in the 1900s), the prisons crisis meant that the concern with delivering systems effects became predominant. The new central government funding was unequivocally an investment in a reductionist strategy. Indeed, the now centrally funded (but still locally organised) 'criminal justice social work' services looked set to follow the 'alternatives to custody' model that had taken root in England and Wales at that time (see Robinson, 2016). The first objective of the *National Objectives and Standards* was 'to enable a reduction in the incidence of custody… where it is used for lack of a suitable, available community based social work disposal' (Social Work Services Group, 1991a, Section 12.1). However, unlike in England and Wales, supervision in Scotland was not required to negotiate the ideological traverse towards punishment in the community. Rather, a focus on *reducing reoffending* was seen as critical to its credibility, on which reduction in the use of custody was thought to depend. Both reducing reoffending *and* reducing the use of custody were to be achieved (as in the mid-twentieth century) by the appliance of science, but now packaged in the form of 'what works?' research (see Social Work Services Group, 1991b). The novel development was the introduction of managerialised discipline (e.g. standardised procedures and interventions, and performance measurement) through which these 'enhanced' techniques could be applied. Late-modern managerialism had indeed arrived in Scottish penalty, but on at least one authoritative account, that managerialism was perhaps intended to *enhance* both professionalism and welfarism rather than to displace them (McAra, 1999).

By the mid-to-late 1990s, there was a growing emphasis on public protection in the UK jurisdictions,[6] coincided with the introduction of significantly higher risk populations to social work caseloads, partly because of new arrangements for the post-release supervision of long-term prisoners (under the Prisoners and Criminal Proceedings Act 1993). As in other jurisdictions (see, e.g. Boone, 2016), scandals occasioned by serious further offences by people subject to supervision played a part in provoking this change. Subsequently, advances in both the rhetoric and the practice of risk management and public protection were rapid (see McIvor & McNeill, 2007; Weaver & McNeill, 2010). For example, in *The Tough Option* (Scottish Office, 1998), it was declared both that 'Our paramount aim is public safety' and that the pursuit of reductions in the use of custody 'must be consistent with the wider objective of promoting public and community safety' (Section 1.2.3). *The Tough Option* also revisited the organisational arrangements for criminal justice social work. Although it raised the possibility of centralising criminal justice social work services, ultimately it led merely to the creation of mechanisms for cooperation across local authority areas in a series of 'groupings'. But this was not to be the last time that re-organisation was to become a policy preoccupation.

Supervision and Scottish Devolution

Although it led to the dissolution of the Scottish Parliament, the terms of the Act of Union in 1707 (which established the United Kingdom under a single monarch) preserved the separate Scottish legal system. However, all laws related to Scotland (and to Scottish criminal justice) had to be passed by the UK Parliament at Westminster.

'Law and order' became a key site of UK political debate in the 1980s but Scottish criminal justice was somewhat protected by its unusual constitutional position. In effect, a quasi-colonial administration through the Scottish Office of the UK Government lacked both (UK) parliamentary time and (Scottish) political and constitutional authority to drive through populist punitive reforms. Indeed, Scotland's odd constitutional position meant that Scottish criminal justice had not suffered the effects of the 'crisis of state sovereignty' that Garland (1996, 2001) had identified in his discussion of the UK and the USA. In the 1980s and 1990s, the Scottish crisis was constitutional. It was not so much that the British state, under the pressures of globalisation was failing and therefore seeking to 'bulk up' its legitimacy by flexing its muscles in the penal sphere. Rather, from the perspective of many Scots, the British state was *already* a failing state in political and constitutional terms. The central issue was not crime; it was politics. More specifically, it was the inability of UK political institutions to reflect and represent the values and aspirations of the Scottish electorate. Consequently, crime and punishment had relatively low political salience during the period when centre-left Scotland was struggling with the depredations of Thatcherism. In that context, civil servants, senior law officers and a variety of professional and academic experts were able to maintain a constraining influence upon penal policymaking (McAra, 2008).

When, in 1999, the Scottish Parliament was restored (following a 1997 referendum vote in favour of devolution), it opened up the possibility of legislating for change. The effects on Scottish criminal justice were profound and paradoxical. Perhaps, more importantly, the new Parliament created space for political debate about – and political capacity building around – questions of crime and justice. The result, according to McAra (2008), was a 'de-tartanisation' of Scottish criminal and youth justice policy – and a form of 'hyper-institutionalism' as the Scottish Parliament and Executive engaged in a frenzied period of debate leading to a proliferation of new policy initiatives, plans, laws and 'quangos'. Though many competing narratives were at play in the new penal politics in Scotland post-devolution, the traditional reductionist narrative was pushed further to the margins. Indeed, five years later, in the 2003 election campaign, the Labour party manifesto adopted an almost expansionist tone:

> *We will set up a single agency – the Correctional Service for Scotland – staffed by professionals and covering prison and community based sentences to maximise the impact of punishment, rehabilitation and protection offered by our justice system. (Scottish Labour, 2003)*

Although the proposed organisational changes were clearly in a more correctional direction and doubtless were intended at least in part as a 'tough on crime' manoeuvre, it is hard to cast them as simply or straightforwardly punitive. The vision of the then First Minister (Jack McConnell) for the future of criminal justice in Scotland retained rehabilitation among his three 'R's ('Respect, Responsibility and Rehabilitation'). In an important speech, McConnell (2003, p. 11) argued that,

There is a balance to be struck. A balance between protection and punishment — and the chance for those who have done wrong to change their behaviour and re-engage with the community as full and productive members. If we don't get that balance right then the system will fail through lack of confidence and trust. Our justice service depends absolutely on ordinary people [...] we need them to be tolerant of the offender who returns to the community because they believe the person truly has been punished and has made amends and they are now ready to give him or her their second chance.

This determination — explicitly in pursuit of credibility and legitimacy — to stress the responsibilisation of the 'offender' but to balance it with notions of tolerance and inclusion had been evident in Scottish penal policy at least since the introduction of the national standards in 1991 (and arguably for over 100 years). The same theme had underpinned the third of the *Criminal Justice Social Work Services: National Priorities for 2001–2002 and onwards*, which was to 'promote the social inclusion of offenders through rehabilitation, so reducing the level of offending' (Justice Department, 2001, p. 3). In this context, rehabilitation was cast as the means of progressing towards two compatible and inter-dependent ends: not only the reduction of reoffending but also the social inclusion of offenders. There was also evidence of a continuing, if more qualified, commitment to penal reductionism, reflected in the second of the *National Priorities*: to 'reduce the use of unnecessary custody by providing effective community disposals' (Justice Department, 2001, p. 3).

After a heated debate about the merits and demerits of a single correctional service, the Management of Offenders Act 2005 represented another compromise solution — and another reorganisation (see McNeill & Whyte, 2007; Morrison, 2015). Scotland's 32 local authorities retained criminal justice social work, but 8 community justice authorities were established to develop and implement multi-agency and multi-authority strategies for reducing reoffending, and a new National Advisory Body on offender management (note the imported and quite un-Scottish terminology) was created to advise the Minister of Justice and to review these strategies.

However, the new system had little time to become established before the election of a Scottish Nationalist Party (SNP) (minority) government in 2007. The SNP government was re-elected (as a majority government) in

2011. Few commentators would dispute that these nationalist administrations have changed the tone and tenor of penal political debates in Scotland. With respect to sentencing and sanctions, their initial move was to appoint an independent commission to examine the use of imprisonment. The resulting McLeish report (Scottish Prisons Commission, 2008), *Scotland's Choice*, was unequivocal that Scotland's comparatively high use of imprisonment was undesirable and unsustainable and that different choices were both possible and necessary. Amongst many far-reaching proposals, the commission suggested the creation of the new single community sentence: the 'Community Payback Order' (discussed previously). As the name suggests, this order was intended to place a new emphasis on reparation, although the report famously made a place for rehabilitation in its contentious claim that 'one of the best ways of paying back is by turning your life around' (Scottish Prisons Commission, 2008, p. 33). The commission's (and subsequently the government's) bold intention was for this new order to displace custody as the default sanction in Scotland.

What is perhaps most interesting about these recent developments is that, although they reproduce Scottish probation's founding reductionist narrative, they clearly invoke the reparative adaptation (Robinson et al., 2013), seeking to allow reparation and redress their places amongst the necessary objectives of supervision, and implicitly, they link legitimacy and credibility to reparation and redress rather than merely to rehabilitation and reducing reoffending. In that sense, it may now (finally) make sense to talk about 'punishment in the community' in Scotland – but probably only if we make clear that 'punishment' need not be 'merely punitive' (cf. Duff, 2001, 2003). The pains of reparative effort are both legitimated and legitimising in this discourse, but they must be constructive rather than destructive, integrative rather than exclusionary and capacity building rather than incapacitating.

However, this is not to say that Scottish social work practitioners have come to own reparation (far less 'punishment') rather than rehabilitation as their primary objective. Indeed, a recent ethnography of the implementation of the Community Payback Order suggests that reparation remains a relatively marginalised aspect of social workers' discourses and practices. Speed and visibility (of community sanctioning) emerge as more important aspects of their accounts of the implementation of the CPO rather than reparation itself, and, in their own direct practice, rehabilitation tends to remain centre stage (see McGuinness, 2014).

Practitioner ambivalence about this new discourse stands at odds with the enthusiasm of the Scottish Government in its reform efforts. Seeking to account for that enthusiasm requires an analysis of the relationships between debates about constitutional change in Scotland and the adaptation and legitimation of supervision.

Constitutional Change, Penal Supervision and Nation Building

As I have already noted, following McAra (2008), devolution settled the constitutional crisis temporarily and changed the salience and dynamics of penal politics. Between 1999 and 2007, for many in the criminal justice system, benign neglect had never looked so attractive. But the 2007 election of the Nationalists – and their plans for an independence referendum – raised the spectre of constitutional change once again. Although this did not lead to an immediate diminution of interest in criminal justice and penal policy, it did inaugurate a new sort of penal politics. As with all other areas of policy, the Nationalists sought to shift the question from 'what's wrong with Scotland?' to 'what might Scotland look like if we were to become independent?' The nationalists switched from an avoidant, risk averse politicking, to one that focused on a new narrative framed in the language of possibility and optimism. In every area of policy, including penal policy, the answers to the second question (about an independent Scotland) needed to be positive for the nationalists to secure their prize.

Although at first sight reparation seems at odds with this discursive shift – since it implies repairing what is broken – in fact, the message of reparation is also that repair is possible. Indeed, one might construct reparation as a process aimed at *social reformation* or at least the reformation of civic social relations and that is exactly the sort of narrative that the Nationalists needed. Political and social reformation was and is, after all, their raison d'être. In this most recent phase therefore, there is evidence of a symbiotic relationship between the legitimation of civic nationalism itself (and the associated case for independence) and progressive penal reform, which aimed to place supervision centre stage.

Lessons from Scottish Supervision: How to Succeed While Failing

At the same time as developing their response to *Scotland's Choice* (2008), the Scottish Government was involved in a parallel consultation about the development of new national outcomes and standards for criminal justice social work services (Scottish Government, 2010[7]). Shortly after the passage of the Criminal Justice and Licensing Act 2010, and in preparation for the implementation of the community payback order, I wrote a briefing chapter for criminal justice social workers exploring the connections between these two parallel developments (McNeill, 2010). I aimed to give some conceptual substance to the notion of Community Payback – seeking to articulate its (potentially) reparative rather than its (potentially) punitive character. The new national outcomes and standards articulated a practice model based on four 'R's: reparation, rehabilitation, restriction and reintegration. Drawing the two sources together, I suggested the following conceptual relationship between the four 'R's (see Figure 15 below).

Here, the primary task for supervision was redefined as reparation, which is seen as a pre-requisite of reintegration. But it is recognised that, for some people, the most appropriate form of reparation might include rehabilitative activities – 'paying back by working at change' – and indeed rehabilitation might also be a necessary process to navigate where criminogenic or social needs represent significant barriers to reintegration. In some more serious cases, some measure of restriction might also be required for public protection. Although submitting to some forms of restriction might not be reparative, it could be part of allowing reparation

Figure 15. The Four Rs.

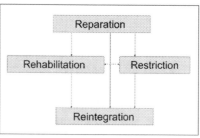

and/or rehabilitation to take place safely in the community. Equally, in some cases, neither rehabilitation nor restriction might be required – here, the reparation might be through apology (although this was not formally addressed in the 2010 Act), through financial compensation or through unpaid work.

Whatever the merits or demerits of this model, it neglects the crucial fifth 'R' – *reductionism* – an objective that was oddly absent from the new national outcomes and standards even though it was *the* central concern of *Scotland's Choice* (2008). Given that the then Justice Secretary, Kenny MacAskill, so often expressed political commitment to reducing the prison population, it would be wrong to read too much into this omission. The same omission is notable in the second phase of the Scottish Government's 'Reducing Reoffending Programme'. Indeed, it is also obvious that the title and content of this key policy programme affecting community punishment stresses *rehabilitative and reintegrative* rather than *reparative* themes, despite the arguments in *Scotland's Choice* (2008).

That said, talk and action are different things. Whatever the shifts in legitimation strategies and narrative reconstructions of supervision, to the extent that this is a history of reframed attempts at penal reductionism, it is also a history of successful failure. The obvious success, in the light of Chapter 3's analysis, rests in the fact that supervision has clearly become a very significant and rapidly expanding feature of the Scottish penal landscape. Yet the failure of supervision to divert is apparent in Chapter 3, in the analysis in *Scotland's Choice* (2008) and in Scotland's continuing high rate of imprisonment; Scottish judges are still choosing to impose more and longer custodial sanctions than many of their European colleagues – at least insofar as this can be judged by relative imprisonment rates.

As I noted in Chapter 3, the simultaneous rise in *both* community supervision *and* custodial sentences in Scotland is partly explained by the dramatic decline in the use of financial penalties – from around 180,000 in 1983 to about 70,000 by 2008– 2009 and less than 50,000 in 2015– 2016.[8]. Although it would take more detailed research to establish the precise relationships between the fates of the three main sorts of penalties (financial, supervisory and custodial), *prima facie*, it seems that supervision's growth has, for the most part, displaced financial penalties rather than custodial sentences.

For example, the Scottish Government commissioned evaluation of Community Payback Orders, [new] Criminal Justice Social Work Reports and the Presumption Against Short Sentences (also recommended by the Scottish Prisons Commission [2008] and introduced by the 2010 Act), concludes that:

> *Sheriffs remain sceptical about the seriousness with which CPOs will be regarded by offenders and their acceptability to the general public. Both factors are potentially important background influences on their own confidence in the appropriateness of the disposal [...] Most [...] considered the presumption [against short custodial sentences] to be of little practical consequence both because of an existing commitment to use community penalties wherever possible and because of the 'inevitability' of a short custodial sentence in a small number of cases (Anderson et al., 2015, pp. 9–10).*

Reading this after more than 100 years of efforts to reduce imprisonment by promoting supervision in Scotland, it is almost as if one can hear the teeth of policymakers grinding on the grit of judicial independence.

It is, of course, possible that the growth of supervision has inhibited what might otherwise have been greater growth in rates of imprisonment. However, administrative data about the criminal histories of people receiving community and custodial sentences in Scotland does not provide strong evidence that community sentences are successfully diverting higher tariff 'offenders';[9] rather, it lends weight to the fear that supervisory sentences are displacing fines.

CONCLUSIONS: REHABILITATIVE REDUCTIONISM AND PENAL EXPANSIONISM

We can perhaps draw some broader lessons about the legitimation of supervision from this elaboration of the Scottish case (see Robinson and McNeill [2015] for case studies from other countries). Certainly, it seems that changes in the constitutional dynamics of the state are likely to have profound effects on the adaptation and legitimation of supervision. Chapter 2 highlighted accounts of the economic, political, cultural and social forces that play a part in shaping penalty; but we also need to recognise that within the broad term 'political', we need to think not just (and perhaps not so much) about the hurly-burly of penal politics (worrisome though that often is) and more about the changing constitutional and institutional dynamics of political fields and penal–political subfields. As we noted in Chapter 2, we need to much more carefully map the shifting contours of the penal state if we are to understand the forms of penalty it nurtures and neglects (Rubin & Phelps, 2017).

We can also see that, in Scotland, the core reductionist narrative for supervision has perhaps changed relatively little – although, crucially, *reductionism* has progressively come to be displaced by another objective that was once its subordinate – *rehabilitation*. In recent decades, the central focus of policy and practice debate and development has been on which objectives, methods and practices (and which organisational arrangements and which practitioners) might supposedly allow supervision to secure credibility by achieving positive rehabilitative effects. Perhaps this is part of the problem. By identifying supervision so closely with rehabilitation, we write out its penal character, blinding ourselves to questions of parsimony and proportionality. Certainly, while there has been concern about supervision's failure to displace imprisonment in Scotland, there has been very little concern about its growth, perhaps because it is (falsely) assumed that it does little harm to its subjects. Thus, it seems that, rather than retarding it, Scottish welfarism contributes to penal growth, partly by disguising it.

Indeed, tracing the shifting discourses that have legitimated supervision in Scotland, the narrative that is missing (for the most part) in the Scottish story has been the punitive one (Robinson et al., 2013). From a primary emphasis on robust supervision (from inception to the 1930s) firstly to a focus on delivering professional social work first to treat delinquency, then to welfarist social education (from the 1930s to the 1970s), then to criminal justice social work as a responsibilising endeavour (in the 1980s and 1990s) and then towards risk management and public protection (in the 1990s and 2000s)(McNeill, 2005), supervision's *penal* character has been continually elided. Arguably even now, whatever its legal status, supervision is not seen as punishment but as an alternative to punishment.

However, while Scotland seems like a paradigmatic case of penal reductionism's tragic quality – with the legitimation and pursuit of 'alternatives' producing a huge expansion of the numbers of people subject to penal control – this tells us little or nothing about the *practice* of supervision and the *experience* of being supervised. That experience is certainly shaped by the institutional imperatives that Norm (in our short story) seems determined to channel. But, like any 'street-level bureaucrat' (Halliday, Burns, Hutton, McNeill, & Tata, 2008; Lipsky, 1980), Pauline clearly contests the sorts of adaptation that Norm is seeking to implement. Thus, contestation and contingency continue all the way down the penal hierarchy, combining to somehow determine how supervision will be experienced by its subjects. It is to those experiences that we now turn since these experiences seem so fundamental to the project of making sense of what 'mass supervision' is and what it means.

NOTES

1. In the 2013 paper, we opted not for the term 'supervision' or 'supervisory sanctions' but rather for the distinctly European label 'community sanctions and measures' (CSM), defined by the Council of Europe as: '[those] which maintain the offender in the community and involve some restriction of his liberty through the imposition of conditions and/or obligations, and which are implemented by bodies designated in law for that purpose. The term designates any sanction imposed by a court or a judge, and any measure taken before or instead of a decision on a sanction as well as ways of enforcing a sentence of imprisonment outside a prison establishment (Council of Europe, 1992, Appendix para. 1)'.

2. There are, in fact, three legal contexts in which community-based supervision can be imposed in Scotland. Scottish public prosecutors (called Procurators Fiscal) can impose certain direct measures in lieu of prosecution. For the most part, direct measures are warnings or financial penalties, but the possibility of diversion, for example, for reparation or mediation or for help with mental health problems, does exist. However, these latter measures are used relatively rarely overall and to quite different extents in different localities (see Bradford & McQueen, 2011), although numbers have grown significant in the few years. Almost 1,700 cases of diversion to such (supervised) measures were commenced in 2012–2013: see Table 1

at http://www.scotland.gov.uk/Resource/0045/00451608.pdf. Since these measures are offered in lieu of prosecution (whether that possibility is deferred or waived entirely), they are not properly considered punishments and so I exclude them from further discussion here.

3. The data used here come from: http://www.gov.scot/Topics/Statistics/ Browse/Crime-Justice/Datasets/SocialWork/CPOs. Accessed on January 30, 2018. Note that the total number of requirements exceeds the number of new orders, since orders can contain multiple requirements.

4. For example, the Glasgow Discharged Prisoners Aid Society was founded in 1856: see http://www.theglasgowstory.com/image.php?inum= TGSG00019. Accessed on January 30, 2018.

5. The Boys' Brigade is a uniformed youth organisation with historical links to Scottish Protestant churches; somewhat similar to the Boy Scouts.

6. For an account of the history of the Scottish Parliament, see: http:// www.parliament.scot/EducationandCommunityPartnershipsresources/ Timeline-English-Nov2016-v5.pdf. Accessed on June 4, 2018.

7. See http://www.scotland.gov.uk/resource/doc/925/0103556.pdf. Accessed on November 28, 2014.

8. Source: http://www.gov.scot/Resource/0052/00528172.pdf. Accessed on January 30, 2018.

9. Personal communications with Peter Conlong, Justice Analytical Services, Scottish Government.

CHAPTER 5

EXPERIENCING MASS SUPERVISION

ANY CHANCE OF A REFILL?

Figure 16. Untitled 6.

Pauline wondered if she had earned the right to ask the next question, and then ploughed ahead:

'Look Joe. Let me be honest with you. I can understand why you were so pissed off with your boss; he sounds like a total dick. And I can see that the red paint made a point about him bleeding you dry over the years. I'm

not saying it was justified but I get it. But – to be blunt – pissing on the reception floor? What was that all about?'

'I know', Joe replied, head in hands and eyes fixed on the bare floorboards below, 'I'm totally mortified about that. I did send Tracey some flowers by way of apology. She's the office cleaner. Lovely woman. I hate the thought of her having to mop that up.'

Joe took a deep breath, lifted his head, looked Pauline in the eye and continued:

'Look, the simple fact was that I had drunk five or six pints winding myself up for the confrontation. Confrontation is just not my thing – nor is beer, it turns out. But, in the heat of the moment, and finding myself with a bladder fit to burst, spraying piss around like Michael Douglas in that movie Wall Street *just seemed like a great way to mess with Steve's massive ego. Needless to say, it didn't look so clever on the CCTV the police showed me – but then none of it did.'*

Pauline smiled and shook her head: 'Pretty moronic, eh? Any chance of a refill?'

While Joe re-boiled the kettle, Pauline studied their surroundings. Joe's place was not, she imagined, a deliberate effort at Scandinavian minimalism taken to extremes; more likely, it revealed that lack of self-care that often accompanies depression. The living room in his one-bedroom apartment boasted only a large beanbag, an easy chair (bottom of the range Ikea) and a small coffee table. An old TV sat on the floor in the corner. The un-curtained window looked out over the courtyard of what was a converted 1920s fire station. A gated community, sealed off from the city life outside. She'd seen much worse places, but she couldn't imagine Joe's kids being keen on sleepovers, unless they shared their dad's newfound ascetic tastes.

Joe placed a fresh cup of instant coffee in front of Pauline and resumed his place awkwardly on the beanbag, sitting cross-legged and trying not to feel like an errant child.

'Anyway', Pauline continued, 'enough about what happened. Let's talk about now. And let's talk about the future. We've got 17 months of this order to get through; and you have the tag[1] and your 7-7 curfew for the next five. I suppose there are really just two or three questions: How do we get you through this without any further bother, and what do you want out of it – what do you want your future to be?'

Joe felt blindsided by the last two questions. The future? What future? He hadn't been able to think clearly since the wheels came off the cart. It wasn't just that he wasn't driving the cart; it was that he hadn't stopped falling since his life crashed. There didn't seem to be any solid ground from which to take a view, just a constant tumble of words and images. Was Pauline going to help him find some solid ground?

'*The first question is a lot easier to answer than the other two. I'm fine with the tag – I haven't had much of a social life since the divorce. It turned out that most of the friendships that we had kept up since we married were my wife's – sorry – ex-wife's. I have a couple of old pals, but we don't see that much of each other; the odd football match or night in the pub – at least, before all this happened. I'm totally off the drink for now – and not missing it. I have the TV and the radio.*'

Joe took a sip of his tea, looked out the window and continued:

'*To be honest, the days are harder than the nights. Work was such a habit that I can't get used to the sheer emptiness of the days. I miss the action and the sense of purpose much more than the money – though my ex and the kids might take a different view about that. I am looking for work, but it's not easy at my age. It's also pretty tricky explaining to your potential future boss why you assaulted your former boss. On the two occasions when I have got as far as interviews, I've seen the colour drain from their faces at that point.*'

'*Work isn't the only possible kind of action and purpose, though, is it?*', *Pauline interjected.*

'*No, I guess not: I still want to be a proper dad, but it's hard when that amounts to a trip to the movies and a KFC Family Bucket once a week.*'

Pauline could feel herself sinking into Joe's hopelessness. The emptiness and desolation of the flat wasn't helping, nor was the sense of being locked in ... but it was giving her the germ of an idea.

'*Look Joe: You're an experienced accountant with a hell of a lot of skills and resources. You're not broke – you still have some redundancy money, even after paying for the office clean-up. You said it yourself: You need some action and some purpose. You need to break out of this cell.*' *A smile crept across her face, and Joe raised an eyebrow in trepidation or curiosity.* '*And I have an idea about how we might spring you ...*'

INTRODUCTION

We've already seen in Chapter 3 that supervision can widen the penal net or divert people out of it. As Jay-Z put it, supervision can be a landmine or a second chance or, in Michele Phelps' (2018) metaphor, it can be a conveyer belt into or an off-ramp out of penal control. The last chapter's exploration of the history of criminal justice social work in Scotland showed that despite an enduring commitment in policy and practice to supervision as a strategy for penal reduction − as an 'off-ramp' to 'second chances' − dramatic growth in the use of supervision has enlarged rather than contracted the size of the penal system.

However, as I noted at the end of the last chapter, neither the numbers analysed in Chapter 3 nor the legitimising narratives discussed in Chapter 4 tell us much about what it is that people under supervision are drawn into. How is supervision experienced? How and to what extent does it hurt, hold and/or help the people that are subject to it (McNeill, 2009)? To put this another way, what exactly is the *penal* character of mass supervision?

In the previous extract, and in the early episodes of the short story, it seems that Pauline is trying to make supervision helpful to Joe, even if she herself feels that she is working within a system that seems to value help and humanity less and less. Joe still seems unsure; he wants to believe that Pauline can and will help him 'find solid ground', but he also feels the precariousness of his situation and he fears the power that she (or the system that she represents) holds over him. While it is not yet clear which way this fictionalised experience of supervision is going to go, it does seem obvious that their relationship is critical to shaping its impacts and effects, for better or worse.

In this chapter, I aim to explore these questions about the penal character of supervision. Though a great deal of criminological research has sought to explore the 'effectiveness' of different kinds of supervision in terms of reoffending (see McNeill, Raynor, & Trotter, 2010; Raynor & Robinson, 2009), much less work has been done on the arguably more fundamental question of how people experience it. I begin by reviewing that limited evidence base before going on to explore innovative research using creative methods (undertaken as part of the COST Action IS1106 on Offender Supervision in Europe[2]) that aimed to make the experience of supervision visible through photography and then audible through songwriting. In the concluding discussion, I analyse and summarise what these various studies and projects reveal about supervision.

EXPERIENCING SUPERVISION

In some respects, it makes little sense to discuss 'experiencing supervision' in general terms. As I have noted in the preceding chapters, supervision comes in many forms and at different stages in the criminal justice process (pre-trial, as a community-based sanction or part of a community-based sanction, or as part of or in conjunction with a custodial sentence). Even focusing on just one stage in the process and just one legal order – for example, the Community Payback Order in Scotland or the Community Order in England and Wales – a wide range of different conditions can be applied that require supervisees to do something (like unpaid work or rehabilitative interventions or drug or alcohol treatment or to reside at a particular address) and/or not to do something (like committing further offences or engaging in certain [otherwise legal] behaviours or socialising with certain people or being in certain places). Clearly, the specific legal form, content and meaning of supervision will influence how it is experienced. At the same time, these different forms of supervision share some important common features; they place an offending citizen under the legal authority of an agent of the state; they confer on that agent an unusual degree of power and influence over the fate of the supervisee; *and* they threaten the supervisee with (further) punishment in the event of non-compliance. In the first extract of the short story (with which I opened Chapter 1), I tried to capture how it might feel to be placed in this position, inspired in part by some of the visual representations of being supervised that I will discuss in more detail in the following section.

Though I focus in what follows on the findings from its studies using creative methods, the COST Action also involved efforts to enhance more conventional survey-based methods for exploring how supervision is experienced. Durnescu, Kennefick, Sucic and Glavak Tkalic (2018) note that such studies have focused on evaluating supervisees' satisfaction with the process of supervision (Abraham, Van Dijk, & Zwaan, 2007; Brandes & Cheung, 2009; Levenson & Prescott, 2009; Mair & Mills, 2009), on more legal or normative aspects of supervision such as procedural fairness (Padfield, 2012) and on the degree of informed consent to supervision and active participation that supervisees are afforded in drafting their individual case *plan* (Sucic, Ricijas, & Glavak Tkalic, 2014).

Durnescu et al. (2018) worked across 8 European countries to develop a questionnaire tool – the Eurobarometer on Experiencing Supervision (EES) – to compare the experience of supervision across jurisdictions. That tool explores supervision in six dimensions: assessing supervision as a general experience, exploring supervisee perceptions of the supervisor and of the relationship between the supervisee and supervisor, examining supervisee views of how compliance and breach have been managed, exploring the relationship between supervision and rehabilitation and assessing the supervisee's degree of involvement in supervision. Although the sample sizes in each country were too small to generate generalisable findings, they provide indicative evidence of some intriguing similarities (and variations) in how people in different systems experience supervision. Crucially, in most countries, supervisees saw supervision as serving *both* punitive *and* rehabilitative purposes, although, overall, they tended to identify the punitive intent more strongly than the rehabilitative.

Indeed, earlier survey research in the USA had suggested that supervision, whatever the durability of its putatively rehabilitative purposes, did not lack penal 'bite'. For example, researchers at the RAND corporation found that there were intermediate supervisory sanctions, which surveyed prisoners equated with prison in terms of punitiveness. For some individuals, intensive forms of probation 'may actually be the more dreaded penalty' (Petersilia & Deschenes, 1994, p. 306; see also May & Wood, 2010; Payne & Gainey, 1998).

In an earlier study, Durnescu (2011) specifically explored the 'pains of probation' as experienced in Romania. Alongside deprivations of time and the other practical and financial costs of compliance, and limitations on their autonomy and privacy, probationers also reported the pain of the 'forced return to the offence' and the pain of a life lived 'under a constant threat'. The threat in question in Durnescu's (2011) study was that of breach or revocation and with it further punishment.

Hayes' (2015) careful study of the pains of probation supervision in England, drawing on interviews with a small number of supervisees and supervisors, similarly reveals six sets of related pains of rehabilitation, liberty deprivation, welfare issues and external agency interventions, as well as process pains and pains associated with stigma. Some of these pains were intensified, some reduced and some unaffected by the supervisory relationship. Hayes (2015, pp. 99–100) concludes that '[...]whether at the level of policy or of individual practise, we must recognise supervised community penalties as systems of 'pain delivery', however benevolent the intention.'

Other recent work in England and Wales (reviewed by Fitzgibbon & Healy, 2017) paints a mixed picture of how supervision is experienced there. King's (2013) respondents suggested that supervision increased their sense of agency, their motivation to change and their problem-solving skills, encouraging them to focus on their futures. However, they were demoralised by the frequency with which they were referred to external agencies for practical help, finding this time-consuming and unhelpful. Probationers in Shapland et al.'s (2012) study did not see their supervisors as likely sources of help. Few of them were taking part in offending behaviour programmes and most thought their probation appointments were too brief and unfocused.

In broad terms, inspection reports in England, since the recent privatisation of much probation and parole work, paint a depressing picture of declining standards in the privatised community rehabilitation companies (see Burke, Collett, & McNeill, 2018); with more reliance on phone contact or automated check-ins and lower levels of human contact. It seems as if 'Transforming Rehabilitation' (as the UK Government's reform programme was called) has, in its implementation, in fact tended to reduce rehabilitation to 'mere' supervision and, in some cases, to not much of that.

My own review of Scottish research on experiencing supervision (based on a range of studies from the 1960s to the current day) led me to conclude that the experience of supervision has been and remains a highly variable and contingent one (McNeill, 2012). Whereas imprisonment is defined – at least to an extent – by an architecture of confinement, supervision is more fluid. The meaning, substance and impact of supervision are constructed somewhere in the interplay between the supervisee's characteristics, attitudes, disposition and situation and *those* of the supervisor. Both *supervisee and supervisor are* influenced by multiple social systems and the resources they afford or deny. For the supervisee, these systems may be personal, familial, peer group related and environmental; for the supervisor, they are personal, professional, team-related and organisational. As I have argued in Chapters 2–4, the wider social context of penalty also influences both the construction of the practice and experience of supervision. Given that the experience of supervision is nested within these various systemic and personal influences, it is perhaps no surprise that it is so contingent in its forms and so vulnerable to personal and social interactions.

However, our grasp of these interacting influences upon supervision – and of the complexities of supervision as a lived experience – has been seriously constrained by methodological limitations of three main sorts that flow from an over-reliance on surveys and interviews in related research (see Durnescu, Enengl, & Grafl, 2013). Firstly, there is a probable selection bias in studies that rely on self-selection of respondents and/or are affected by low response rates. Even where they present negative findings, there is reason to believe that the picture of supervision that they present is likely to be skewed towards those with more favourable supervision experiences, who are more likely to be in contact with services, to be traced easily by researchers and to respond favourably to research access requests. Secondly, most studies are relatively insensitive to issues of diversity and how they impact on supervision, tending to treat supervisees as a relatively homogeneous group. Thirdly, interview- and survey-based studies necessarily rely on *accounts* of supervision rather than on *observations* of supervision. These accounts may be influenced by social desirability biases (e.g. anticipating that the researcher expects positive responses, or wishing the interview to reflect favourably on the supervisor) and perhaps by anxiety about reporting adverse experiences (where to do so might be perceived as risking negative reactions and adverse consequences from supervisors). These limitations may tend to produce an artificially or at least unrepresentatively positive account of supervision.

By implication, a clearer (and more accurate) grasp of the lived experience of supervision seems to require the development of more fully ethnographic studies, which take diversity seriously and which are specifically prospective in nature, observing and engaging with the experience as it happens, rather than relying on retrospective accounts of it. Only such an approach seems capable of generating a properly cultural account of supervision as a lived experience in its interpersonal, social and organisational contexts. It is to such studies that I turn next.

ETHNOGRAPHIES OF SUPERVISION

Whereas ethnographies of penal supervision are a relatively recent addition to criminological and sociological research and remain rare, prison ethnography is so well established that it might be considered almost a sub-discipline (Drake, Earle, & Sloan, 2015). In both custodial and community contexts, ethnographic research has tended to be more thoroughly theorised than work based on interviews and surveys.

As I noted in Chapter 2, the notion of disciplinary power has been central to explaining the evolution of punishment in general and probation and parole in particular (see Cohen, 1985; Garland, 1985; Simon, 1993), connoting terms like surveillance, observation and supervision as methods of mastering or training the human body, not via the use of force or constraint but by influencing or training 'the soul'.

I also noted in Chapter 2 that the ways in which these disciplinary mechanisms have evolved or been supplanted in late-modern societies is, of course, a matter of much debate. Deleuze (1990) has drawn attention to the shift from disciplinary societies to 'societies of control' in which rather than being moulded by a disciplinary 'cast', our behaviour is controlled by modulation, 'like a sieve whose mesh will transmute from point to point' (Deleuze, 1990, p. 4). Both this invocation of more fluid, shifting and interminable forms of control and Deleuze's analysis of how they operate on 'dividuals' (as units of a mass that is to be controlled, rather than as individualized subjects of discipline) in many ways seem consistent with contemporary accounts of penal control.

Drawing on these sorts of ideas, his own important recent prison ethnography (Crewe, 2009) and earlier work by Downes (1988), King and McDermott (1995), Crewe (2011) has helped to clarify the penal character of contemporary imprisonment in England and Wales. He distinguishes between the depth, weight and tightness of imprisonment. Depth refers to degree of physical security to which one is subject and to the distance from release and from the outside world that this implies, represents and constitutes. Weight refers to the psychological burdens of imprisonment; to how heavily it bears down upon prisoners. Tightness is the dimension that Crewe adds:

> *The term 'tightness' captures the feelings of tension and anxiety generated by uncertainty (Freeman & Seymour, 2010), and the*

*sense of not knowing which way to move, for fear of getting
things wrong. It conveys the way that power operates both
closely and anonymously, working like an invisible harness on
the self. It is all-encompassing and invasive, in that it promotes
the self-regulation of all aspects of conduct, addressing both the
psyche and the body. (Crewe, 2011, p. 522)*

In Crewe's analysis, tightness relates to the pains of indeterminacy, of
psychological assessment and of self-government that have become apparent in modern prisons (especially for those serving longer sentences). The
concept of tightness describes the psychological straitjacket created by
correctional regimes – one which, paradoxically, must be continuously
woven and re-woven if 'freedom' is to be secured. Crewe (2011) prefers
Weber's metaphor of the 'shell as hard as steel' created by the bureaucratic
machinery of corrections – something other than us that confines us and,
in so doing, becomes part of us. As such, it has a certain degree of malle-
ability and permits its wearer some motility, but it travels with him or her.
As Crewe elaborates:

*The shell of soft power is similar. At best, the prisoner can
jettison some of its psychological weight, but he or she cannot
simply detach it. The shell also represents the identity that the
institution assigns to the prisoner, which has to be carried for
the remainder of the sentence. (Crewe, 2011, p. 523)*

Although his focus is squarely on imprisonment, Crewe (2011) does
allude briefly to the 'tightening' nature of post-release supervision in the
community. The shell of soft power may need to be carried long after the
custodial part of the sentence, through the licence period, if recall to prison
is to be avoided. This is a shell from which the supervisee can only break
free when the licence period ends. For those subject to life-time restrictions, penal control is legally and literally interminable.

In somewhat similar vein, several excellent recent ethnographic
explorations of re-entry to and supervision in the community have begun
to paint a more complex and fine-grained picture of the penal character of
these experiences, particularly in the UK and the USA. Many of these
studies have focused not on supervision per se but rather, like Crewe
(2011), on the pains of rehabilitation in its current risk-focused guise
(e.g. Shammas, 2014). The late-modern penal subject is, it seems,

compelled not just to internalise the 'shell as hard as steel' but to *display* how it has re-fashioned his or her riskiness; thus *performing* the internalised containment of risk. Official recognition and endorsement of this performance is key to progression, release and then also to the maintenance of the supervisee's semi-freedom.

For example, Lacombe's (2008) ethnographic study of an English prison-based sex offender programme revealed the ways in which risk-based rehabilitation invited people serving time for sex offences to contort their perceptions *and* presentations of self in line with the requirements of the programme to which they were subject. Digard's (2010, 2014) English study of the experiences of post-release supervision for people convicted of sexual offences makes clear that these performances must continue long after release; the failure to perform appropriately and convincingly results in the system biting back in ways that are often experienced as illegitimate and procedurally unfair, for example, through recall to custody or the imposition of further conditions on licenses.

Cox's (2011, 2013, 2017) ethnographic study of young people (between the ages and 15 and 24 years and mainly from minority ethnic communities) involved with the juvenile and adult justice systems of New York State tells a similar story. In a chapter that vividly describes the dilemmas that the young people face in participating in treatment programmes, Cox concludes that

> [...] *young people's aspirations for wholeness may result in their domination by the behavioural change practices which are said to liberate them. This form of domination encourages them to express self-discipline and control, yet provides them with few opportunities for an exercise of such forms of control [...].*
> (Cox, 2011, p. 604, *emphases in original*)

Cox's references to 'domination' and her analysis of the ironies of being required to perform 'agency' in the context of overwhelming structural constraints perhaps invoke Bourdieusian notions of symbolic violence as much as Foucauldian disciplinary power.

In similar vein, Reuben Miller reveals how responsibility for eliciting these performances of personal transformation is increasingly being devolved beyond the penal state's agents (prison, probation and parole officers). Miller's (2014) fascinating ethnography of the re-entry experiences of men (most of whom identified as African American) in Chicago's west side shows how:

> *Reentry organizations, while not acknowledging this, engage in a logic in which former prisoners 'prove' their submission to a program of personal transformation by (1) completing programs designed to broker within them an ethic of transformation; and (2) sharing in treatment groups the kinds of struggles on which they are working. Thus, a changed life is one of constant (re) evaluation, (re) discovery, and above all consistent progress toward the moving target of personal transformation. Unwillingness to transform is disciplined by service providers who facilitate reentry programs, and by former prisoners participating in these groups themselves. (Miller, 2014, p. 325)*

Thus, responsibility for rehabilitation and re-entry is devolved to the para-professionalised resources of low-income communities themselves. The re-entry organisations in these communities work on and with what they can; they work on and with the ex-prisoners who come to them. The consequence is that the socio-structural dynamics of rehabilitation, re-entry and reintegration are neglected. Rehabilitation here can only be a personal project of transformation, not a social one.

Werth's (2011, 2013) exploration of the experiences of parolees in California also produces broadly similar findings, but sheds light on how the parolees resist and subvert their domination and subjugation. In a recent chapter, Werth (2016) argues that many of the parolees were committed to 'straightening [themselves] out', but on their own terms – rejecting externally imposed demands to remake themselves on the system's terms and in its image. Werth interprets this as a form of resistance to the 'logic' of parole, one that assumes its subjects to lack the capacity to manage themselves and their lives ethically. Their rule-breaking is thus cast as a form of resistance to what they perceive as the excessive and punitive regulation of their lives, an assertion of autonomy in determining how to live well or how to go 'straight'. Yet, as Werth notes, even this resistance remains vulnerable and subordinate to penal power (via revocation). It also reveals, in some senses, the internalisation of discipline through the operation of 'power-at-a-distance'. Despite resisting the (parole-imposed) *terms* of their remaking, the parolees accept the *need* for their remaking, suggesting the ways in which such subjectivities may be engendered by penal power.

SUPERVISIBLE: MAKING SUPERVISION VISIBLE

These ethnographies of re-entry and supervision paint a much more detailed picture of how supervision is experienced; one which is both bleak and concerning. Informed by this recent ethnographic work, but also eager to find new ways to study and represent supervision, and to address its relative invisibility, in the COST Action's *'Supervisible'* pilot study, we used visual methods to explore people's thoughts and feelings about being supervised (see Fitzgibbon et al., 2017 for a fuller account of this project's methods and findings). Broadly speaking, there is evidence that more creative research methods can enable participants to increase their self-esteem and self-confidence, as well as develop new skills with which to communicate and share their emotions and experiences with others (Palibroda, Krieg, Murdock, & Havelock, 2009).

Here – once again to provide some continuity with preceding chapters – I focus mainly on the Scottish part of the pilot study. This involved seven men and three women, all of them White. Their ages ranged from 20 to 60 years and collectively they had experience of very diverse forms of supervision ranging from Community Payback Orders to life licence parole supervision. We ran two Scottish workshops: one with seven participants recruited through a local criminal justice social work team and the other with three people recruited through social media and an advocacy organisation of and for people with convictions.

In both workshops, an artist and photographer (Jenny Wicks) provided a basic briefing on photographic techniques and I explained the aims and focus of the project. Participants were then given about 90 minutes to take photographs (using disposable cameras) that somehow reflected their experiences of supervision. The cameras were then collected and the films developed while we shared lunch together. We then collected the pictures and returned them to each participant. In a focus group discussion, we shared and discussed the pictures with one another. The data analysis involved both an examination of the visual data (i.e. of the 160 photographs produced) and an examination of the transcripts of the two focus groups (and one follow-up interview with a participant, who had to leave one of the workshops early).

Because the focus group discussions took place immediately after the pictures were developed, the process of interpreting the meaning of the images was collaborative. While each photographer was able to explain what they *intended* to communicate, the others involved could also contribute their readings of one another's pictures; this often elicited new or refined interpretations that were interesting to the producer of the image. Later, I tried to cluster the 160 images in relation to the objects or scenes that they depicted and the themes that they seemed to imply. In this task, I was guided by the initial focus group discussions. Broadly, the images clustered into five groups.

Some images focused on positive development or change. For example, some people simply took pictures of the buildings where they received help or experienced supervision, and then spoke about the type of help they received. Others took pictures of bridges, roads, paths or scaffolding to metaphorically illustrate support on a journey or project of life reconstruction. Similar themes were also apparent in growth-related images of the natural world from nearby parks or beaches (trees, bushes and flowers; sand, sky and sea).

A second group of images were focused on time, often referring to lost, wasted or suspended time. These included images of watches and clocks, but also of long shadows and park benches (perhaps implying waiting).

A third set of images seemed to imply constraint. These included images of locks, chains, doors, gates and walls, but also of dogs on leashes, surveillance cameras and of people or objects left hanging in a state of suspension.

A fourth set of images centred on waste. These include images of broken bottles, litter, burning garden refuse, recycling bins, drains and toilets. In discussion, these images were often related to supervisees' feeling judged, labelled or stereotyped.

Finally, there were images that used signs and words, for example, road signs (no entry or one way) and road markings (yellow lines), as well as advertising posters and signs with prohibitions (telling us what not to do) and prescriptions (telling us what to do). These images often pointed to supervisees' sense of being subject to direction or discipline.

One of the benefits of using the pictures was that they often allowed for these themes to be represented and combined in subtle and complex ways, defying any simple presentation of supervision as *either* 'bad' or

Figure 17. Untitled 7.

Source: By 'Bob Hope'.

'good' or as *either* 'helpful' or 'hurtful'. For example, 'Bob Hope' chose to share both the picture shown in **Figure 17** (above) and a second picture of a war memorial outside the social work office he regularly attended (not shown).

He explained:

> *This is my first picture, it's a padlocked fence, it just kind of, just kind of spoke to me because you're kind of chained to the supervision order whether you like it or not [...] The second one I brought is actually the [...] monument at the front [of the building where the supervision agency is based], and what it says to me is it's kind of ironic that you've got a monument of war and freedom right next to a building that you're going to be chained to, and there is bugger all you can do about it for the next however long [...]*

Another participant, a young man subject to a Community Payback Order took this picture the picture below (in **Figure 18**). He explained:

> *[...] my first picture is just a picture of the beach, going up to the beach right there. A woman walking her dog. For me it kind of*

Figure 18. The Long Walk by 'Messiah 10'.

relates prison and probation and stuff. Whereas it's the kind of
relationship is one's the boss. One's the obedient one: the dog.
[Murmurs of agreement from the group]. It depends how you're
treated. The dog looked happy on a walk, obviously treated
well, that's the first one.

This image then is clearly one of constraint; punishment demands
'obedience' as he says. In both prisons and probation, there are bosses
who must be obeyed. However, although we might focus on the dehumanisation implicit in identifying with the dog, 'Messiah 10' offers a more
complex reading, suggesting perhaps that the extent of dehumanisation is
contingent on *how* he is constrained, not simply on the *fact* of his being
constrained. Being treated well makes constraint more endurable. In
discussing a second image (of two ships in the distance), he elucidates this
further, implying that the development of shared understanding with a
supervisor might also mitigate the pains of being compelled or constrained
to obey her authority.

Similarly, apparently positive images of development or growth could
also be ambiguous. For example, 'Elvis' provided an image of a small tree
or bush, surrounded by a protective cage (see **Figure 19** below).

Figure 19. Untitled 8.

Source: By 'Elvis'.

However, rather than stressing the merits of this sort of protection, he intended to convey how protection can inhibit growth and distort development:

> *Elvis: The wee tree in the cage is sort of being restricted to where it can go without a cage, a kind of obstacle round it. So it's still got the walls but it's not got its freedom [...] It's confined within its areas [...] because it is it's restricted and that. If you look at that [other tree] behind it, there's nothing round that. That's a free tree, do you know what I mean, that's going where it's meant to go.*

To me, these images and the discussions of them are both fascinating and revealing. Despite significant differences in the three countries in which the pilot took place (England, Germany and Scotland) and in the forms of supervision involved, Fitzgibbon et al. (2017) identified clear, common and recurring themes revealing the relationships between supervision and constraint, time (lost or suspended), waste, judgement and growth or hope.

As Fitzgibbon et al. (2017) note that, and in common with the ethnographies discussed previously, these representations challenge the findings of more conventional research on supervision. For example, the English language literatures both on supervision practice and on experiences of supervision tend to focus on supervisory meetings, assuming that it is in these encounters that supervision 'happens'. Our findings suggested that the experience of supervision is much more diffuse and pervasive; it seems to extend in time and in impact across the life of the supervisee. Crucially, this pervasiveness is very often experienced as painful. The pains of supervision consist largely in being both (continually) judged and constrained over time in the omnipresence of a suspended threat.

However, the *Supervisible* pilot also highlighted the complexity and ambiguity within supervision. Most of the major themes – constraint, time, waste and growth/hope – were neither inherently and inescapably negative nor positive. In many respects, this underlines the possibility that supervision can be productive *at the same time as* being painful. The broader findings of the pilot (and of the COST Action overall, on which see McNeill and Beyens, 2016) suggest that being treated fairly and being given meaningful help may moderate the pains of supervision and maximise its positive potential. But it is important to acknowledge that even when supervision is positive and productive, *it still hurts*. The key contribution of the *Supervisible* project was to help communicate and represent these pains (and to a certain extent the positive potential of supervision) more effectively.

SEEN *AND* HEARD: MAKING SUPERVISION AUDIBLE

Towards the end of the COST Action, we decided to take our engagement with creative research methods one step further, developing a project called '*Mass Supervision: Seen and Heard*'.[3] As the name suggests, Seen and Heard combined the visual representations from Supervisible with an attempt to make supervision audible. With respect to the visual, we collaborated with another artist, Carolyne Kardia, to curate an exhibition of photographs from the Supervisible project and from its sister pilot project 'Picturing Probation'[4] (which involved supervisors in taking photographs to represent their work; see Worrall et al., 2017). With respect to the auditory, we collaborated with Vox Liminis, a Scottish arts organisation, in running a two-day workshop in Glasgow that aimed to enable participants to write songs inspired by some of the pictures selected for the exhibition.

At our final conference in Brussels in March 2016 and at other events since, we have exhibited the images and invited musicians to perform some of the songs live (or we have used recordings). Vox Liminis also released an EP featuring some of the songs.

The songwriting workshop brought together former or current supervisees, supervisors, supervision researchers and a radio producer to work with professional musicians to write original songs reflecting on supervision. It took place in a city centre bar and music venue; one that opened only in the evenings and so was ours to use during the two days.

The musicians leading the workshop began by performing (unplugged) a few songs written in previous 'Vox [song-writing] sessions' in prisons. In the process, they demonstrated their gifts as interpreter-performers and provided impressive and moving examples of what might be achieved in the next couple of days. In my previous experiences of similar songwriting sessions, I had noted how these strikingly vulnerable and beautiful unplugged performances seemed to create a particular 'affective atmosphere' (Anderson, 2009); one in which people become willing to risk both emotionality and creativity and to recognise and support one another in taking these risks.

I briefly explained supervision as the theme of the workshop – making the links to the *Supervisible* project's aspiration to explore people's thoughts and feelings about supervision through photography – but making clear that the participants could interpret the theme in any way and write about whatever they wished. With the organisers, I had selected and hung around the room's walls 12 images from the exhibition. The images were selected simply because we found them evocative, powerful or ambiguous; drawing on our experience of previous Vox sessions, we had some sense of the sorts of images that might best elicit creative responses. Because the workshop was over-subscribed, and because I had some previous experience of songwriting in similar workshops, my role changed unexpectedly from that of participant (writing about my own experiences as a former supervisor and current researcher) to musician/facilitator, helping two participants to write songs. The two songs tell very different stories about supervision.

Initially, the participants were invited to pair up, and then to look at and discuss the images, noting any words or phrases that they conjured up on the flipchart chapter on which the pictures were posted. This is a common technique using in Vox sessions to generate words and phrases that might help participants create song titles or lyrics, as well as helping them think about the session theme. The musician-facilitators led a range of other exercises to help the participants understand aspects of the craft of songwriting.

I was initially paired with 'Teejay' (the only person other than me to participate in both the photography and songwriting workshops). Much later in the same session, and in much greater haste, I helped John, another supervisee who had missed the first day of the workshop, to write a song reflecting on his experiences. John and I had met before; we were both involved in working with Vox Liminis and had already co-written a song in an earlier prison-based workshop.

'Blankface'

Teejay is a small and wiry man, grey and balding and with sunken cheeks, but his eyes are bright and brim with intelligence (and sometimes a little mischief). He is middle-aged – maybe in his mid-50s. He seems to embody a shrewd and sinewy resilience, born of hard and long experience. Although Teejay is a born sceptic, he is friendly and easy company. He is also the subject of a parole life licence. Having completed the custodial part of his life sentence more than a decade before, Teejay remains subject to post-release supervision by a criminal justice social worker.

Just as when I initially met him in the photography workshop, I was impressed by Teejay's creativity, reflectiveness and by his eye for a metaphor. In the song-writing process, he revealed a gift for crafting narrative connections across images. On one of the walls, we had hung four pictures side by side. One showed a digital clock at midnight: 0:00. Another pictured a woman probation officer sitting at the far side of a desk, staring absently past the camera and, it might be assumed, towards an off-camera supervisee. A third image showed the closed sliding glass doors of a probation office. The fourth showed a children's climbing frame and the shadows cast by it and by the two adults atop it. This last image is reproduced as shown in **Figure 20** (below).

Teejay immediately connected these four images, weaving them into a story of supervision. Many of the themes found in his own *Supervisible* photographs (see McNeill, 2018) recurred in this simple story: the clock

Figure 20. Untitled 9.

Source: By 'Jack Clements'.

signified the supervisee being required to start over yet again, without much hope of success. In the probation officer, Teejay thought he recognised the blank face of bureaucratic indifference; the kind of weary disinterest that would elicit, he expected, an equally weary and disinterested response from the supervisee. The failure of these two people to connect and engage would inevitably result in breach or revocation. Teejay saw the sliding doors as the entrance to the prison to which the supervisee would be returned. The climbing frame represented a spider's web binding *both* the humans it confined: the (higher) supervisor and the (lower) supervisee. He explained: 'The criminal justice system is like a spider's web. The more you struggle, the more tightly it grips you.'

From these initial observations, we worked first independently and then together to write lyrics. Teejay provided the song's narrative structure and all its metaphorical allusions. My role was limited to tidying up metre and rhyme, with minimal contributions to the formation of the ideas and words themselves. When it came to putting the words to music, Teejay played me a song from his mobile phone; I can't recall the artist or the song, but I remember that we described it as a sort of 'rising lament' and so that was the sort of music that I tried to write to accompany his words. Over the course of several hours, we settled on chords and a melody. On the second day, we rehearsed and eventually recorded the song together.

The lyrics of the song 'Blankface' are reproduced as follows. It can be played freely here: https://voxliminis.bandcamp.com/album/seen-and-heard-ep, in a version recorded later by one of the musicians that led the workshop, Louis Abbott. Intriguingly, although this is essentially a post hoc cover version, Louis's interpretation and performance of the song came closer to conveying Teejay's meaning than he and I were (musically) able to.

Blankface

The clock spins, zero hour begins
This is the end, the end again
Here sits Blankface and she spins my tale
I've stopped listening now I know that I'll fail

Tick by tick and line by line
Thread by thread now you weave mine
A web of shadows, a silk spun tomb
A windowless room, windowless room

Sliding doors open and they welcome me in
This is the place, the place we pay for sin
These four seasons they reflect in glass
Trapped in a jar here where the time will not pass

Tick by tick and line by line
Thread by thread now you weave mine
A web of shadows, a silk spun tomb
A windowless room, windowless room

One day ending, a new day begins
Tick says 'he'll do it', again and again and again
You see what you want but I know it's not real
Anyone out there who can feel what I feel?

Working through this writing, rehearsing and recording process provided an opportunity for me to learn more about Teejay's experiences of supervision and to reflect on my own, both as a researcher and as a former criminal justice social worker. Unlike more conventional forms of research like interviewing, we learned not by me questioning him but rather in our collaborative consideration of how and where our experiences fitted into or informed the narrative we wanted to convey. For example, Teejay talked about how he recognised 'Blankface's' expression, having seen it many times across the interview room desk, and how he had mirrored that expression back to countless supervisors in the past. In forming the song's chorus, we spoke about how it feels to have your (his)story 'spun' by a supervisor 'tick by tick'-ing boxes to complete forms and how shrunken and drained (like the desiccated prey of a spider) this can make a person feel. As a practitioner, this editorial power was something I had reflected on and about which I often felt uncomfortable.

Teejay's weariness with a life lived under supervision surfaced in the final verse, just as it did in some of his *Supervisible* photographs (see McNeill, 2018). However, his weariness was not, as I had assumed, with the requirements and intrusions of submitting to supervision. Indeed, after 10 years of being free from any trouble, he could have applied to have the requirement to meet with a social worker lifted. I struggled for some time to understand why Teejay couldn't see the point in making that application. Now, I think I understand that Teejay's weariness was about still being construed as a subject requiring supervision, a construction he rejects in the song's penultimate line: 'You see what you want, but I know it's not real.'

The pain that he articulates in the song then was not primarily the pain of being surveilled and disciplined, it was the pain of being interminably ('tick by tick', but now in the sense of time passing) misrecognised as someone who (still) needs to be surveilled. As Teejay had asked in our brief meeting to discuss his photographs: 'You see me [as I am] coming across to you? Am I a risk in any way that you see?' What Teejay most wanted was to be recognised and trusted as a person worthy of unsupervised freedom.

'Helping Hand'

I spent much less time with John than with Teejay. He could attend only the second and final day of the workshop and – having taken part in workshops previously – he initially worked independently to develop his own song. It was only under the pressure of the clock ticking down to the time to record the song that I recognised the need to help him out a little, since the other musicians were busy.

John is in his 30s, and, having served a long (but unlike Teejay) deter-minate prison sentence, he is now subject to post-release supervision. At the time of the workshop, he had been out of prison for about 18 months. He had over five years of his post-release supervision period still ahead.

It was clear from the outset that John wanted to write a positive and upbeat song. He said that he had a good relationship with his social worker and appreciated the support and encouragement that the super-visor provided. Supervision wasn't easy – particularly in terms of the ways that it interfered with his freedom of association with friends and family – and it hadn't helped him navigate the labour market exclusion that most concerned him at the time. Even so, he valued the chance to talk to someone about the issues he faced. Perhaps unlike Teejay and perhaps because his supervision was relatively recent and was time-limited, he accepted its legitimacy as part of his sentence; a sentence that he felt he deserved.

I don't recall John making much reference to the pictures in developing his lyrics. Rather, he had settled on a simple chronological structure reflecting his past, present and future and the role of supervision and sup-port (or the lack of supervision and support) in it. The help that I provided again centred on helping him with metre and rhyme, and in putting the words to music. John likes country music. In the absence of more expert musical help and under pressure of time, we settled on a simple folk-country melody and chord structure; a kind of travelling song that con-veyed both journeying and reflecting on the journey at the same time. In the absence of a publicly available recording, the lyrics are reproduced as follows.

Helping hand

Was going down a rocky road
No one to help me on my way
I wish I'd had you by my side
Stop these feelings deep inside

Hold my hand and let me go
The things I know, I can't unknow
Let me go, please hold my hand
It's time to fly, I know I can
It's time to fly, I know I can

Now I have you by my side
Making sure I do no wrong
I am glad that you are in my life
Though it's only for so long

Hold my hand and let me go
The things I know, I can't unknow
Let me go, please hold my hand
It's time to fly, I know I can
It's time to fly, I know I can

Time to move on in my life
I'll take the next steps on my own
I will take you with me, in my heart
That way I'll never be alone

At the time, John wrote this about the song's meaning:

This song is about not having someone there that could have
helped me in a time of need in the past. Verse 2 is about how
grateful I am about having someone who is here in my present.
The last verse is about how I would like to move on in the
future – not needing a helping hand – but still taking in the
things that I have learned.

Clearly, this reflects a much more positive and optimistic take on supervision than Teejay's. John welcomed the help he was receiving – and
wished it had been available to him earlier in life, before he got into trouble. Even so, there is obvious ambivalence in the chorus lines 'Hold my
hand and let me go' and 'Let me go, please hold my hand'. These lines
convey both the comfort and reassurance of being held and the desire to
be more fully free and independent. Even so, this is essentially a song
about helpful and legitimate supervision and support.

The other songs written in the workshop approached (or departed
from) the theme of supervision in very diverse ways. From those still available alongside 'Blankface' on the EP,[5] 'You're Waiting' by Richard Bull (a
radio producer) co-written with Louis Abbott, reflects on Richard's (supervisory) role as the father of an adolescent daughter. In 'There's Always a
Way', Gordon McKean (a criminal justice social worker), again co-writing
with Louis Abbott, explores the possibilities of apology and redemption.

'Five Days', by Chris McBrearty (a former supervisee) and Gordon McKean explore the crisis point of arrest and police detention as the trigger for a process of recovery. In several songs, the formal institutional lines between policing, courts, probation, parole and prisons blur into more generalised reflections on lives affected by criminal justice, for better or worse.

CONCLUSIONS: SUPERVISION, RECOGNITION AND MISRECOGNITION

In different ways, these representations of supervision in photography and song illustrate the themes of many of the ethnographic studies discussed previously. For example, Teejay's experience seems to have much in common with the parolees in Werth's study; perhaps partly because of the similarities in the terms of their involvement with criminal justice; that is, as people who have progressed beyond release but not to freedom. However, unlike Werth's participants, Teejay doesn't seem to be actively engaged in a struggle with the system's *disciplinary* power; from his perspective, personal transformation had already happened by his own effort and on his own terms, years before. John is in a different position – he sees himself as being in a process of transition if not transformation – and he is differently disposed to a related exercise of penal power that he sees as legitimate.

Both Teejay and John ultimately want dominion over their own lives. The problem for Teejay is that he knows this will never be granted. Yet, rather than allowing his sense of who he is to be subjugated by the system's logic, Teejay is highly reflective about his situation and both dismissive and critical of it. In formal terms, he does what he has to do; he complies. But in his pictures and in 'Blankface', he actively disputes and contests the legitimacy of his continuing misrecognition as a subject in need of supervision. By contrast, John recognises himself as the subject of legitimate supervision on a journey to his eventual and complete liberation from penal control.

Although it would be foolish to over-generalise from these experiences, placing them in the context of the other studies reported previously suggests that *both* the symbolic and the material aspects of being gripped tightly by the penal state's processes and agents hurt penal subjects in significant ways but also that these pains can be moderated by helpful and legitimate supervision.

The pains of 'judgment' – and the limits of judgemental authority – play a key role here. Indeed, as I noted previously, in the Supervisible project more generally, 'judgment' was a very prominent theme in the pictures from all three jurisdictions. To give one further example of this theme (from Fitzgibbon et al., 2017), a German supervisee living under supervision (in a kind of halfway house) shared a picture of a chest of drawers with the lowest drawer open. In explaining this picture's intended meaning, he referred to the German term 'Schubladendenken' (literally: drawer thinking), a compartmentalised and stereotyped way of thinking that might be translated as 'pigeonholing'.

> *Each time I see my probation officer – they have these*
> *predefined questionnaires, these ones they use. [...] And I am,*
> *for instance, I am in the drawer* [figurative for: category]
> *'without social contacts', 'without work'.*

He illustrated this giving an example of his probation officer reacting to the news that the supervisee had lost his job:

> *He didn't ask me how I felt in this moment without work. All he*
> *was concerned about was that when [it] all goes wrong for me*
> *that I could ricochet* [figuratively: reoffend]. *[...] Another*
> *stabilizing factor has disappeared.*

For this German supervisee, as for Teejay in Scotland, the penal apparatus of mass supervision in and through which they suffer *mis*-recognises them and *mis*-judges them; for the German supervisee, it also *mis*-construes his struggle for work as a risk factor rather than a human need.

In a recent paper based mainly on my encounters with Teejay in *Supervisible* and in *Seen and Heard* (McNeill, 2018), I suggest that institutional forms and processes of mass supervision that generate these forms of misrecognition might be conceptualised better as a 'Malopticon' than as a Panopticon. I argue that in the metaphorical Malopticon:

> *penal subjects suffer not hyper- or super-visibility; rather, they*
> *suffer the pain of not being seen; at least not as they would*
> *recognise themselves [...] The Blankfaced officers of the*
> *Malopticon stare at the supervisee, but they do not see* him or

her *at all; their gaze fails to individualise him or to discern him.*
But not only is the subject of the Malopticon seen badly; he is
she is seen as bad [...] Worse still, the Malopticon projects this
dubious assessment – socially and temporally: 'Tick says he'll
do it, again and again'. Merely by virtue of its insistence on
supervising them, the Malopticon represents and projects its
subjects as untrustworthy. So, while in its rhetoric it sometimes
calls for their reintegration and re-entry, it simultaneously
undermines confidence in their redeemability by perennially
misrecognising and discrediting them. When they resist, the
Malopticon uses this as 'evidence' to confirm the veracity of its
constructions, tightening its grip on its subjects and projecting its
reified misrepresentations more intently. (McNeill, 2018,
pp. 19–20)

Teejay's representations of maloptical supervision are more concerned
with its *persistence* and with its *construction* of him, rather than with its
penetration into his 'soul' or psyche. These are pains associated as much
with civic degradation as with penal discipline. So long as a person is
under supervision, he or she is constructed as untrustworthy; as unworthy
of dominion. John accepts and tolerates this (for now) as part of a propor-
tionate and time-limited punishment; he wants his supervisor's help and he
accepts the need to earn his trust. By contrast Teejay refuses to accept a
permanently discredited and diminished status and a process of supervision from which there is no prospect of release.

The comparison sheds light on the crucial importance of supervision's
legitimacy in the eyes of its subjects, a legitimacy that is related to the
extent to which they can or cannot recognise themselves in the ways that
the system sees them. Gwen Robinson and I have written elsewhere about
how and why the legitimacy of supervision has a liquid quality; under different circumstances, it can flow into or ebb away from supervision.
Often, the organisational imperative to seek political and public legitimacy
acts in ways that can undermine the practical legitimacy (with supervisees)
on which supervision's helpfulness and usefulness depends (McNeill &
Robinson, 2012).

The temporal dimensions of supervision are also important to its legitimacy. Whereas John can see himself *being* who he is and *becoming* who
he aspires to be *through* supervision, there is literally no life *beyond*

supervision for Teejay. So, the only way for him to preserve his self-respect and to assert his vision of himself as a man who has settled his debts and learned his lessons is to dispute and resist how indefinite supervision portrays him.

Teejay's acute sense of grievance about this situation and the wider dangers associated with mass supervision's capacity for misrecognition point me towards Nancy Fraser's wide-ranging work on social in/justice. Fraser (2007) explores the relationships between recognition of status, redistribution of economic resources and representation in political terms. Misrecognition for Fraser is a problem for *social* justice because:

> [...] *people can also be prevented from interacting on terms of parity by institutionalized hierarchies of cultural value that deny them the requisite standing; in that case, they suffer from status inequality or misrecognition.* (Fraser, 2007, p. 20)

Drawing also on Honneth's (1995) work, Ruth Lister (2007) suggests the need to recognise *both* the social consequences of misrecognition *and* its psychological effects. She illustrates this powerfully with reference to empirical studies of the experiences of people in poverty and of people seeking asylum. In similar vein, Wacquant's (2011) analysis of 'Urban Denigration and Symbolic Desolation in the Hyperghetto' points out the ways in which these forces come to be concentrated in particular places and spaces and on particular populations in what he terms the 'dualizing metropolis' of advanced societies. The analysis in Chapter 3 has already drawn attention to the ways in which mass supervision is both pervasive and concentrated in particular places and amongst particular social groups.

In turn, this points us beyond the social and psychological and towards the political dimensions of misrecognition. As I have argued elsewhere,

> In 'advanced societies', the degradation of certain social groups (asylum seekers, migrants, 'felons', ghetto-dwellers) serves a common purpose; these degraded groups can be put beyond the pale and behind the veil; the deprivation or diminution of their citizenship serves to minimize the neo-liberal state's liabilities (see Barker, 2017). The Malopticon strips them of entitlement to support by projecting them both as threats to be managed and as objects of control (Miller & Stuart, 2017). The dispersal (and

concentration) of degradation through the Malopticon is thus part of the inter-connected welfare retrenchment and penal expansion that Wacquant (2009) described. When set alongside the findings of other studies, this analysis suggest that we need to map and challenge mass supervision not just as the 'dispersal of discipline' of which Cohen (1985) and others warned, but also – within 'societies of control' (Deleuze, 1990) – as the 'dispersal of degradation.' (McNeill, 2018, p. 20)

The next chapter turns to the question of how we might best resist such a dispersal of degradation by engaging in public and professional debate about supervision's proper limits, its legitimacy and its helpfulness. In other words, it is time to explore how to clear landmines and create second chances.

NOTES

1. The term refers to a device worn on the ankle that electronically monitors the wearer's compliance with a curfew.

2. See www.offendersupervision.eu. Accessed on 11 March 2018.

3. Pictures from the exhibition are available here: http://www.offendersupervision.eu/supervisible. Accessed on 19 February 2018 and the resultant EP can be found here: https://voxliminis.bandcamp.com/album/seen-and-heard-ep. Accessed on 19 February, 2018. Although *Seen and Heard* was initially seen as a 'knowledge exchange' (or dissemination) project rather than as (more) research, it produced significant further evidence and learning about the penal character of supervision. Since we secured fully informed consent to record both the processes and the outcomes of the songwriting workshop, and to put the songs into the public domain (with anonymity protected, where requested), I include discussion of this supplementary project here.

4. I am very grateful to Nicola Carr, Gwen Robinson, Anne Worrall and their colleagues in the 'Picturing Probation' project for permission to reproduce some of the photographs they collected in this book.

5. See: https://voxliminis.bandcamp.com/album/seen-and-heard-ep. Accessed on 20 February 2018.

CHAPTER 6

SEEING MASS SUPERVISION

A STRANGELY APPEALING ASSEMBLY

Joe couldn't quite get his head around this place or these people. In fact, he felt a bit dazed. Or maybe dazzled. The meeting room was bristling with energy. The people were like fireflies alight with friction; sparks looking for tinder. He wasn't sure whether to be excited or just plain terrified. Probably both.

Figure 21. Untitled 10.

Pauline had introduced Joe to Petra the week before, describing her as the convenor of the 'Conviction Collective'. Petra said the collective was 'part self-help group, part social movement' (though Joe thought it sounded more like a 70s folk-rock super-group). The only membership qualifications, she said, were a criminal conviction and a personal conviction, born of experience, that the justice system needed to change. Most of the fireflies in the room had both kinds of conviction, but they welcomed a few 'associates' – community activists, social workers, students and academics – who could boast only the second sort.

To be honest, Joe was sold on neither self-help nor social movements (nor 70s folk-rock super-groups), but Petra wasn't the sort of person to take 'no' for an answer, and their initial conversation had piqued his curiosity. When she told him her own story – and the story of the group's genesis – it made him realise that he had been so busy trying to cope with his own spectacular and self-propelled fall from grace, that he hadn't stopped to think that there were other people in his situation, also subject to the vagaries of the 'system' in which he found himself entangled.

Petra had spoken so passionately and so practically about the obstacles put in the way of re-building a life during and after punishment, and how things could and should be done better, that – for the first time since the incident – Joe felt the stirrings of interest in something beyond his personal troubles.

So, he had agreed to come to the meeting … and now he wondered if he regretted it. He felt uncomfortable, uncertain and ill-at-ease. The incessant din of chatter and laughter was giving him a headache. It had been a while since he had been around so many people. They could certainly be described as a motley crew, but they were also a strangely appealing assembly of diverse characters, perhaps held together only by their shared convictions. A little like a church without religion, Joe thought, still figuring out its doctrine and its rituals; a fellowship connected by a common hope for change.

Petra looked across at him and smiled encouragingly. Joe felt the same unnerving sensation that he often experienced with Pauline; they both made him feel as if his thoughts were appearing as subtitles on his forehead.

A little later, as they tidied up the room, Petra asked:

'So, what do you reckon, Joe? I know that it can be a bit of a brain-melt, but if this collective is going to achieve anything, we're going to need a fund-raiser and a treasurer. You've got the skills and qualifications –

and Pauline says you need a project if you're ever going to get your head out of your arse. As someone once said, 'From each according to his ability, to each according to his need'. What do you say? You up for it?'

INTRODUCTION

The last two chapters of this book take us in a different direction from the first five. Chapter 1 briefly introduced the issues and questions about pervasive punishment and mass supervision that the book aims to address. Chapter 2 reviewed different theoretical accounts of how and why punishment changes, setting these out as resources for making sense of the emergence of mass supervision. In Chapters 3–5, I have called on those resources from time to time to examine and (to some extent) explain the scale and social distribution of supervision, its legitimation and adaptation in late modernity, and its penal character as a lived experience.

In this chapter, I begin by briefly reviewing and consolidating our progress in Chapters 3–5 towards making sense of 'mass supervision'. Then, in this and the final chapter, I want to consider how we might use this analysis in seeking to do something about it. I defer any of my own predictions about and prescriptions for supervision's future until the final chapter. Here, I want first to explore contemporary debates about both public criminology and visual criminology to consider whether and how we might best challenge the invisibility of 'mass supervision', making it the subject of public and democratic dialogue and deliberation. I end this chapter by considering the potential risks and benefits of doing so.

MAKING SENSE OF 'MASS SUPERVISION'

Chapter 2's review of a range of different attempts to make sense of penal change concluded that doing so requires us to analyse the penal impact of wider economic, social, cultural and political changes in the societies whose penal systems interest us. But I argued that, in addition to exploring these *distal influences* on penalty, we need to examine the more *proximate influences* represented in more particular ways of ordering penal states and systems. This means attending carefully to variations between penal states in the ways in which penal power is generated and circumscribed, governed and deployed (Garland, 2013b). It also necessitates a close examination of state-level political and institutional dynamics; infrastructure and resources; law and policy; organisational structures and professional organisations and unions; and wider civil society engagement in the penal system.

However, even if we regard these characteristics of the penal state as important proximate influences on how penalty develops in policy and practice, then to increase the granularity of our analysis, we will also need to zoom in on *local influences*. Here, the effects of distal and proximate influences are moderated by even more specific and peculiar characteristics; for example, by the acquired dispositions and habits of local actors (e.g. judges, prosecutors, probation and parole staff, and each of their professional associations) and by the distribution of capital within the (local) penal field (Page, 2013), whether in the form of material resources, cultural capital, social networks or the power that status, recognition or distinction confers. The potency of 'happenstance', of historical path dependencies and of human agency (Brangan, 2013) is also keenly felt at the local level where unforeseen events, problems and situations command a response from local actors.

Indeed, the contestation that Goodman et al. (2017) identify as being so central in the production of penal change (*and* during periods of apparent penal stability) may be most apparent at the local level, although local- and state-level penal contestation are interrelated and mutually constitutive. The kinds of penal states that develop through these processes may also exercise some reciprocal influence even on the distal factors that reflect the wider social change. The local changes the state just as the state changes the local, and punishment changes society, just as society changes punishment.

Chapter 3's analysis of the scale and social distribution of 'mass supervision' illustrates some of these points. Firstly, it confronts us with the unavoidable reality that explaining the penal change, penal states and penal fields requires us, as Phelps (2017b) urges, to consider not just *how much* but also *how* we punish differently in different states and at different times. This second question – about the *forms* of punishment that evolve – underlines the folly of trying to make sense of penal change *without* making sense of supervision, not just in terms of its volume and distribution but also in terms of its penal character. To do so is like trying to explain the evolution of health care only by looking at the historical development and contemporary forms of hospitals. In punishment, as in health care, most of the action that needs to be accounted for is elsewhere – beyond not behind the walls – extraneous but symbiotically related to the architectures and institutions that are too readily mistaken as definitive and representative of the field.

Both in the USA and in Scotland, the distal influences on penalty remain important in making sense not just of the growth of supervision but also of its social distribution, particularly in relation to ethnicity and class, although these demographics play differently in the two cases. Crucially, Phelps's (2017b) work shows us that in the USA, between 1980 and 2010, state-level probation populations expanded at very different and unpredictable rates. Distal influences cannot account for this. Rather, a closer reading of proximate and local influences is required if we are to understand how some states target probation more effectively than others, and how some states deliver it more constructively than others, sometimes allowing for diversion rather than net-widening.

Chapter 4 aims to provide one such close reading of the development of supervision in a small nation: Scotland. That analysis applies but extends Robinson et al.'s (2013) account of how probation systems have thrived in late modernity through four forms of adaptation and legitimation – managerial, punitive, rehabilitative and reparative. I showed how penal reductionism has been discursively interwoven with rehabilitation, reparation and managerialism (but not punitiveness) at different times in the history of supervision in Scotland. Recalling the evidence of Chapter 3, I concluded that Scottish penal reductionism is a story of successful failure; producing a huge expansion in rates of supervision but having little impact on imprisonment rates. More generally, making sense of Scotland's enduring but flawed and fragile welfarism requires analysis of contestation within a penal state that has been constitutionally unsettled, producing turbulence within the penal field. However, I also presented evidence that the (proximate) institutional policy-level contestation apparent in legitimation struggles maps only imperfectly onto how (local) practice is constructed. Penal contestation must, therefore, be analysed 'all the way down' to the levels of practice and experience if we are to understand what penalty is, what it means and how it is changing. This is as true of supervision as it is of imprisonment.

To examine supervision as a lived experience (and indirectly, from the receiving end, as a constructed practice), Chapter 5 reviews a range of forms of relevant research before focusing on new findings from two creative projects – *Supervisible* and *Seen and Heard* – that explored how supervisees chose to represent their experiences of supervision in pictures and in songs. These findings have much in common with a wider range of recent ethnographies of supervision that are highly revealing. Taken together, these studies draw attention to the pervasiveness and painfulness of supervision as a lived experience, even if some studies also suggest that these pains may be moderated if supervision is experienced as legitimate, helpful and time-limited. In my own analysis (McNeill, 2018), absent these three conditions, mass supervision develops 'maloptical' qualities, representing a form of pervasive penal control that disperses degradation and disqualification as much as discipline, diminishing its subjects' civic standing and rights and thus the state's responsibilities to and liabilities for them. It is through the analysis of highly localised experiences of mass supervision that perhaps we can see and confront most clearly the impacts and effects of distal influences on penalty.

It seems then that 'mass supervision' can be understood in several interrelated ways. The term refers to very large increases in the scale of supervision such that it is much more pervasive in society, yet it remains primarily concentrated amongst structurally disadvantaged communities. These increases in scale need to analysed and understood both with reference to variations across and within penal states over time, and in comparison with other forms of penal action (primarily custodial and financial penalties). The ways in which the emergence of mass supervision has been legitimated and engineered – often but not always as a putative vehicle for rehabilitation or penal reductionism – also require careful and critical scrutiny. Not least, we need to explore the disjuncture between the arguments used to advocate for supervision (as a diversion) and the evidence about its systemic effects (as expansion) and its individual impacts (as degradation and discipline).

This analysis suggests that any project of challenging mass supervision requires at least three interrelated strategies: the first focused on scaling down supervision, the second focused on clarifying and circumscribing its legitimate purposes and role, and the third (within these constraints) focused on developing and delivering it constructively. But before we can even begin to discuss and develop these strategies in the final chapter, there are some prior questions to consider: How do we get mass supervision on the agenda in terms of public debate and democratic deliberation, why should we do so and what might be the costs and benefits of doing so?

SEEING AND NOT SEEING 'MASS SUPERVISION'

In the introduction, I referred to Gwen Robinson's (2016) characterisation of supervisory sanctions as the 'Cinderella' of 'Punishment and Society' studies, marginalised as 'a neglected and under-theorised zone' (Robinson, 2016, p. 101). In the preceding chapters, I have tried to make my own contribution to enhancing the academic dialogue between accounts of penal change and mass supervision. However, important though it is to advance and improve scholarship in this area, the aspiration to do something about mass supervision also requires engagement and dialogue beyond the academy. The quality of that dialogue matters a great deal. As Chapter 3's analysis makes clear, it has often been *progressive* policy-makers and practitioners who have, unwittingly, driven the expansion of penal control, partly by failing to properly police the boundaries between diversion and net-widening, both in the ways that supervision is imposed and in the ways that it is delivered, despite the warnings of some prescient scholars (e.g. Cohen, 1985). At the very least, that suggests a troubling problem in the conversation between theory, research, policy and practice.

But I think this problem extends even further into the public sphere. There, widespread ignorance of and apathy or cynicism about supervisory sanctions may be an even greater challenge. Research tends to suggest that public understanding of and confidence in supervisory sanctions like probation and parole is very low (Hough & Park, 2002), even if there is some evidence that engagement in deliberative processes that invoke 'redemption' narratives may support shifts in attitude (Maruna & King, 2008). In broad terms, public understanding of supervision seems to be hamstrung by limited and inadequate media coverage (Maguire & Carr, 2013) that tends to characterise non-custodial sanctions as inherently inferior to the prison (Hayes, 2013) – the penal institution that dominates our penal landscape and imaginations (Brown, 2009). Indeed, it might be argued that one reason for supervision's perennial struggle for legitimacy (discussed in Chapter 4) is that, despite the crucial and often observed importance of punishment's expressive aspects (Freiberg, 2001), it is not clear what supervisory sanctions communicate, for whose benefit and to whom (McNeill & Dawson, 2014).

One innovative and recent Scottish study sought to explore the communication processes by which media shape public understanding and attitudes towards community sanctions and to examine how these processes promote or undermine their legitimacy (Happer, McGuinness, McNeill, & Tiripelli, 2018). Rather than focusing on the content of media reporting, the study examined the dynamic processes and practices through which audiences select, access and evaluate media reports, and whether these practices tended to confirm or challenge their penal predispositions. The methodology involved immersing focus groups in a multi-media environment constructed around news reporting on community sanctions. The focus groups involved 27 people (15 men and 12 women), all local to Glasgow but drawn from different occupational groups. The three-stage process involved (1) examining the nature of and sources for participants' beliefs and opinions in relation to crime and punishment and, in particular, community sanctions; (2) immersing participants in the constructed news environment to illuminate their processes of engagement with the media; (3) exploring the impact of immersion by asking participants to discuss their views about and responses to particular stories and to identify any shifts in their beliefs and attitudes.

Happer et al.'s (2018) study was small-scale and exploratory, but its findings are salutary. In sum, they find that 'moral censure remains a key feature of late modern penal tastes and community sanctions – even when cast in the language of 'payback' – do not seem to satisfy [these tastes]' (p16). This finding was consistent across respondents with different media preferences and different forms of media engagement. 'Traditionalists' mainly relied on newspapers and TV whereas 'convergers' also used social media. Broadly speaking, traditionalists rejected stories about community sanctions because of a perceived lack of censure and punishment; convergers rejected the same stories because the stories seemed to lack critical distance; they were suspicious of being manipulated by 'humanising' stories about the recipients of community sanctions. Both groups, therefore, seemed to opt-in to familiar penal narratives and out of discomfiting ones, thus tending to reinforce their existing, settled penal tastes.

Happer et al. (2018, p. 17) conclude that:

To encourage a more informed dialogue about the legitimacy or illegitimacy of different forms of punishment (whether imprisonment or community sanctions) may require us to move beyond the top-down approaches of 'better' penal reform campaigns or 'better' public relations strategies for probation. Rather, our findings suggest the need for a much deeper deliberative dialogue about punishment which has the potential to better exercise and develop our penal tastes; dialogue that allows us to recognise when satiating our appetites and indulging our tastes might in fact harm us and others (cf. Loader, 2009). The echo chambers created by both traditionalists and convergers mean that the news media may not be the best arena in which to foster such dialogue.

SUPERVISION, IMAGINARIES AND IMAGINATION

The problem of supervision's invisibility does not begin and end with academic neglect and public mis/understandings. Throughout this book, I have also tried to highlight a gap between what policymakers and practitioners *think* they are doing in promoting and practising supervision and different kinds of evidence about its systemic and human effects. In these contexts, the problem is not perhaps one of invisibility so much as one of distortion or lack of perspective. For example, in Chapter 3, drawing on the work of Michelle Phelps, I highlighted the gap between what policymakers and practitioners imagine that probation might do in terms of diversion from penal control and the evidence of its contradictory, net-widening effects. In Chapter 4, I extended this analysis, outlining the remarkable persistence of supervision's discursive association with penal reductionism in Scotland, despite the evidence of its huge contribution to Scottish penal expansion. In Chapter 5, I drew on different forms of evidence to show that supervision's impact on the lives of supervisees often differs markedly not just from how it is commonly misrepresented in the press (as 'walking free from court'), but also from how it is imagined by those of its practitioners committed to rehabilitation (and supporting 'second chances').

Pat Carlen's (2008) notion of 'penal imaginaries' is instructive in this context. The origins of the term lie in her observations of how the rehabilitative ethos of prisons has been hollowed out in recent decades. Under the assault of social and economic pressures associated with late modernity, the focus has shifted from a serious effort at *social* reintegration to preoccupations with risk management and (sometimes) an associated demand for *personal* transformation. Carlen (2008) argues that prison staff collude in a charade. They know that social reintegration has become well-nigh impossible in these conditions, but sustain a rehabilitative fiction or imaginary in and through their professional or occupational discourses and practices.

In the decade since Carlen's important contribution, the situation for probation staff in England and Wales has become much more difficult – and much more market-driven (Burke, Collett, & McNeill, 2018). The part-privatization of probation services under the UK Government's *Transforming Rehabilitation* initiative has resulted in profound organisational and professional ruptures, including the creation of a new National Probation Service (NPS) dealing with higher risk cases and the contracting out of the rest of the work to 21 Community Rehabilitation Companies (CRCs), entailing the splitting of existing staff between these two new practice contexts. Drawing on Carlen's thinking, we might fear that staff of the public NPS are now thoroughly subject to what Carlen (2008) calls 'risk-crazed governance', whilst staff of the private CRCs are subject to market-driven imperatives to drive costs down.

Indeed, Burke et al. (2018) – reviewing evidence from studies of the impact of these reforms and from recent inspection reports – argue that the reforms have indeed fragmented probation, undermining its legitimacy (with judges and perhaps with supervisees) and producing changes in organisations and practices that seem inimical to those values and approaches that once characterised probation. Nonetheless, the evidence does not suggest that probation staff in England and Wales, at least for the most part, are in active collusion with these processes; indeed, perhaps contrary to Carlen's view, it would seem to suggest that many of them are both tormented by them and resistant to them.

In one sense, this is hardly surprising. There is ample evidence that probation staff – perhaps particularly in jurisdictions where they are university-educated professionals – are critically reflexive about their work. And there are many studies of their sophisticated resistance to and adaptation of, for example, punitive or risk-based logics (McNeill et al., 2009; Robinson & McNeill, 2004). More generally, at least in the UK, probation researchers, educators and practitioners have actively debated the politics and ethics of their work for decades, not least in the Probation Journal (which has been published since 1929 and has a long association with the National Association of Probation Officers).

That said, there remain good reasons to heed Carlen's (2008) warning that we must resist the power of established penal imaginaries to restrain and disable critique; and, crucially, to inhibit the imagining of something better. I offer one salutary example, based on my own experience as a criminal justice social worker turned researcher. Despite the fact that I have been engaged in one way or another with supervision since the early 1990s, it has taken me decades to confront its *penal* character, as outlined in Chapter 5. Indeed, it was only the combination of the gentle persistence of more critical European and American colleagues (who were, crucially, less professionally and personally associated with proba-tion) and the vivid force of the images produced by supervisees in the *Supervisible* project, that propelled me towards that recognition. Indeed, much of the impetus for this book comes from a single and, with hind-sight, blindingly obvious insight generated by that project — that supervi-sion consists of much more than meetings between supervisors and supervisees.

The Anglophone literature on probation focuses on supervisory encounters and relationships for very good reasons; this is where con-structive work might be done to support reintegration and reduce re-offending. In other words, the focus on supervisory encounters unwittingly reflects a practitioner perspective (this *is* where supervision happens for them) and a specific associated research interest; in what works to reduce reoffending. But, as the evidence of Chapter 5 reveals, this focus creates a kind of tunnel vision in the supervisory imaginary; there is much, much more to the penal experience of supervision than these encounters.

If this personal example is salutary, it also offers some hope. Carlen (2008) is as concerned with finding new ways of imagining punishment — or alternatives to punishment — as she is in exposing penal imaginaries.

Indeed, the two projects are linked; it is by recognising these imaginaries that we liberate our imaginations. As she writes:

> *[...] the same knowledges that are incorporated into imaginary penalities are also those which, re-imagined differently, might one day give birth to new, more democratic and more socially enhancing responses to crime and security threats. (Carlen, 2008, p. xxiv)*

Since I think it was no accident that it was supervisees' pictures (and not words) that creatively disrupted my own imaginary of supervision, I turn now to the promise of creative, 'counter-visual criminology'.

COUNTER-VISUALISING SUPERVISION

In spite of its apparent privileging of the visual, visual criminology is in fact concerned with all forms of academic, policy, professional, media and cultural representations of crime and punishment:

> *Criminological and criminal justice optics are incredibly powerful in the ways in which they facilitate practices of seeing and not seeing, practices that have the ability to render people, harm and control visible and invisible, apparent or disappeared [...]. (Brown & Carrabine, 2017, p. 6)*

Carlen's (2008) concept of 'penal imaginaries' also focuses on the distorted 'optics' at play in criminal justice policy and practice discourses, but our earlier discussion of media representations of community sentences is equally pertinent here. I have already shown how, in both contexts – professional and public – invisibility and distortion exercise important limiting effects on dialogue and deliberation about supervision.

The project of *counter-visual criminology* (Schept, 2017) offers one way to address these problems. Counter-visual criminology is 'about the deployment of a politics of visibility for change and transformation' (Brown & Carrabine, 2017, p. 6). In other words, it seeks to help us 'unsee' or 'see through' familiar misrepresentations of crime and punishment, so that it becomes possible to see these issues differently, to ask new questions, to offer new critiques and, equally importantly, to construct new ways of seeing.

In broad terms, the COST Action on Offender Supervision in Europe itself was a 'counter-visual' criminological research network. Even if we did not know or use the term at the time, we were working together to develop new ways of challenging a fundamental misrepresentation of punishment; the focusing of our penal imaginaries *and* imaginations in and on the prison.

More specifically – and more intentionally – in the *Supervisible*, *Picturing Probation* and *Seen and Heard* projects (discussed in Chapter 5), we developed an 'emic' approach, focusing on how people within a culture (or in this case an institutionalised form of punishment) themselves saw it and chose to represent it. Our counter-visual intention was to bring these visual representations directly into academic, professional and public conversations. Rather than offering an 'etic' (or outsider) interpretations of other people's experiences of supervision, we wanted to exploit the polysemic character of pictures and songs as engaging and vivid means of inviting meaning-making with and from the perspectives of both their 'authors' and their 'readers' or 'listeners'. This approach also reflected our intention to treat participants as 'knowledgeable informants' and partners in the process, not as mere producers of objects that we claimed the authority to interpret (see Pauwels, 2017).

Two of the most important qualities of creative representations of human experience are their ambiguous, open texture and their resistance to closure. Often, they require both the creator to review and make sense of their experience and the viewer or listener to make their own sense of what they see or hear. Leaving space for that sense-making seems crucial since it is in and through that process that the viewer-reader is invited to engage and even identify with the creator's experience; and often to *feel* it or be *affected* by it. If interpretation and sense-making generate an affective connection between an image, a song or a story and its viewers, listeners or readers, then these visual, literary and auditory representations perhaps do more than making supervision seen and heard; they may make aspects of an unfamiliar experience more 'feel-able'. In other words, they invite the viewer, reader or listener into *both* a cognitive *and* an affective engagement with the experience represented, perhaps exemplifying a sensory criminology as much as a counter-visual criminology. That engagement is likely to be partial, attenuated or mediated in important ways (e.g. by a musician performing a song, or a curator exhibiting a photograph); it is not a direct encounter between the author and audience of the representation. Nonetheless, in the process of the viewer, reader or listener attending to the representation, its author may become less of a 'moral stranger' (Loewy, 1997) and as we become better morally acquainted through these forms of representation and engagement, indifference to one another's fates, or even the hostility reserved for outsiders, may be undermined (Bauman, 2016).

It is for these reasons that, particularly with respect to its commitment to social transformation, participatory arts approaches may have much to offer a sensory or counter-visual criminology. For example, the broad literature on participative music-making, reveals how community music activities may have positive effects in the development of communication and awareness skills, supporting the ability to think and act creatively (Rimmer, Higham, & Brown, 2014), fostering self-confidence and building positive links between individuals and wider communities (DCMS, 1999; Jermyn, 2001). Beyond these effects on individuals' capacities and skills for engaging with one another, there is some evidence that such activities can also have wider social effects; improving cohesion, community empowerment, self-determination and inclusion (Jermyn, 2004). With regards to audiences who engage with the songs created in such contexts, researchers have suggested that popular music can influence affective aspects of political processes, functioning as a social force connecting the political aspirations and activities of audiences, opening up semi-autonomous 'spaces' in public settings, fostering opportunities for resistance to social conditioning and for mediation of socially accepted and socially proscribed values (e.g. Lipsitz, 1994; Pratt, 1990).

These processes and effects may be influenced by the peculiarly informal nature of the learning that occurs through popular music (Green, 2002). Song-writing activities show some potential to create 'enclaves of autonomy' within larger institutions or power structures (Dougan, 1999). Sharing music is also social and collaborative in nature (Anderson, 2013; Small, 1998). More broadly, popular music also represents a non-representative form of tacit knowledge and therefore a potential means of expression that overcomes 'hermeneutical injustice'; meaning the injustice attendant on our inability to understand another person's lived experience because of a paucity of shared resources for expressing, hearing and understanding it (Fricker, 2007). The song 'Blankface', discussed in Chapter 5, perhaps exemplifies the capacity of music and song to vividly express and render intelligible Teejay's suffering; to help the rest of us see, hear or sense it. In so doing, it begins to chip away at the injustice represented in our failure to take seriously such supervision-related suffering.

MASS SUPERVISION, PUBLIC CRIMINOLOGY AND DEMOCRATIC DIALOGUE

If visual criminology is concerned with analysing, challenging and re-imagining how punishment is represented, public criminology is concerned with analysing, challenging and reimagining how crime and punishment are discussed and debated, particularly in democratic societies.

In their engaging and provocative introductory text on 'Public Criminology?', Ian Loader's and Richard Sparks' (2010) introduce five endearing (and sometimes) infuriating protagonists — a series of ideal-type criminologists who represent different possible forms of engagements with politics and policy. The titles of these characters reveal both the identities and the tactics implied; the 'scientific expert', the 'policy advisor', the 'observer-turned-player', the 'social movement theorist/activist' and the 'lonely prophet'. In seeking to challenge the rising temperature of contemporary penal politics (which seems to offer more heat than light), two of these characters might be seen as penal climate change activists. Both the 'lonely prophet' and the 'social movement theorist' share an unwillingness to accept how things are. Both insist on the need for fundamental social change if penal politics are to cool down. By contrast, the 'scientific experts', 'policy advisers' and 'observers turned players' are pragmatists, working to use evidence about 'what works', new technologies and techniques, or legal structures and constraints in the meantime to insulate penal policy from the political heat.

While they want to stress the complementarities between these approaches, ultimately, Loader and Sparks argue that the tactical de-politicisation of crime and penal policy — for example, by allowing a body of independent experts to set the penal equivalent of the Bank of England's interest rate (Lacey, 2008) — is neither feasible nor desirable. Rather, they argue that criminology needs to fashion itself as a 'democratic under-labourer' (a term borrowed from John Locke, the seventeenth-century English political philosopher). By this, they have in mind a sensibility or a disposition that criminologists (of any and every hue) should seek to develop; one that reflectively and actively contributes to the development of a 'better politics of crime and regulation' (Loader & Sparks, 2010, p. 117). For Loader and Sparks (2010) this requires 'criminologists to cultivate greater humility in the face of democratic politics' (p. 119), to understand 'the circumstances of politics', to better appreciate the need to build consensus and support collective decision making. This is not, they argue, to cede too much to the multiple problems of contemporary politics (and the threats to democracy that these problems bring). Rather, it is to play a part in addressing and challenging them. To do so requires criminologists not to argue that as 'experts' they know best and should be left to get on with the job, but rather to bring criminological knowledge to the negotiating table, as it were, alongside other legitimate interests and forms of knowledge.

In this context, democratic under-labouring involves three 'moments': the moment of discovery (of new knowledge about and constructions of 'problems' and 'solutions'), the institutional-critical moment (which generates new knowledge that challenges existing systems, cultures and practices), and the normative moment (which engages with the moral dimensions of and value judgements at stake in criminal justice). In terms of this book's interests in 'pervasive punishment' and 'mass supervision', it seems possible to extend the claims that criminology has perhaps arrived at moments of discovery in relation to mass supervision and its human effects; and at institutional-critical moments, in relation to the institutional, legal, fiscal and organisational structures that shape it. These 'moments' clearly generate a number of questions about penal values, but I defer this book's 'normative moment' until the next and final chapter.

Loader and Sparks' (2010) book has attracted considerable attention, some of it critical. For example, Loic Wacquant's (2011) review essay remarks somewhat caustically:

> I will make my remarks brief and pointed for the sake of
> provoking and then reorienting the discussion away from
> textualist disquisitions on the hoary label of 'public' (enter
> discipline) and towards the political economy of the production,
> circulation and consumption of criminological knowledge in the

age of escalating inequality and pornographic penality.
(Wacquant, 2011, p. 438)

In other words, we should spend less time and effort on analysing what criminologists have to say about criminology and its public role, and more analysing the social and structural conditions that shape and skew both criminology and its political reception or rejection.

Similarly, Elizabeth Turner (2016) notes that Loader and Sparks (2010) admit that they have not explored the circumstances of reception of criminological knowledge, not least in 'a far from ideal "actually existing public sphere" [where] democratic principles can be subverted and social inequalities obscured and mystified, whilst the rich and powerful casually and unapologetically break the law, often without fear of coming under scrutiny' (Turner, 2016, p. 156). Her charge is that while Loader and Sparks (2010) have helped us to better articulate what public criminology might do, 'they have not provided a convincing account of how criminologists as 'bearers and interpreters' of knowledge' can realistically and democratically hope to contribute to a 'better politics' of crime and criminal justice under contemporary socio-political conditions' (Turner, 2016, p. 157).

Turner's (2016, p. 163) own prescription is that criminologists must move beyond the Weberian distinction between 'facts' and 'values' (and the modernist 'constitution' of the dubious distinction between them). Instead, 'we both can and should engage in informed and constructive deliberations (with each other and with the wider public) about the 'value' of different ways of representing, constructing and knowing reality [...]' In other words, while criminologists are not experts in possession of 'facts' that might act like 'trumps' in a penal–political card-game, they *do* have particular skills and forms of knowledge that can enable complex dialogue about crime and punishment, how we see them and how we respond to them.

Vincenzo Ruggiero (2012, p. 153), however, cautions against the 'unjustified moral superiority' implied by a public sociology (or criminology) 'from above' that 'is tantamount to claiming a leadership no one suffering problems would dream of bestowing on academics':

In this sense, the 'arrogance' detected by Tittle (2004) in public
sociology denotes, in fact, most criminology, a discipline which

> *needs 'informants' not peers, a type of social inquiry that needs to teach others in what contexts they are situated, which the others presumably ignore. Criminologists, Olympian observers, believe they can see the whole picture [...] As Bauman (2011, p. 163) has contended, our objects of study are not dumb by nature, but in order to retain our status 'and to secure the sovereign authority of our pronouncements, the objects to which our pronouncements refer need first to be made dumb.*
> *(Ruggiero, 2012, p. 156)*

He also decries the tendency of some criminologists to study marginalised people and communities 'with a missionary zeal and a honeyed paternalism', suggesting that, '[s]uch criminologists need their objects of study more than the objects need them' (Ruggiero, 2012, p. 156). Only in the abolitionist movement does he find a public criminology worthy of the name; one premised on collective action bringing change from below, its sociological analysis rooted in and with social movements. To be properly integrated within a social movement is, he argues, necessarily to reject the role of mediator between 'the socially excluded' and 'the authorities'. In the role of the mediator, it is much too tempting and easy to claim the right to speak *for* others, ultimately undermining cooperative mobilisation and expression of feelings of injustice.

Neither Loader and Sparks (2010) nor Turner (2016) advocates a public criminology from above. In both cases, the claims they would make for 'democratic under-labourers' or (in Turner's phrase) 'pragmatic, flexible, knowledge diplomats' are much more circumspect. In neither case would these public criminologists seek to speak for 'the excluded' to 'the authorities' or vice versa.

In more recent work, Loader and Sparks (2012 and forthcoming) and with Albert Dzur (Dzur, Loader, & Sparks, 2016), have risen to the challenge of more clearly articulating the kinds of resources required for a 'better penal politics'. In particular, they have sought to move 'beyond lamentation' (Loader & Sparks, 2012), that is, beyond questions of critique or strategies of penal restraint, looking instead to democratic theory itself as a resource for reconstructing responses to crime. They argue that much recent criminological work, including some of the best of it, has been so pessimistic about our bleak penal prospects as to abandon any hope of imagining something better. To move beyond these 'criminologies of disappointment', Loader and Sparks have begun to identify 'resources of hope'. Perhaps the most intriguing of these, particularly in light of Turner's (2016) criticism, relates to the promise found in better understanding how, where and when legitimate social arrangements can create space for dialogue and deliberation that might inform penal policies and practices.

In this regard, Loader and Sparks (forthcoming) revisit the pragmatism of John Dewey and his view of democratic decision-making as the 'joint exercise of practical intelligence by citizens at large [...] as cooperative social experimentation' (Anderson, 2006, p. 14). Social sciences, such as criminology, have a key role to play in these processes but, as Roberto Unger has argued:

> *The fundamental problem with the social sciences today is that they have severed the link between insight into what exists and imagination of what might exist at the next step [...] The vocation of social science is to help us understand how we came to be in this present situation, in such a fashion that our understanding of our circumstance, rather than putting is to sleep and inducing this fatalistic superstition, awakens us to the imagination of the adjacent possible.*[1]

That we have settled too readily for a merely critical social science is only part of the problem here. In addition, and particularly in the UK and the USA, we have elevated and privileged a form of political communication that is both adversarial rather than cooperative and exclusionary rather than inclusionary. Here, the default form of communication on social and political issues tends to be debate rather than dialogue – the literal meaning of which is 'to beat down'. Communication scholarship has shown consistently that this is often counterproductive (Tannen, 1999), sometimes leading to oversimplification, stereotyping, polarisation, confrontation and ultimately disaffection from political life and subsequent loss of social capital (Escobar, 2011; Mutz, 2006). As an adversarial mode of communication, debate can also make public spaces inaccessible and unappealing to citizens less accustomed to or adept at certain forms of public speaking, working to disadvantage the least privileged sections of society (Young, 2001).

In contrast, dialogical approaches can foster a range of individual, community and democratic goods, particularly in relation to hotly contested and divisive topics like crime and punishment (Forester, 2009; Littlejohn & Domenici, 2001). The etymology of dialogue implies 'a flow of meaning'. As Escobar (2011, p. 20) outlines, it aims to build understanding and relationships through communication that is 'mutually responsive, free-flowing, open-ended, and oriented to the exploration and co-creation of meanings'. It implies a quality of meeting between human subjects characterised by collaborative engagement. For these reasons, it seems obvious why dialogue rather than debate might help us collectively imagine Unger's 'adjacent possible' rather than merely defending entrenched positions for or against any status quo.

However, dialogue is not easy. It takes time and commitment, its impact is not always immediate or apparent, it entails a degree of trust and hence vulnerability, and it is often undermined by problems of power and inequalities (Escobar, 2012). Even so, effective and legitimate democratic deliberation is impossible without it. If we have not co-constructed our understandings of the issues at stake and of the 'adjacent possible', then the process of deliberation about how we address them will revert swiftly to resolution through factional debate in which established hierarchies will likely be re-asserted.

Hence for Roberto Gargarella (2016), what we require is 'Democracy all the way down'. For him, the case for deliberative democracy rests finally not in its pragmatic utility but in the ways in which it honours our equal moral dignity. As he argues:

> We live in unjust and unequal societies, and it is simply not acceptable to have our criminal norms created, applied and interpreted by an elite that benefits from this situation, and (quite possibly) is never affected by those coercive powers that they administer. Hopefully, in future, not-so-remote circumstances, things will be diverse [...] democracy needs to preserve and protect as rich treasures the voices of those who dissent, voices that sometimes carry messages we dislike, in forms that we dislike, but finally messages through which learn how to live together. (Gargarella, 2016, pp. 321–322)

Gargarella's insistence on the importance of dissent and of attending carefully to the voices we are most inclined to ignore or silence is as important in its implications for discussing supervision as it is in any other area of public policy. In simple terms, the argument of this chapter and of this book is that *we need to talk about supervision*; and, in that dialogue, we need to listen to those most intimately involved in it – supervisors and supervisees. Moreover, our dialogue will likely be enabled and enhanced by creative practices, processes, representations and responses that help us see, hear and sense supervision.

CONCLUSION: THE RISKS AND REWARDS OF SURFACING 'MASS SUPERVISION'

At the beginning of this chapter, the short story extract revealed Joe moving into the dialogic space created by the Conviction Collective. Surfacing from submersion in his private troubles, he seems to be on the brink of exploring how his experiences and the meanings he makes from them might relate to the experiences and meanings of others; collectively, they are forming convictions about social issues and questions through dialogue.

By contrast, the evidence we reviewed about public understandings of and appetites for community sentences seemed to suggest that penal tastes might be difficult to change. Partly, this may be accounted for by the ways in which our penal imaginaries have been framed and formed by certain cultural, political and professional representations. These imaginaries may both comfort and constrain us; perhaps they sustain a comfortingly familiar and self-justifying world view – basically of the good 'us' and the bad 'them' – but they also stifle our abilities to see and to steer towards a different world of adjacent possibilities.

Counter-visual and other sensory criminologies have the potential to disrupt our imaginaries, and – perhaps particularly where they draw on creative representations (as illustrated in Chapter 5) – to stimulate our imaginations. As Emily Dickinson wrote:

The Possible's slow fuse is lit

By the Imagination

Emily Dickinson (1924: 1687.J, unknown date)

Taking Teejay's lead, for example, creative representations might unsettle *both* the mis-representation of supervision as an 'alternative' to incarceration *and* the internal ideologies and practices of supervision that distort, degrade and disqualify its subjects. Equally importantly, by so doing, they invite us to imagine how supervision might be reconstructed to make it less maloptical and to deliver it in ways that better recognise and support its subjects.

Public criminology seems to need counter-visual criminology. In particular, creative and reconstructive forms of sensory criminology might better allow for the flows of meaning that democratic dialogue requires. Crucially, creative methods seem to have some potential for enabling penal subjects both to speak for themselves and to be heard in ways that might very significantly enrich penal–political discourse. Public criminologists might be 'under-labourers' or 'diplomats' or facilitators in such a process, but they should not be 'mediators' between 'the authorities' and 'the excluded'. Rather, we might see ourselves better as fellow citizens (with our own peculiar skills and particular interests) engaged with others in forming and supporting social movements that contribute to democratic dialogue and deliberation.

Undoubtedly, there are risks in surfacing supervision politically. Some have argued that penal policy has been more moderate where it has flown beneath the radar of public-professional interest (McAra, 1999, 2008) and that mechanisms must be found for insulating penal policy from the heat of political battle (Lacey, 2008). Whilst sympathetic to the intent behind these arguments, I take the opposite view for both principled and pragmatic reasons. Pragmatically, the 'expert' view of supervision has not in fact moderated its growth; indeed, it may have contributed to it. And, in principle, if that growth has not served the public interest – if it has contributed to criminal *injustice* – then we all need to talk about supervision.

NOTE

1. From https://www.socialsciencespace.com/2014/01/roberto-manga-beira-unger-what-is-wrong-with-the-social-sciences-today/. Accessed on 4 June 2018.

CHAPTER 7

SUPERVISION: UNLEASHED OR RESTRAINED?

INTRODUCTION: A TALE WITH TWO ENDINGS

At the beginning of the last chapter, I reviewed the analysis of 'mass supervision' developed in Chapters 3–5, summarising its scale and social distribution, its legitimation and adaptation in late-modern societies and its penal character as a lived experience. Chapter 6 added an analysis of supervision's relative invisibility in the public and political spheres but, perhaps more importantly, it also moved beyond analysis and into questions of action and activism, examining how we might tackle that invisibility and unsettle the sorts of 'penal imaginaries' that have enabled *both* mass incarceration *and* mass supervision. I argued that a sensory and 'counter-visual criminology' could and should play a role in fostering a deeper and more affective democratic dialogue about punishment – including supervisory forms of punishment in the community.

In this final chapter, my aim is to contribute to the development of that dialogue by imagining and examining two possible futures for supervision. I do so both by offering two endings to the short story that has evolved throughout this book and by engaging briefly with some of the normative questions that this book and these two visions raise. There is no intention here to offer a compelling or comprehensive set of principles to guide supervision's reform. This chapter does not attempt to offer a philosophy of penal supervision (as a strand of the philosophy of punishment). That would require another book – and perhaps a very different book.

However, this final chapter does begin to sketch out some of the conceptual and practical challenges with which such a philosophy would need to engage. The first of the imagined futures that follow is intended as a warning of what may happen if we continue to allow the pervasiveness of punishment to spread, both within the social body and in the lives of those subject to supervision. The other future, with which the book ends, offers a glimpse of the possibilities that might exist if we take seriously the need to restrain and reframe supervision.

SUPERVISION UNLEASHED

Administering Shocks and Sickness

[12 months later]

Joe heard two sounds as he woke: his own low moan and the insistent, monotonous electronic bell tolling from his ankle bracelet. He fumbled for the clock — it read 08.01 — he had 59 minutes to get to the probation office for his check-in. He knew that somewhere, somehow, some algorithm had determined that this was the moment to test his commitment, to strengthen his resolve, to keep him from temptation. At least that was how Norm had explained it, but Joe saw that the bracelet-bell was a call to worship, an invitation to obey. He pressed the button to acknowledge the signal and the bell stopped.

Joe washed and dressed cautiously, taking care not to let his sock break the contact between bracelet and skin. He knew that any interruption in the signal that allowed remote biometric analysis of his pulse and sweat could constitute an infraction. He had no wish to repeat his recent experience of a weekend in the compliance cells as part of the new SaCS (Swift and Certain Sanction) approach. That had been a high price to pay for trying to use ice cubes and hypoallergenic wipes to relieve the skin irritation that the bracelet caused.

Forty minutes later, Joe was glad to find a reporting booth empty at the probation office. It looked like a cross between an arcade game, a confessional and an upright coffin. He took a deep breath and sat inside, pulling the black curtain across. The touchscreen invited him to provide his hand-print while the retinal scan double checked and confirmed his identity. When prompted, Joe put on the virtual reality headset and was met by the smiling face of 'Virpro', the virtual probation officer. She spoke in slow, soft, maternal tones:

'Good morning, Joe. Well done. You have arrived on time and drug- and alcohol-free. We have no record of adverse contact with the author- ities since your last appointment. There are four months and two weeks of your revised order remaining to be served. The conditions remain the same. Would you like me to remind you of them?'

'No, thank you', Joe replied.

'That is your choice. Do you require any support or counselling at this time?'

'No, thank you', Joe replied. He guessed he should probably show will- ing but couldn't get out of the booth quickly enough. He already felt suffocated.

'That is your choice. Please wait for a message from future Joe, after which you are free to go'.

This part always freaked Joe out. Virpro smiled her farewell and faded from view; in her place came an avatar of Joe, looking a few years older but well-groomed, confident, contented, suited and booted. His 'brief motivational intervention' was becoming as predictable as it was sinister:

'Hi Joe. I'm proud of you. You've done so well since that last infrac- tion. The Swift and Certain Sanction really seems to have worked for you. You're back on track, pal. And there are only a few months to go until you are a free man. Just keep at it. Keep your head down. Keep away from troublemakers'.

Future Joe paused for effect, losing his saccharine smile and replacing it with the furrowed brow of his most earnest expression. Though his intense stare met Joe's eyes, it also seemed to look right through him, somewhere into the middle distance.

'Joe: remember, you can become me, if you want it enough, if you really commit. I can be your future. Meantime, take care and look after us both'.

Outside, Joe steadied himself on the railing, taking in as much air as he could. As he walked away, he wondered what Pauline was doing now. He hadn't expected to miss her this much.

…

Upstairs, Norm looked at the three huge screens in front of him: 59's green flag caught his eye. One of Pauline's cases, he recalled. He had to admit that he kind of missed the lifers. The office was quiet without them. Still, Norm took some pride in that fact that he was now managing 412 low-medium risk cases himself; or rather, he was maintaining and monitoring the system that was managing them. It was remarkably efficient now that it was up and running, even if it would take 25 years (with caseloads at current levels) to recoup the installation costs. In the long run, it was worth it. Now that the infrastructure existed, the possibilities of combining remote biometric monitoring with VR and AI were limitless.

That said, Norm still harboured doubts. The newly proposed GATE (Geo-Aversion Tag Enhancer) tech troubled him. These tags could respond to remote signals by releasing nausea-inducing drugs implanted in pellets under the offender's skin. In an emergency, they could issue taser-style shocks. Both measures disabled offenders who strayed beyond their permitted spaces, or showed the classic signs of over-stimulation associated with imminent risk of offending.

Norm had a lot of sympathy for the argument that GATE allowed high risk offenders to be managed safely in the community. As the marketing slogan put it, 'GATE retrains and restrains'. The pilot studies seemed promising, despite one or two admittedly very unfortunate cases. Yet, even though the offenders would have to consent to GATE and even though they signed the relevant disclaimers, he didn't much like the idea that he would be the one administering shocks and causing sickness, or even administering a system that did so. He tried to reassure himself that GATE wasn't about punishment; it was just doing what was necessary for public safety. And he wasn't being asked to press those buttons yet.

Norm thought it was probably best to keep his doubts to himself.

MASS SUPERVISION, ELECTRONIC MONITORING AND 'TECHNO-CORRECTIONS'

Some well-informed readers will perhaps have been wondering why this book has had relatively little to say about electronic monitoring and other recent technological innovations. One doesn't have to look too far − in either the academic literature (for example, Roberts, 2004), in journalistic writing or in science fiction − to find significant interest in the ways in which new technologies are re-shaping punishment and may further re-shape it. For example, in November 2017, ScopeNI[1] published an article entitled: 'The future of punishment: prisons without bars and hell on earth'.[2] The article reports the comments of a researcher (DM Martin) to a US congressional hearing in 1966:

> *We may reach the point where it will be permissible to allow*
> *some emotionally ill people the freedom of the streets, providing*
> *they are effectively 'defused' through chemical agents. The task,*
> *then for the computer linked sensors would be to telemeter, not*
> *their emotional states, but simply the sufficiency of the*
> *concentration of the chemical agent to ensure an*
> *acceptable emotional state. I am not prepared to speculate*
> *whether such a situation would increase or decrease the personal*
> *freedom of the emotionally ill person.*

Although such a vision may have seemed far-fetched in 1966, the notion of narcotic-induced compliance with the law and social norms had already been explored in Anthony Burgess' novel *A Clockwork Orange*, which was published in 1962. Stanley Kubrick's infamous film of the same title followed in 1971. The book and film depicted a dystopian future in which *both* 'rehabilitation' *and* decarceration were delivered through a brutal form of aversion therapy that associated states of violent and sexual arousal with crippling nausea that aimed to make offending physically impossible.

But whereas the 'Ludovico Method' relied on behaviourally training its recipients to internalise an embodied form of social control, my own dys-topia above (and Martin's testimony) alludes to something different; a form of technologically mediated control that physically restrains and retrains simultaneously. Thus, it need not rely merely on the subject's psychological internalisation of the association between non-compliance and pain. Rather, this can be supplemented by the technology's ability to *physically* disable. If retraining fails, then restraint kicks in and that restraint itself might perhaps retrain its subject to comply next time.

At least in some respects, 1960s science fiction has become present-day reality. As I have written recently (McNeill, 2017b), many of us accept and employ our smart phones as 'guide, guard and glue'; they monitor and inform our movements, our health and habits, our purchases and preferences. Indeed, they both enable and encode many of our personal and social activities. Of course, most of us can and do make choices about the extent to which we allow our lives to be technologically mediated in these ways.

As Mike Nellis (2018) has recently argued, when similar technologies are applied in the penal sphere, a form of 'coercive connectivity' is imposed. In the ScopeNI article referred to above, Nellis is quoted as arguing that probation professionals and penal reform groups must engage with the possibilities and the pitfalls of new technologies:

> They must recognise that [...] [the technology] is merely an affordance, a customised coercive form of the ubiquitous digital connectedness that characterises our age, and engage more actively in shaping the wise use of monitoring technology [...] [they have] signally failed to grasp the importance of reconfiguring EM as a safe, legitimate application of digital technology in the struggle to create safe communities and reduce prison numbers.

Nellis (2010) has argued previously that the reticence of UK-based probation professionals and penal reform groups to engage constructively with EM effectively cleared the way for privatisation of this increasingly important aspect of punishment. In so doing, they also undermined the possibilities of creatively and constructively combining electronic and traditional, human supervision in ways that might support both rehabilitation and community safety, whilst also restraining penal growth.

Despite the importance of these issues, there are several reasons why I have deferred discussion of 'techno-corrections' until now. The first is that our fascination with technological innovation and its possibilities can and does sometimes serve to further marginalise (and render invisible) more established forms of 'human supervision' (for example, probation and parole). For example, although I agree about the importance of analysing EM as 'coercive connectivity', this seems to me to be a digital form of a very old-fashioned 'analogue' practice. In the oral history of Scottish probation in the 1960s referred to in Chapter 4 (McNeill, 2009); one respondent vividly described the network of connections (his mother, his school teacher, his priest and the local beat police officer) mobilised by his probation officer to monitor and control him as a teenager. This then common-place practice — of using and fusing formal and informal social control — might be read as a pre-digital form of 'coercive connectivity'; one which certainly endures in the practice of 'human' supervision in some jurisdictions today. Admittedly, EM may significantly enhance the 'network coverage' as it were, collecting and processing more data without reliance on fallible, sympathetic or collusive human actors. But, at the same time, human supervisors may provide less data but more information, as well as employing more subjective judgements, for better or worse. Thus, it is not immediately obvious that the 'coercive connectivity' of EM is inherently more intrusive or demanding than that implied in human supervision; it may entail a 'broader' experience of supervision, but not necessarily a 'deeper' one, as it were (Crewe, Liebling, & Hulley, 2014). Much depends on what data are collected through EM, on how it is interpreted and used both by systems and by human actors like monitoring officers, probation staff and judges. Much also depends on how human supervision is constructed (including through technologies other than EM: see McNeill, 2017b).

The second reason for this book's limited attention to EM rests in the fact that, in most (or perhaps even all) jurisdictions, the numbers subject to EM-based supervision remain only a small fraction of all of those supervised. For example, in Chapter 3, I reported that in 2015–2016 in Scotland, 19,410 new community payback orders were issued. In the same period, the number of new restriction of liberty orders (which impose electronically monitored curfews as a community sentence) was just 1,646.[3] Likewise, whereas in 2015–2016, the total criminal justice social work caseload of those subject to compulsory forms of post-release supervision stood at 2,500, the number subject to Home Detention Curfews (which impose electronically monitored curfews as a condition of early release) stands today at just under 300.[4]

A third practical problem in seeking to properly integrate EM within a discussion of 'mass supervision' relates to the paucity of available data. A recent comparative study into the development of EM in five European jurisdictions (Belgium, England and Wales, Germany, the Netherlands and Scotland) found that available data on EM are very limited. That said, Hucklesby et al. (2016) also found that EM is used extensively and for diverse purposes and that, of the five countries, its use was greatest in England and Wales, with a daily population of about 12,000 subjects to some kind of EM. This is five times the rate of the next highest user, Belgium (1,700). In Germany, the least frequent user of EM, the daily population of monitored individuals stood at just over 100. Importantly, Hucklesby et al. (2016) found that *less* extensive use of EM is associated with longer term reductions in prison populations and lower imprisonment rates.

It is even harder to estimate the changing scale of the use of EM in the USA, but Lilly and Nellis' (2012) overview concludes that 'For all that it was born in the USA, EM has not wrought major changes in US penal policies [...] [it] may have been held in check by a deeper and more pervasive commitment to mass incarceration'. Indeed, in light of the work of Michelle Phelps (reviewed in Chapter 3), it may be that it is not just 'mass incarceration' but also 'mass [human] supervision' and 'mass probation' that have restrained EM's growth in the USA, although clearly the empirical case for such an argument has yet to be made.

For all the allure of technological innovation then, these low numbers suggest that we should not give undue prominence to EM in our analyses of mass supervision; at least, not yet. There are signs that the use of EM is growing, or is set to grow in some jurisdictions. To give just one current example, it seems likely that plans in Scotland to limit the use of prison sentences of less than 1 year will lead to an increase in conditional or community sentences involving EM. The current Scottish Government tender document for the next contract to deliver EM from 1 April 2020[5] offers an estimated total value of £35 million over seven years. The current contract was valued at £13 million over five years at its inception in 2013.

However, the relationships between human and technological forms or aspects of mass supervision might evolve, it seems obvious that we must remain alert both to the dangers of supervision's unrestrained growth and to the consequences of its growth for those subject to its intrusions. Examining how those intrusions are mediated by human supervisors and by technology should be part of that vigilance. But perhaps the first and most pressing task is to articulate how and why supervision must be constrained, not just in its scale but also in its severity.

THE PENAL SEVERITY OF SUPERVISION

In a recent conference paper, David Hayes and I began to develop a conceptual analysis of how we might examine the relative severity of EM and 'human supervision' (Hayes & McNeill, 2017). We argued that such an examination was necessary not just to inform deliberation about parsimony and proportionality in punishment but also to help us think about its claims to humanity and legitimacy. Drawing on Hayes' (2015) earlier work, we employed a subjective, inductive and evaluative conception of penal severity; that is, rather than thinking only about what sentencing *intends*, we insisted on attending carefully and critically to what penal subjects tell us about what sanctions do to them and for them. Thinking about the severity of sanctions in this way requires consideration not just of the *incidence* of the associated pains (which pains and how many?) but also of their *magnitude* (how painful?).

One common feature of EM and human supervision is their delivery of some form of oversight. Probation and parole practitioners and advocates have tended to assume that human supervision is more benign than EM, perhaps partly because EM has more often been cast as a punitive measure explicitly intended to mirror and displace the deprivation of liberty that follows imprisonment, or as a measure of control, rather than being directed at rehabilitation (Nellis, 2009). Since their inception, probation and parole, by contrast, have often been defined as essentially rehabilitative or reformative (e.g. Canton, 2018; Duff, 2001; McNeill, 2006), even if, as we saw in Chapter 4, they have increasingly been associated with risk management, public protection and even punitiveness (Robinson et al., 2013).

These differences in the purposes of the two forms of supervision are to some extent reflected in a series of related but sometimes different pains of supervision evidenced in various studies (on EM – Gainey & Paine, 2000; Mair & Nee, 1990, Nellis, 2009, 2010; Payne & Gainey, 1998, 2004; Vanhaelemeesch, 2015; on probation and parole – Durnescu, 2011, Hayes, 2015; Fitzgibbon et al., 2017). Whereas EM intrudes on the privacy of its subjects by collecting data about them and requiring certain behavioural changes to sustain compliance, human supervision often entails 'pains of rehabilitation'; here, deeper personal and wider lifestyle changes are elicited and evaluated not through digital technology but through 'treatment' programmes or casework relationships. Human supervision may also bring with it vulnerability to the punitive or even abusive impulses of some supervisors (see McNeill, 2009).

Both EM and human supervision entail deprivations of liberty and autonomy, requiring penal subjects to be at certain places at certain times.

These requirements often entail incidental financial and social costs, as well as opportunity costs, for example, affecting work, leisure and family activities.

These intrusions and requirements can also affect supervisees' health, welfare and well-being. For EM's subjects, this extends beyond effects on family, social and work life; there may be physical discomfort associated with wearing the tag (as depicted in the story above). While human supervision has no direct physical effect, its subjects may be more anxious than EM subjects about the intrusions of state authorities into their lives and homes; for example, parents on supervision may fear referral of their children to social services.

We argued that both forms of supervision also entailed 'process pains'. For EM's subjects, these include the fear of equipment failure, of visits by monitoring officers and, more generally, of their increased 'telematic' visibility. For subjects of human supervision, as we saw in Chapter 5, there are pains associated with the suspended threat of further punishment and with 'proving' oneself, as well as related fears around enforcement, whether fair or unfair.

Both forms of supervision also produce potentially stigmatising effects. For instance, in EM, stigmatising reactions from strangers, occasioned by the sort of *Scarlet Letter* effect of wearing a visible tag, are sometimes described as one of the worst aspects of the experience. Human supervision involves no physical mark, but family, friends and employers often know about it, and the experience of meeting the supervisor may itself be experienced as a stigmatising one (as the first episode of the short story depicted).

Importantly, Hayes' (2015) earlier work, based on analysing experiences of probation supervision, suggested that loss of time, money and freedom may be experienced as *less* severe than the 'process pains' of supervision, its impact on family relationships and its production of shame. While Hayes (2015) also noted that the severity of these pains is contingent on the attitudes and resources of penal subjects and those around them, on the qualities of the supervisory relationship and on the formal requirements of the order, it is notable that the more severe pains seem to be incidental rather than intended aspects of supervision.

Our chapter also paid attention to the potential 'gains' of supervision (Hayes & McNeill, 2017). In part, these relate to whether supervision is associated with the avoidance of imprisonment, at least where it is assumed that this is a worse fate. That avoidance, for example, may allow for sustaining and even improving family relationships and home life, as well as employment opportunities. Second, being known, by whether technological or human means, can sometimes afford protection and security. The tag may help prove its wearer's innocence. The supervisor may vouch for the supervisee. Third, supervision can provide its subjects with reasons (or excuses) for avoiding risky situations (e.g. 'I can't come out because of the tag'; 'I can't come out because my PO is on my case'). Fourth, supervision in either form might help to motivate change. The tag might function much in the way that a weight or activity tracking app can enhance motivation to eat healthily or take more exercise. Extending the analogy, human supervision might motivate in a manner more akin to that of a personal fitness trainer. Fifth, supervision might reduce perceived opportunities for offending (particularly in the case of EM), and/or, in the case of human supervision, enhance positive opportunities by providing access to services to support finances, employment, housing, family life, health and mental health or substance use issues (e.g. see Maguire & Raynor, 2006, 2017). Sixth, supervision might develop its subjects' capacities and capabilities: EM might help people practice self-control albeit under an external threat, whereas human supervision might add educational aspects, supporting the development of new attitudes and skills.

In broad terms, it might be argued that one of the 'gains' and limitations of (standalone) EM is that it allows freedom from compulsory engagement with human supervision (and all of its attended psycho-social intrusions). Conversely, human supervision at its best offers practical and professional help in navigating towards social reintegration, but it does so within the context of penal compulsion (Burke et al., 2018; McNeill, 2009).

Crucially, for present purposes and as I argued in Chapter 5, these potential 'gains' do not nullify the 'pains' of supervision. They may sometimes accompany and even moderate those pains, but that depends on how supervision is constructed and administered by probation and parole agencies and practitioners.

SUPERVISION CONSTRAINED

In the first chapter of this book, I suggested that one of the reasons for supervision's invisibility *as punishment* (Robinson, 2016) rests in its history in many jurisdictions as a suspension of, or alternative to, or curtailment of punishment. In the last chapter, I discussed Carlen's (2008) concept of 'imaginary penalties', referring to stubborn misrepresentations or fictions that sustain the logics and legitimacy of penal institutions in the face of evidence of their absurdity or illegitimacy. The durability of the misconception that penal supervision is not punishment has likely contributed to a lack of normative theorising[6] about whether, how, when and to what extent it can be morally justified *as punishment*, although a few scholars have attended carefully to these questions (Hayes, 2015, 2016; Rotman, 1989; Snacken & McNeill, 2012; van Zyl Smit, 1993; van Zyl Smit et al., 2015).

In the Final Report of the COST Action on Offender Supervision in Europe, we argued that two key principles should guide our thinking about supervision:

(1) Since supervision hurts, decisions about imposing and revoking supervision must be bound by considerations of proportionality. No one should be subject to more demanding or intrusive supervision than their offending deserves.

(2) Supervision must be delivered in ways that actively minimize unintended and unnecessary pains both for those subject to supervision and for others affected by it (for example, family members)' (McNeill and Beyens, 2016, p. 9).

In the last few pages of this book, I want to briefly elaborate and extend these two principles by suggesting that any legitimate development of supervision, like any legitimate development of punishment (Loader, 2010), must be bound by three 'P's: *parsimony*, *proportionality* and *productiveness*. The articulation of these arguments is not just a matter for philosophers of punishment and legal scholars. Since it is impossible to properly apply parsimony and proportionality in the absence of knowledge about how supervision is experienced in terms of its demands and intrusions, it is crucial that the lived experience of supervision should inform these discussions. Without that knowledge, provided directly by people with relevant life experience and indirectly through criminological and sociological research, the calculus of parsimony and proportionality can only be uninformed, abstract guesswork (see Hayes, 2016, for a justification of an intersubjective measurement of penal severity).

THE THREE 'P'S: PARSIMONY, PROPORTIONALITY AND PRODUCTIVENESS IN SUPERVISION

Barbara Hudson (1996) concluded her discussion of justice in similarly inter-disciplinary terms:

> *Punishment cannot [...] be used as a synonym for justice. The weakness in the philosophical approaches, the insights of the sociological approaches, the challenges of abolitionism and of feminist jurisprudence should mean that punishment is restricted and reduced. Rather than imposing penalties with self-righteous confidence, we should always punish with a bad conscience.*
> *(p. 151)*

In sum, Hudson argues that all of our attempts to justify the infliction of pain on those who offend (whether as retribution or deterrence or denunciation or for public protection or rehabilitation) have flaws and limitations; that sociological analyses of punishment suggest both that the pains we inflict often extend far beyond those that we intend (and might see as legitimate; and that those pains are distributed and experienced unevenly, falling most often and most harshly on those who are already on the receiving end of social inequality and injustice. Accordingly, we should be profoundly uneasy about state-administered punishment in general and therefore should approach it with caution and restraint.

The principle of parsimony recognises these arguments, treating the suffering that punishment imposes as a necessary evil. Whether or not we agree that penal suffering is necessary, we should make every possible effort to ensure that it does not exceed – in type or duration or impact – that which is intended.

Parsimony finds itself expressed in different ways in the adult and juvenile justice systems of most liberal democracies. For example, in the Scottish Hearings System (which deals with children and young people in trouble), there is a 'no order principle' which stipulates that: 'The children's hearing may make, vary or continue the order [...] only if [it] considers that it would be better for the child if the order [...] were in force than not' (section 28[2] of Children's Hearing [Scotland] Act 2011). In other words, no compulsory measures – no mandatory state intervention – should be imposed unless compulsion and mandate is necessary.

Admittedly, this principle applies to a system which accords primacy and judges necessity with reference to the welfare of children and young people. But in an (adult) justice system deliberating about supervision, we might amend the principle, judging the necessity as a question of justice rather than welfare, as follows:

> No court may make, vary or continue a compulsory supervision order unless it considers that it is more just that the order be made, varied or continued than not.

In other words, the state's exercise of penal power (i.e. compulsion) must always be justified as a matter of justice; no expansion of *penal* compulsion should be justified as being, for example, in the supposed best interests of the offender. The same principle might be elaborated so that the court is obliged to justify why, in the interests of justice, it is necessary to curtail liberty (and which liberties), to restrict autonomy (in which ways), to invade privacy (to what degree) or indeed to interfere with any other human or civil rights. In sum, the case for penal supervision requires a justification of why, how and to what extent any diminution of or disqualification from ordinary citizenship is to be imposed in and through it.

If we must pursue parsimony in the use of supervision, then clearly we will also need to engage with questions of the *proportionality* of supervision's demands. The logic of proportionality (that the punishment should somehow 'fit' the crime), at least within 'limiting retributivism' (Morris, 1974), requires that the severity of the punishment should somehow match the severity of the crime and the culpability of the offender. In relation to imprisonment, the quantum of time informs the judicial calculus; more severe crimes by more culpable offenders deserve longer prison sentences.

However, as we saw in Chapter 5, sociologists of imprisonment have increasingly explored not just the effects (or severity) of imprisonment's duration, but also of its 'depth, weight and tightness' (Crewe, 2011). These other dimensions also surfaced in the analysis of the penal character of supervision offered in that chapter, along with the question of degradation. It follows that a proper assessment of supervision's proportionality would require consideration not just of the length of time a person spends subject to supervision, but also of the depth of the supervision's interference with autonomy, the weight of its burdens, the tightness of its controls, and the degradations of status attendant upon it. Once again, deliberations about proportionality would need to consider not just the intended pains of supervision, but also any other reasonably foreseeable (even if unintended) consequences (Hayes, 2018).

If the principles of parsimony and proportionality operate negatively, seeking mainly to restrain the intended suffering that supervisory punishment entails, then the principle of *productiveness* (in the design and delivery of supervision) operates positively, seeking to actively address injustices that may precede or attend punishment. In one sense, striving to make supervision productive (maximising the 'gains' identified previously) can be seen as a logical consequence of parsimony and proportionality. The requirement for productiveness follows from the responsibilities of courts and agencies of supervision for bringing just punishment to an end when putative debts are settled. If we punish with a bad conscience, uncertain about our capacity to do justice ethically and effectively, then we must accept a responsibility for ensuring that punishment ends at the earliest possible opportunity, without imposing one ounce of additional (and therefore illegitimate) or unnecessary suffering.

This also requires acknowledgement of a positive right to re/integration that should influence the administration of punishment throughout and beyond supervision. That acknowledgement requires, in turn, the honouring of the punished citizen's claim for access to services during supervision that may develop human potential and citizenship capabilities and for access to material resources and opportunities necessary for social re/integration. Broadly, this entails a focus during supervision on supporting and securing timely access to full civic requalification at the end of the punishment; as I have said, the concern for requalification is entailed by a commitment to parsimony. No one should be civically degraded, diminished or disqualified in any way more than or for one second longer than just punishment requires. A productive approach to supervision also requires and responds to respect for the dignity of supervised persons, reflected in commitments to treat them fairly (i.e. in line with the requirements of legitimacy and procedural justice, on which see McNeill & Robinson, 2012) and (again in line with the parsimonious use of penal power) to seek to maximise their voluntary participation and to minimise coercion in supervisory processes.

Attending seriously to these three principles, not just in individual judicial decision-making but also in the design of supervision laws, policies and practices, might do much to properly guard the entry points into supervision, to effectively guide supervision's administration (including crucially in relation to enforcement) and to glue it into a properly restrained yet constructive system of criminal justice. Whether supervision can go further — contributing to the development of a just society, as opposed to reinforcing existing inequalities — is a still more complex and challenging question (on which see Burke et al., 2018).

CONCLUSION: REHABILITATING SUPERVISION

In certain respects, the three 'P's mentioned above echo existing European norms and standards about the development of probation or community sanctions and measures (on which see, for example, Morgenstern & Larrauri, 2013; van Zyl Smit et al., 2015). Some scholars have explicitly linked the development of such standards to the values that define the European project and, within it, a distinctively European approach to penal moderation (Snacken, 2010). But van Zyl Smit et al. (2015) have also warned that recent revisions of these standards have tended to marginalise the crucial focus on reducing the scale and extent of penal control by focusing too much on promoting 'what works' and on the development of probation services. They argue that:

> With the extra money and resources being invested in community sanctions and measures, pressures to propagate probation are greater than ever. The distance between the 1992 commitment to (incremental) abolitionism and the modern state of play in Europe — which is swiftly approaching a state of 'mass supervision' (McNeill & Beyens, 2013) — ought not to be understated.
>
> Under these circumstances, the time is ripe to critically re-evaluate arguments from the perspectives of liberal scepticism and radical non-interventionism that were made in the past, as well as those from a human rights perspective, in order to ensure that probation, as it has now evolved, does not become an unnecessarily restrictive response. (van Zyl Smit et al., 2015, p. 18)

In the USA, calls for principled probation and parole reform are also gathering pace. For example, in 2017, a group of probation and parole officers and executives, prosecutors, judges, policy-makers, reformers and academics, organised through the Harvard Kennedy School's Executive Session on Community Corrections, produced a consensus document entitled 'Towards An Approach to Community Corrections for the twenty-first century.'[7] Their approach was consciously rooted in foundational US principles and values − including life, liberty and equality before the law. Their four guiding principles were as follows:

(1) to promote the well-being and safety of communities;

(2) to use the capacity to arrest, discipline, and incarcerate parsimoniously;

(3) to recognise the worth of justice-involved individuals; and

(4) to promote the rule of law, respecting the human dignity of people under supervision and treating them as citizens in a democratic society.

Indeed, they go so far as to explicitly advocate a shift from 'mass supervision to focused supervision', calling for an end to the use of probation for low-level offenses and for a radical reimagining of how individuals are treated on community supervision, with a new emphasis on promoting success, providing meaningful assistance and emphasising dignity and respect.

As Michelle Phelps comments:

> Bringing community supervision out of the shadows and centered in criminal justice reform is critical if we are to dramatically reduce the scale of imprisonment without transferring those populations onto community supervision. In addition, such an upheaval of the justice system has the potential to bring real improvements to the lives of families in distressed communities, where criminal justice control has been far too extensive and repressive.[8]

The challenges of promoting such a necessary 'upheaval' should not be underestimated. In April 2018 (just a few weeks ago as I write this), the hip-hop artist Meek Mill was released from prison. He had served about

5 months for the alleged probation violations discussed in the introduction to Chapter 2. Just before his release, he was interviewed in prison by telephone by CNN's Don Lemon.[9] In a mainstream news feature that directly addressed mass supervision as a public issue, and as a question of racialised *injustice*, Meek Mill said:

> *A lot of people, they get locked up for technical violations [...] They lose their jobs, and they lose their family. Their kids go fatherless for months, years at a time, over small mistakes, not committing crimes.*

Towards the end of the interview, Lemon asked Mill whether he had a message for young black men who may come into contact with the justice system, like two innocent men who had recently been arrested merely for sitting in a Starbucks waiting to meet a friend. Mill replied:

> *Be careful [...] young minorities. I call it target practice. When you're already a target and you're in high-risk neighbourhoods, where people go to jail a lot, be careful, watch the way you move, you could be caught up in a situation like this [...]*
>
> *The most important thing I want to say is: Vote. When it's time to vote for governor, when it's time to vote for judges, DAs: Vote. Let's vote for people that's into justice reform and helping the urban communities.*

Perhaps the time is not so far away when a counter-visual, sensory, public criminology of mass supervision can contribute to serious political engagement with the issues this book has tried to render more visible, to analyze and to begin to address. A different future might just be imaginable. Supervision can and must be restrained and rehabilitated. We all need to watch the way that criminal justice moves and that means looking beyond the prison.

Rehabilitating Norm(s)

[12 months later]
Norm heard two sounds as he woke: his own low moan and the insistent, monotonous electronic bell tolling from his alarm clock. It read 08.01 —

he had 59 minutes to get ready and catch that train. Today was the day of the Justice Committee hearing on the future of supervision.

Norm hadn't slept well, though already he couldn't quite recollect the plots and sub-plots of the anxiety dreams that had plagued him in the night. Did Joe bring a tin of red paint to the hearing in one version? Did Petra accuse the parliamentarians of 'techno-fascism' in another? He was pretty sure Pauline had been late in every scenario his unconscious had so kindly visualised for him.

The old Norm would have run for cover long before now but, despite his fears, the new Norm was excited about the day ahead. There was no doubt that the past 12 months had changed him. As he looked in the mirror, tying his tie, he admitted that he liked what he was becoming better than what he had been.

His first encounter with the Conviction Collective – at Pauline's insistence – had left him unconvinced. Initially, he was sceptical about the willingness and ability of people under supervision to provide meaningful and effective peer support. But he reasoned that if the Collective was a free supplement to formal services, then why not give it a chance? To offset any risk to his personal reputation and standing in the Company, Norm made clear that it was Pauline's initiative and Pauline's responsibility.

Within weeks though, seeing the glint in her eye and the spring in her step, he decided he should attend the weekly gathering and see what was going on. At first the answer seemed to be: 'Not much'. About 12–15 people met and shared some pizza (it was never clear who paid for it, but Norm suspected Pauline). They talked together, sometimes they walked together. Someone found an old table tennis table and they played.

But, they also got organised. Ever the accountant, Joe had been instrumental in persuading them to identify, recognise and detail all the forms of 'capital' that they held. He made an inventory of their skills, resources and contacts. They started to exchange goods, services and introductions for one another – from each according to their abilities, to each according to their needs. The group grew and so did the inventory. The founding members invested more of themselves, the new members brought new assets and abilities. In sum, they advised, assisted and befriended one another.

Group members also began to share more and more of their experiences – both good and bad – of the justice system. They invited other 'expert witnesses' to plug the gaps in their understanding;

criminologists, lawyers, sociologists – even a historian. Norm himself had been invited to explain the logic of the current supervision system. That had been quite a challenge and quite a grilling. Soon, the Collective had written a manifesto, naming it: 'Just Conviction, Fair Supervision'. Norm didn't agree with all its prescriptions, but he admired its clarity, its use of evidence and the force of its arguments.

The press soon took an interest. Petra turned out to be quite an operator; proving more than adept at handling everything from hostile questions from cynical political hacks to irate callers on early morning phone-ins. Surprisingly perhaps, listening to Petra and the others, people seemed to become more cautious and more curious about what court sentences did to people and about what they achieved or failed to achieve for society.

Initially, Norm's bosses had liked the positive PR that came with supporting the Collective; they thought it made them look progressive. They hadn't been so happy about 'Just Conviction, Fair Supervision' – worried about their market share, he supposed, if those proposals were ever to be implemented. That said, Norm and Joe didn't have to work too hard to convince the Company that excessive supervision wasn't especially lucrative; not at least while there were stubbornly high revocation and reconviction rates.

The Company also knew that re-nationalisation was back on the political agenda; it was time to look for better business opportunities elsewhere. At the very least, Joe had argued, working with the government and the courts to scale down supervision and to deliver better results might minimise losses in the meantime. And in reputational terms, it also meant that the Company wasn't left carrying the can on its own.

It was now Norm's job to lead the Ministry-sanctioned local pilot of 'Just Conviction, Fair Supervision'. And the very early results of the pilot had led to the invitation to Norm, Petra, Pauline and Joe to give evidence to the Committee today.

The gang of four met at the coffee stall in the train station. Even Pauline was on time. They greeted one another as old friends, collected their orders and, as was their habit, made for the front carriage. They knew they were going to be in a hurry when they arrived in the capital. They had already come a long way together in a short time, but there was a lot of work still to be done.

NOTES

1. ScopeNI is a web-based resource: see http://scopeni.nicva.org/. Accessed on 14 May 2018. The site states that 'Our mission is to provide the voluntary and community sector and other interested parties with clear, incisive news, information and analysis on public policy and important developments that affect organisations in the sector and the people they work with.'

2. See http://scopeni.nicva.org/article/the-future-of-punishment-prisons-without-bars-and-hell-on-earth. Accessed on 14 May 2018.

3. Data from Table 7a in http://www.gov.scot/Topics/Statistics/Browse/Crime-Justice/Datasets/DatasetsCrimProc/CPtab16. Accessed on 14 May 2018.

4. Data from Scottish Prison Service website, http://www.sps.gov.uk/Corporate/Information/SPSPopulation.aspx. Accessed on 14 May 2018.

5. See http://www.gov.scot/Topics/Justice/policies/reducing-reoffending/Electronic-Monitoring/EMContract. Accessed on 14 May 2018.

6. I suspect that this omission is most glaring in the English-language literature, since our continental European colleagues have a longer and stronger track record of normative theorising on such questions (cf. Morgenstern & Larrauri, 2013).

7. See https://www.hks.harvard.edu/centers/wiener/programs/criminaljustice/research-publications/executive-session-on-community-corrections/publications/toward-an-approach-to-community-corrections-for-the-21st-century. Accessed on 14 May 2018. This work has now moved to Columbia University, with Bruce Western who co-leads their 'Justice Lab' with Vinny Schiraldi. For a recent example of their work, see http://justice-lab.iserp.columbia.edu/toobigtosucceed.html. Accessed on 5 June 2018.

8. See https://injusticetoday.com/to-fix-the-justice-system-shrink-and-reform-community-supervision-f53a0e46f88b. Accessed on 14 May 2018.

9. See https://youtu.be/K7JZgmz566Q. Accessed on 14 May 2018.

POSTSCRIPT: MAKING STORIES AND SONGS FROM SUPERVISION

Jo Collinson Scott and Fergus McNeill

INTRODUCTION

In this short postscript to *Pervasive Punishment*, we aim to provide a brief and mainly descriptive account of the processes by which we produced two of the more unusual elements of the project's output: the short story that features in the book in episodic form (and is reproduced as a whole in the Appendix) and the EP of four original songs that accompanies it. Chapter 6 of the book has already provided an explanation of why we think it is necessary and important to work in creative ways (e.g. with pictures, stories and songs) to make supervision visible, but we are aware that, for many readers within criminology and the social sciences more generally, the processes of doing so – both as practice and as 'practice-based research' – may be less familiar.

In the first section, Fergus explains why and how he wrote 'The Invisible Collar' and why he invited Jo to make an EP of songs in response entitled 'System Hold'. In the second section, Jo describes how she took on that task. 'System Hold' can be accessed here: https://www.pervasivepunishment.com/system-hold-ep/ using the password 'The_Invisible_Collar'.

MAKING STORIES FROM SUPERVISION

Fergus McNeill

Beginnings

Given that the relative invisibility of penal supervision in the public sphere was one of my main reasons for writing this book, I was concerned from the outset to try to make the book accessible and intelligible to lay readers as well as academics and other criminal justice 'insiders'.

My partner is a primary (or elementary) school teacher and an avid reader of fiction, with limited interest in criminal justice and, therefore, in most of what I have written before. Back when I started writing the book, we had a conversation that went something like this:

> *'Are you going to read this book that I'm writing?'*
>
> *Her answer was a question of her own: 'Are you going to make it interesting?'*
>
> *'What would make it interesting?', I replied.*
>
> *'I like stories', she said.*

I mulled over that brief conversation on a long train journey from Glasgow to Cardiff (where I attended the European Society Criminology conference in September 2017). On the equally long journey back, I decided to shed my academic (and personal) inhibitions and write her a story, or at least the beginning of one. I spent several hours drafting the few hundred words that comprised the first draft of the first episode of 'The Invisible Collar'. When I got back to Glasgow, I asked her to read it. She said:

> *OK. I'm interested. I want to know more about these characters and the relationship that develops between them.*

I thought this was an auspicious beginning. She now had characters forming in her mind and she was curious about what might happen to them and between them. She was beginning to imagine the supervisory relationship and how that might feel for the (at that stage) unnamed male supervisee and his female supervisor. It occurred to me that this capacity to invite imaginings was important and valuable. Perhaps it would draw readers into the more conventional academic writing and, even if not, readers only of the story might engage with a kind of distilled and re-crafted version of the academic work.

Once the project blog was established (www.pervasivepunishment. com), I began sharing draft episodes of the story as they were written, noticing that these sometimes elicited more interest on Twitter (and more comments on the blog) than other posts. Admittedly, much of this interest and commentary came from other academics (staff and students) and from criminal justice practitioners, sometimes comparing what was depicted with their own experiences. But I became convinced that the story was working broadly as I hoped: that is, it was sparking and interacting with people's imaginations and generating dialogue.

Characters and Contexts

Several readers have asked me about Joe and why I chose to centre the story on such an apparently atypical supervisee. Joe is middle-aged and middle-class and has few previous convictions. A more statistically repre-sentative character might have been, for example, a relatively young, poor man with a substance use problem and a significant history of offending.

While I could have written the story around such a supervisee, I felt uncomfortable about doing so. I feared it would lack authenticity and might come across as patronizing or even stigmatizing in some way. I thought that I would create a more convincing or believable character if I could relate to him. In one sense then, Joe is a middle-aged, middle-class man because I am. What is happening to him is something that, I can imagine, could be happening to me. I realise that this also poses risks. In particular, it pro-duces a story that reflects my position and my partialities – and some of my privilege. That said, any character that I created would reflect my situation and my limitations – and any single story of supervision is necessarily bound to be partial. In the end, I decided that the story needed depth rather than breadth, and authenticity rather than representativeness.

To add to his 'imagine-abilty', I put Joe in places that were familiar to me. Thus, the waiting room that is the scene of the first episode, in my mind at least, is the waiting room of the criminal justice social work office where I worked in the 1990s, in the east end of Glasgow. His flat (or apartment), which is the venue for episode 4, is my old flat in Glasgow's west end. The station that he and the others are leaving from in the final episode is Glasgow's Queen Street station.

That said, these places are all re-imagined in my writing. The version of the waiting room in which Joe waits is also coloured by my recollections of visiting numerous probation offices in several countries in the course of my academic career and by the pictures of waiting rooms provided in the *Picturing Probation* project. My depiction of his experience of waiting is also inspired by the photographs and findings of the *Supervisible* project.

Pauline is a composite of many social workers and probation officers that I have met during both my practice and research careers. Norm's characterization of her as a 'lifer' is a direct reference to work on the occupational identities of English probation workers by Mawby and Worrall (2014). 'Lifers' are career probation officers who see their work as a vocation. More generally, my portrayal of Pauline's position and disposition tries to convey the sort of tormented habitus generated by a changing criminal justice field (as suggested, e.g. by McNeill et al., 2009; Deering, 2011). Her name is also significant. Like many probation workers (and like her namesake the Apostle Paul), Pauline might say: 'I have become all things to all people so that by all possible means I might save some' (1 Corinthians 9: 22, New International Version).

The character of Norm is perhaps less rooted in my personal experience of probation and criminal justice social work managers. Rather, he is an archetype, personifying the pragmatic, managerialist ideal, defined in implicit contrast to Pauline's traditional humanism (McWilliams, 1987). In my mind's eye, Norm is a young, lean and ambitious first line manager. But I have tried not to depict him as a pantomime villain. He does have values. He is a true-believer in modernization, convinced that the pursuit of 'evidence-based' efficiency and effectiveness serves the public interest better than Pauline's 'tea and sympathy' (see the fourth episode). His name is also significant. Norm is a zealous normalizer, imposing discipline on his workforce through surveillance. He expects his disciplinary power to extend indirectly to their supervisees. That said, Norm is without neither doubt nor curiosity as the story's alternative endings in Chapter 7 reveal. He too is human and, therefore, capable of change.

Petra is the rock on which a movement is being built. Naming it the 'Conviction Collective' is a sociological pun, referencing Durkheim's idea of the 'conscience collective' but subverting it to suggest that shared morality might be re-discovered amongst stigmatized 'offenders'. Again, Petra is a composite character based on several people I know who have developed organisations of and for people with convictions (like 'Positive Prison? Positive Futures […]' in Scotland and User Voice in England) committed to supporting one another and challenging the status quo in criminal justice. The description of the Conviction Collective's meeting in the sixth episode draws directly on my experience of meetings convened by 'Positive Prison? Positive Futures […]'

Settings and Plotlines

Although I have drawn on people, places, experiences and academic literature in writing the story, I did not set it consciously in any specific jurisdiction or at any precise moment in time. The institutional form of supervision that it depicts is perhaps closest to the current situation in community rehabilitation companies in England and Wales (Burke et al., 2018). Indeed, some English managers and practitioners have identified painfully closely with some aspects of the story. If there is a temporal setting, it is the near future.

The plotline was written with the pre-existing structure of the book in mind. I wanted each episode to speak to the issues raised in the chapter within which it sits. In all but the final chapter, the fictional episode precedes the academic writing and is then referred to within it. My intention in this was to grab the reader's interest, to vividly highlight the importance of the issues addressed in that chapter and to draw her or him into engagement with the academic writing. Perhaps most fundamentally, I tried to stick to my partner's advice, refining the characters and depicting their relationships as a way of sustaining interest in the book's themes and argument.

Given the myriad possible ways of engaging with those themes (respectively, pervasiveness and invisibility, change, numbers, legitimation, experiences, making visible and future possibilities), it did not feel like much of constraint to develop the story with them in mind. Indeed, I found it helpful to anchor my writing in a theme and a place and with a character or an encounter between characters and then to see what happened. Most often, I didn't know what was going to happen in the episode until I sat down to write it. In this sense, the plot was produced by the characters in my imagination. Thus, for example, in the fifth episode, all I did was arrange the home visit: It was Pauline that then became concerned about

Joe's mental health and social isolation and, in the end, formed an idea of how she might help him address both issues. I didn't know what that idea was — so I published the fifth episode on the blog and invited readers to suggest what might happen next. The sixth episode and the two endings were thus informed by readers' suggestions (and thanks are due in particular to Hannah Graham and Kirstin Anderson).

The way that the story sits in Chapter 7 is a little different. Here, I settled on writing two episodes that offered different possible endings. Chapter 7 opens with a dystopian ending and ends with a utopian alternative. The dystopian ending may read as being a little more like science fiction than the rest of the story, but I am reliably informed that all of the technology that it introduces either exists or is imaginable. For example, probation reporting booths already exist (as an alternative to or supplement for 'human' supervision) and I have myself been at a meeting where Dutch technologists discussing their efforts to design a virtual reality headset that allows for its wearer to be 'counselled' by a future self, although I should stress that my dystopian imagining of 'Future Joe' is not what they had in mind. Transdermal devices that test the wearer's sweat for evidence of alcohol use also exist and are in operation in some justice systems.[1] The utopian ending also represents the more hopeful sort of 'adjacent possible' discussed in Chapter 6, in so much as I have given evidence at Parliamentary Committees (in Scotland) alongside people with convictions whose experience and expertise appeared to be recognized and respected at least by the parliamentarians involved.

Offering these two endings was a helpful way of inviting the reader to think about what kinds of choices might propel us away from one and towards the other. Thus, the conventional academic part of Chapter 7 is sandwiched between these two possible worlds, hoping to help steer is onto what I argue is the better path.

Substance and Style

Perhaps that last admission — about Chapter 7 — raises the obvious question of whether what I have written in the story is an example of instrumentalising 'art' (or at least my fictional writing) as a kind of propaganda. It is obviously the case that I wrote the story with a purpose and even a message in mind, though I would argue that my intention was simply to help readers imagine and think about supervision (and especially *being* supervised), rather than to persuade them *what* to think about it.

There is developing interest in 'creative non-fiction' and in 'faction'. How these terms are defined seems to vary but the former term generally refers to writing that applies the techniques of fiction to writing from personal experience, for example in the forms of memoir or meditation or commentary. Barrie Jean Borich writes that:

> *We begin a work of creative nonfiction not with the imaginary but with the actual, with what actually is or actually was, or what actually happened. From this point we might move in any direction, but the actual is our touchstone.*[2]

'Faction' refers to the fictionalization of real events and characters, for example, in historical novels like the work of Hilary Mantel. S.K. Nicholls offers the example of Norman Mailer's 'Armies of the Night' as a critically appreciated non-fiction novel, using his personal experience of the 1967 march on the Pentagon, but recounting the story in the third person.[3]

As a short story, I think that 'The Invisible Collar' is neither creative non-fiction nor faction. It is not rooted in any specific historical events or characters that I am trying to reconstruct imaginatively. Rather, like all fiction, it draws on the writer's experiences to imagine its own events, people and places. However, in this case, the fiction is very consciously rooted in practice and research and, as such, I was committed to a kind of 'critical realism' in writing it, 'realistic' in the sense of being faithful to personal experiences and/or research findings, 'critical' in admitting that I can only imagine from the position that I occupy (and the positions that I have occupied) and with all the partialities that I have.

Rather than creative non-fiction or faction then, I think what I was trying to do in 'The Invisible Collar' perhaps owes more to the work of the filmmaker Ken Loach. His film-making was inspired by the determination to document and represent the ordinary working-class lives and struggles that he felt were being neglected in mainstream cinema. Some of his films, especially those set in Scotland (Carla's Song, 1996; My Name is Joe, 1998; Sweet Sixteen, 2002; Ae Fond Kiss, 2004; The Angel's Share, 2012) have made a significant impression on me, helping me to imagine (and care about) lives that were at the same time close to mine and very distant from it.

I am not for a moment arguing that 'The Invisible Collar' stands along-side or even in the tradition of Loach's films, either as art or in political terms; only that it was driven by a similar frustration. In my case, the frus-tration was that much of the ordinary and routine but pervasive and pain-ful business of punishment was not being seen or heard and therefore was not being discussed and debated.

'The Invisible Collar' is the first story I have written since High School (that is, in more than 30 years). Unlike Jo, I am not a trained or profes-sional artist with an established practice. Fictional writing is not my craft. I am sure that there is plenty wrong with 'The Invisible Collar' as a short story and that there are many problems with the process by which I wrote it. If I persist with creative writing and get better at it, I may well become embarrassed that I put it in this book. But in the final analysis, if I want other people to imagine supervision, then I think I have to be prepared to imagine it myself. Indeed, I think the conversation about supervision will be much more serious, meaningful and productive if we all use our imagi-nations and risk sharing our imaginings.

MAKING SONGS FROM SUPERVISION

Jo Collinson Scott

Purpose

When Fergus first approached me with the idea that his book might have an EP of tracks to accompany it (as it did a short story), we reflected together on what the nature of those tracks might be, how they might be created and for what purpose. We considered that songs could be co-created with those who had lived experience of supervision and use song-writing to explore this directly. However, we decided that this process had already been undertaken very skilfully in the *Seen and Heard* project and that an EP of those songs was already available.[4] We also agreed that it would be good to add to the rich variety of forms of exploration of the research questions here by presenting music that reflected not on direct, primary lived experience of supervision, but on the wider understandings of pervasive punishment as discussed in this book. This opens out the potential for the EP not only to present deeper aspects of what it feels like, sounds like, or means for an individual to be supervised, but also to reflect on the broader structures and concepts surrounding it and the societal impact of mass supervision. To ask collaborators to each have read the entirety of the book and have considered it in the light of other sources was unrealistic, and therefore, we decided that the EP would be developed by myself as principle songwriter and performer, working in conjunction with other artists selected for their particular musical skills and aesthetic. The songs and the sounds of the recorded tracks were created in conjunction with these collaborators in a way that was intended to best compliment the role of the music to explore and make audible crucial aspects of this material.

In my work over a number of years with Fergus, he has always understood and respected that my practice resists the instrumentalisation of music. That is, the tendency to look at music primarily as a potential tool to be used, for example, to add emotional force (or indeed a bit of fun) to the communication of specific subjects, or as an add-on intended merely to attract a wider or non-academic audience. With that in mind, the EP was not created with the intention of setting the story or the book to music, nor to communicate it to an audience in a different way. The use of music in this context, as it is in all my work, is for the purposes of exploring and researching a subject from a different (creative) perspective, by different means and with different results. The songs, I hope, are not simply a form of communication of Fergus' research but are embodied examples of a research process themselves. They do ask what it feels like to experience supervision, and they do so in a rich way that uses the experience of songwriters and performers in tapping in to points of shared humanity of a broad range of listeners, but they also ask: What does a creative and musical mind draw out from the collected information as key points of interest in this regard? What does this sound like (and what has this sounded like in the past)? Where are the resonances within this and between this and other texts? What is missing from this exploration and how does music help us imagine differently? As the reader may have noted, there is often an over-emphasis on seeing when it comes to knowledge (e.g. in the name of the fields of 'visual sociology' or 'visual criminology') and because the ways that we talk about punishment are a crucial part of 'penal imaginaries', this means that music — as a way of 'hearing differently' — is a particularly fresh way of helping us to do this.

The arts are a crucial way to foster imagination and imagination is central to a number of the most important aspects of what Fergus explores here. For example, the process of rehabilitation is an act of imagination, as is reimagining the future of supervision and community justice (as he does in the final chapter, and in the two versions of the future of supervision his story presents). Indeed, Jacques Attali contends in his influential future-focused text *Noise* that 'music is prophecy [...]. It makes audible the new world that will gradually become visible' (Attali, 1977, p. 11). Attali discusses art music, but popular music has also been explored in this way too. For example, ecomusicologists have been grappling with music's role in imagining a different future (an environmentally sustainable one) for a number of years, and in doing so, Mark Pedelty suggests that popular music can be helpful in reimagining futures in three main ways. Firstly, as communication (music as a means of mediating issues), secondly as art (as 'creative, aesthetic, symbolic and affective' expression of meanings related to the subject) and thirdly, as advocacy (an attempt to 'inform, inspire and persuade audiences') (Pedelty, 2012, p. 7) The third of these, if treated as the sole focus, can result in extremely boring art (propaganda, as Fergus discusses previously) and as Pedelty notes, 'music is about affect rather than effect' (p. 203). Consequently, we decided that the first two rather than the third of these aims constituted the focus here.

Authenticity

Having made these decisions about the nature of the EP and in the process of developing the tracks along these lines, I have been reflecting frequently on the issue of authenticity. As Fergus notes, this is a consideration that is seen as particularly relevant to creative endeavours such as short story writing, and even more so in relation to popular music, especially where songs are performed by the individuals who wrote them. I have no direct experience with being supervised or with supervising (as Fergus does) and I did not directly carry out research with those that do. This will raise questions about what grounds I have in order to speak about these experiences. I do bring my experience of having worked for many years as a community music practitioner and having led workshops in prison and community justice settings, helping those who do have such experience to communicate that through music-making and songwriting. I also work as a co-investigator on a collaborative action research project (*Distant Voices: Coming Home*) alongside co-researchers who have past and ongoing experience of supervision or monitoring – both supervising and being supervised – and I have worked collaboratively with a number of them to explore related experiences.

In addition to this, I bring my expertise as a creative practitioner to bear on this project, which means that I have spent many years developing skills in either imagining and then representing the experiences of others, or in combining what I know of those experiences with some of my own in order to construct and perform new possible perspectives that I expect will generate understanding, connection, potential empathy or even challenge for a listener. Indeed, part of what songs do so well is to complicate narratives and to leave space for listeners to use songs to embody their own perspectives or encompass their own experience, rather than laying out a specific version of that experience. It is also the case that, despite appearances, popular music does not always arise from personal experience or communicate current personal feeling. The music press and a large number of artists tend to play to (and often have inculcated in them) long-standing romanticized images of the creative process (Brennan, 2006; McIntyre, 2008; Scott, 2017; Shuker, 1994; Wicke, 1990). This includes the idea that creativity is untrammelled personal outpouring of the life experiences of the performer and is related to the erroneous assumption that all songwriters and musicians must be plagued with personal difficulties and dark emotional troubles in order to write or perform well and/or that they only sing autobiographically (Bilton, 2013; Burnard, 2012; McIntyre, 2008). This is not at all the case and – like in scriptwriting for film or theatre – musicians frequently write or perform from the imagined perspective of others and are skilled and trained in attempting to explore experiences that are not their own within their work. Many professional songwriters, for example, go their whole careers rarely, if ever, writing a song for themselves or from their own perspective, always writing for other performers' personas or perceived interests.

Having said that, despite this being the case from the point of view of professional practice, these are still widespread perceptions that have an effect on the reception of popular music by audiences. For this reason, I was mindful of the fact that it would be me performing these songs on the recordings, and developing them within my own genre or field of practice and that this would mean that the results would in some sense 'sound like me'. The most obvious implication of this is with relation to gender. It is clear from my voice that I am female, and having a female voice sing certain words or narratives brings inevitable questions with relation to the portrayal of certain viewpoints. It is also the case that although the sub-genre in which I work (alt-folk) does draw on genres that have been considered to be founded in more structurally disadvantaged communities (e.g. country- and folk-related music), its current manifestation is certainly a sound that has a largely middle-class audience, and therefore does not communicate to or from an audience that is most likely to be under mass supervision. This was clear from the practice review that I carried out, where I attempted to source a range of popular music tracks addressing supervision. Having done my own research, and asked within my networks of popular music scholars, it was clear that this subject is – as Fergus highlights – largely invisible. Where it is addressed in popular music, this is mostly in hip-hop (for a key example, listen to Tee Grizzley's track 'First Day Out', a later version of which features Meek Mill, the subject of Jay-Z's New York Times piece decrying the US probation and parole system), and even then, very sparsely. There are isolated examples in country music and in rock, but with the latter, these appear to be mainly appropriative of the subject in order to build a persona or image related to risk and deviance (for example, Motörhead's 'On Parole').

Perspective(s)

With these considerations in mind, I decided that I would concentrate on taking oblique or broadened viewpoints in developing the tracks. Originally I had considered the possibility of writing one track from the viewpoint of each of the characters in the 'The Invisible Collar' – Joe, Pauline and Norm – but having broadened my perspective, through the process described previously, the tracks now reflect something of each of these characters but from alternative perspectives and alongside the exploration of other concepts. For example, in discussing the characters in the story with award-winning novelist Martin Cathcart Fródén (co-writer of 'Tightness' along with Lucy Cathcart Froden) we began to wonder – if Joe was supervisee number 59, then who were the other 58? This began to widen our focus to include the characters only implied in the story (or obliquely mentioned). One of the resonances I then encountered when reading other creative representations of supervision in preparation for

developing the musical material was in descriptions of the wives or partners of men on parole in Edward Bunker's book *No Beast So Fierce*. In
this brilliant semi-autobiographical account of being released from prison
and being subject to supervision, these minor characters frequently
absorbed me more than the main drivers of the narrative. They were
depicted as suffering greatly – living in poverty, uncertainty and with even
less control over the fate of those on whom they and their children
depended than the supervisees themselves. They weren't numbers 1–58,
but they were certainly anonymous and invisible others within the system.

Where my voice might not easily embody the experience of a middle-
class man like Joe, it could certainly explore the perspective of a partner or
daughter. 'Weight', therefore, is written from the perspective of a family
member of someone under supervision. The narrator of the song – much
like the narrator of Dolly Parton's song 'Jolene' – sees their 'stranger'
(parole/probation officer) as a threat to her way of life and a threat that is
at a complete remove from anything she can control or interact with. She
feels the need to plead with them for leniency and empathy. In this sense,
'Weight' can be seen to explore Norm's character and role within the
story – the regulation-driven, relatively invisible person behind the frontline who enforces compliance and whose decisions pervade far beyond the
supervisor and supervisee themselves – but through the eyes of another.
This song was co-written with musician A. Wesley Chung, an American
musician, who brings embodied knowledge of American (alt) country music
and the exploration of cultural ideas related to US systems in this context.

'Depth', on the other hand, appears more directly to explore the experience of a Joe-type character, but the use of second person perspective directly challenges the listener to question themselves, and as such, makes
them a subject of the song. This raises the possibility of listeners putting
themselves in the place of the person described and therefore empathetic-
ally imagining the experiences related to supervision that are described. At
the same time, it makes the narrator of the song hold no claim to personal
experience except the ability to ask critical questions, whilst still allowing
for emotional engagement. 'Tightness', as a third example, takes an
oblique perspective on the character of Pauline, by exploring the Pauline
of the future, who (according to the dystopian ending to the story) may
indeed be a technological substitution. In this song, my co-writers and
I attempted to write from the perspective of a camera or a robotic

monitoring technology and to imagine what that eye would see and understand of a supervisee. This approach resulted in ambiguities that mean the perspective of this song could also encompass more broadly the public who are themselves monitored or monitoring (for example by CCTV) within the same system. Indeed the refrain 'also of we that system holds' invites the question as to who else is held by this system and how.

Depth, Weight, Tightness and Suspension

As may be clear from the titles of the songs on the EP, I found some of the most resonant concepts that were explored in this book to be those described by Ben Crewe as the 'pains of imprisonment' and extended by Fergus to help us understand the pains of supervision – 'depth', 'weight' and 'tightness' (Crewe, 2011). After talking to Fergus about those as exploratory headings for the work, we added 'suspension' to this list as an important addition. The tracks 'Weight', and to a certain extent 'Tightness', also explore what might be described as the 'breadth' of supervision, i.e., the spread of the pains of punishment beyond the supervisee themselves (Cohen, 1985; Crewe, 2011).

Depth, weight, tightness and suspension are all terms that are very evocative in a musical sense as they relate to timbre, time, style and performative gesture amongst other things. It was under these headings that I began to coalesce and develop my lyrical and musical ideas relating to the themes explored in the book and the characters in the story. I did not set out to represent or 'communicate' these concepts, but rather it was the case that beginning to explore these terms and their creative resonances foregrounded a number of other key concepts and related practices including identity, the pains of self-supervising and the representation of failure.

Sound

There is no more space to describe in any detail the specific ways in which the tracks on the EP explore the audibility of these subjects. But it might be good before I finish to discuss something more with relation to the specific sound of the EP and how this was developed. In exploring what sounds might best be employed to expand understandings of mass supervision, I struck upon the area of 'glitch' music. 'Glitch' is a genre of music associated with a popular production trend of the 1990s, in which musical failure is foregrounded and celebrated as an aesthetic ideal. Glitch is the word used to describe a small hitch of some kind in the playback or recording of sound. A key example of this might be the sound that is made when a CD skips whilst playing or that a speaker makes when a mobile phone is held near it while transmitting signal. There are numerous means by which digital glitches are made too, including malfunctions in music production software that generate unwanted noise. Glitch music celebrates these noises to such an extent that they become ubiquitous to the sound of the genre. In this sense, a glitch can be seen to be a form of redemption of the failure of the system within which it is created (Bates, 2004; Hainge, 2007; Hofer, 2006; Sangild, 2004). 'Swift and certain' is how the response to failure is described in the US parole and probation system. And yet, in the creative process, failure is often one of the most potent sites of potential for breakthrough and advancement. As such, an intersection of the glitch genre with music such as my own seems a productive (and somewhat subversive) place to begin an aural exploration of such a system. As one of the key names in the burgeoning of the folktronica movement in the UK, the producer here (Adem Ilhan) has been well placed to help explore the combination of my signature alt-folk sound with aspects of glitch and electronic music in order to make these concepts more audible.

The research that is presented in the rest of this book moves towards an understanding of the identity of both the supervisee and the supervisor that is complex, wound up in many systems other than simple personal choice, and bound to failures, both personal and systemic on a number of levels. In this sense, it seems highly appropriate to use glitch as a means to explore this musically. Glitch music, in turning up the sound of failures in the recording systems we use, brings to light the real identity of music recordings – not as transparent reproductions but as wound up in many other forms of sounds and systems. For this reason, I have worked with the producer of the tracks to try and rejoice aesthetically in glitches, failures and the noise inherent in home recorded music. This has involved exploring, amongst other things: slightly nudging keyboard tracks out of sync with each other, enhancing and playing with the sound that splicing two vocal takes together makes (a sound that is normally smoothed out with production software), reincorporating the noise of recording back into the tracks and celebrating skipping and jolting of all kinds by employing these rhythmically.

FINAL THOUGHTS

Much more could be written about the processes of writing the short story and the songs on the EP and, indeed, we hope to elaborate on this initial account in our future writing. Perhaps more importantly, bearing in mind our shared interest in creatively mediated dialogue, we also hope that we will be able to reflect on and write about what we learn from how the story and songs are received. With that in mind, if you would like to respond in some way to the story or the songs, including critically, please do get in touch.

We also want to encourage you to engage with the story and songs and to use and share them in some way, if you like – whether as an educator, a practitioner or simply as a citizen. All we ask is that you let us know how you use them and what happens. Having shared something of our differently rooted, generated and presented imaginings of supervision, we are keen to know what imaginings they prompt in others.

So please: listen, look, imagine and share.

NOTES

1. See https://www.youtube.com/watch?v=KYHRvhE_hqE. Accessed on 11 June 2018.

2. See http://barriejeanborich.com/what-is-creative-nonfiction-an-introduction/. Accessed on 11 June 2018.

3. See https://sknicholls.wordpress.com/2013/08/04/what-is-faction/. Accessed on 11 June 2018.

4. The Seen and Heard EP can be found at https://voxliminis.bandcamp.com/album/seen-and-heard-ep. Accessed on 19 February 2018.

APPENDIX: THE INVISIBLE COLLAR (A STORY ABOUT SUPERVISION)

THE WAITING ROOM

Joe sat on the bench in the waiting room. Looking down, he noticed that the bench was screwed to the floor. Not even the furniture here was free. Perspex screens and locked doors separated him and the others waiting from those for whom they waited; the veils between the untrustworthy and those to whom they were entrusted. Joe absent-mindedly read the graffiti carved into the bench; testimonies of resistance that made the place feel even more desperate.

Joe scanned the postered walls, shouting their messages in pastel shades and bold print. Problems with drugs? Problems with alcohol? Problems with anger? Stay calm. Apparently, help was at hand – or at the end of a phone-line. But meanwhile remember that abusive language and aggressive behaviour will not be tolerated. Not in this room that itself felt like an installation of abuse and aggression. To Joe it said 'You are pathetic, desperate or dangerous. You are not to be trusted. You must wait'.

He fidgeted and returned his eyes to the floor, downcast by the weight of the room's assault, avoiding contact, avoiding hassle, staying as unknown as possible in this shame pit. Better to be out of place here than to belong. This was no place to make connections.

Joe wondered what she would be like – Pauline – the unknown woman who now held the keys to his freedom. Her word had become his law: This was an 'order' after all. He was to be the rule-keeper, she the ruler – cruel, capricious or kind. She might hold the leash lightly or she might drag him to heel.

Instinctively, he lifted his hand to his neck, but no one can loosen an invisible collar. At least it was not a noose. Joe swallowed uncomfortably, noticing the dryness of his mouth and the churning in his gut. He was not condemned to hang. He was condemned to be left hanging.

Joe wondered what Pauline would be like.

SCREEN-WEARY EYES

Pauline put down the phone. The new guy, the 59th on her caseload, was 15 minutes early. A sign of eagerness maybe, but also an irritation. She had too many other things to do and hadn't had time to prep yet. She took off her glasses, rubbed her screen-weary eyes and gulped another mouthful of her now-cold coffee (black, of course; no one in the office brought in milk anymore). Replacing her glasses in the twin dents on the bridge of her nose, she resumed her screen gaze, clicking the 'casefiles' icon and opening up no. 59 for the first time.

Joseph Earnshaw, aged 49 years, divorced father of two. Two previous convictions – possession of cannabis and public affray ... but these dated from almost 30 years ago. The indiscretions of his youth perhaps? The standard format court report was light on detail and substance, but the account of his offence was interesting.

Having been made redundant two weeks before the incident, Earnshaw had returned to the offices of the accountancy firm where he had worked for 15 years. He was drunk and abusive, and proceeded to spray piss around the reception area before daubing the boss's office door with the one-word epithet: 'BLOODSUCKER'. The red paint had also found its way all over his former boss's designer suit in the scuffle that ensued.

The report said that Earnshaw scored 'low-risk' on the Offender Assessment Triage System (OATS). Pauline raised a single eyebrow; she was long enough in the tooth to be wary of that. She knew that these scores didn't save probation officers from shouldering the blame when things went wrong. Funny how the scoring system itself could never be at fault.

Joseph Earnshaw was either a bad case of an embarrassing and brief mid-life crisis or a man on the edge of a potentially violent meltdown who might lose Pauline her job. Maybe the court expected her to figure out which during the next 18 months.

Pauline sighed. When she had started out back in the 90s, she might have had the energy and enthusiasm – and the time – to suss him out and maybe even to help him get his head back together and his life on track. But caseloads back then were in the 20s or 30s not the 50s or 60s, and the bosses cared about and supported that sort of work. Now they cared only about targets.

She cast her eyes across to Norm's 'pod', wondering if her supervisor was even now watching her screen on his, or analysing the IT system's reports of the time she had spent in each of her casefiles in the last month. Glancing at her watch, she realized that she was probably already a quarter way through the monthly time allowance for a 'low-risk' case. She'd better go and see the guy before his time was up.

She just hoped he wasn't going to be a pain in the arse. She had enough of those to deal with already, with Norm top of the list.

17 MINUTES AND 14 SECONDS WASTED

Norman stopped the video clip and lent back in his chair, stretching his back and trying to unfurrow his brow. He clicked open Pauline's quarterly appraisal form, took a deep breath and contemplated the section of the pro-forma entitled *Video Practice Quality Audit*.

1. **Relational Skills** (To what extent does the worker demonstrate an ability to develop a strong and appropriate professional working relationship with the offender?)[Rate on a 5-point scale, where 5 is 'fully demonstrated' and 1 is 'not demonstrated' at all].

2. **Structuring Skills** (To what extent does the worker keep the interview focused on addressing needs and risks related to reducing reoffending, using appropriate techniques to motivate, rehearse and reinforce prosocial behaviours and to challenge antisocial behaviours?) [Rate on a 5-point scale, where 5 is 'fully focused' and 1 is 'not focused' at all].

3. **Use of authority** (To what extent does the worker maintain appropriate professional boundaries using their authority to promote and enforce compliance with supervision?) [Rate on a 5-point scale, where 5 is 'fully maintained' and 1 is 'not maintained' at all].

4. **Brokerage** (To what extent does the worker ensure that the offender is appropriately signposted to relevant services relevant to addressing needs and risks?) [Rate on a 5-point scale, where 5 is 'fully ensured' and 1 is 'not ensured' at all].

Norman sighed. Pauline's performance in 59's induction interview was typical of the problems associated with 'lifers'[1] (as he liked to refer to his more 'experienced' staff). He admitted that she was a #4 for 'relational'. She put 59 at ease straight away – as simple as a warm smile, the offer of a hot drink and a firm but welcoming handshake (despite, he noted disapprovingly, the latest health and safety memo about avoiding the winter vomiting bug).

The issue was that, like most of her peers, her interviews often lacked appropriate focus and purpose. True to form, she had let 59 talk too much, wasting time, instead of cutting to the chase. Did she really need to know the ins and outs of his divorce or his worries about how the court case would affect his struggle to see his kids? Worse still, letting him bleat on about the injustices of his dismissal from his job just gave him time and space to repeat excuses for his offences instead of taking responsibility. If ever there was a moment for an 'appropriate challenge' of his 'cognitive distortions' that was it – and Pauline had either missed it or bottled it. At best a #2 for 'structuring'.

The lifers were stuck in their ways; ironic, he thought, since they considered themselves the experts at supporting change, always stressing their hard-earned experience at the frontline. But what good was decades of experience of doing things badly – or, at best, inefficiently? He had done the courses and read the correctional research. Most low-moderate risk offenders need, at most, brief, focused and structured interventions with prompt onward referral to interventions and services that addressed any 'criminogenic' factors. It wasn't rocket science ... Nor was it social work, whatever the old-timers thought.

No, it was court-ordered supervision and its purpose was simple; reduced reoffending at reduced cost. 59 just needed to know what to do, what not to do, who to go and see, and who to keep away from. Cheerily telling 59 to keep out of trouble didn't cut it. It was a #1 for authority then. The risk assessment score justified only the most minimal intervention – and it was blindingly obvious that, if anything, he needed a few sessions of anger management. For now, the tag[2] could take care of keeping him away from his ex-boss, his ex-wife and his ex-life.

Norman re-opened the video file and checked the clock-counter. 37 minutes and 14 seconds. The contract allowed 1 hour of contact time per month for low-moderate cases. And, instead of referring him on, Pauline had promised to visit 59 at home in a few days. So, it was a #1 for 'brokerage' then. The home visit was another health and safety issue — and another waste of precious time.

Norman totted up Pauline's score. Nine out of a possible 20. He'd have to talk to her. This appraisal wasn't going to end well. Norman needed 75% of his staff scoring 15 or better in these audits to trigger the results-related bonus payment. For that he needed fresher, younger and hungrier staff. Pragmatists not puritans.

No wonder the furrow in his brow had become a trench.

WE'RE NOT HERE TO BUILD THE COMMUNITY, WE'RE HERE TO PROTECT IT

Pauline noticed too late that Norm had directed her to the seat furthest from the door of the meeting room, placing himself between her and the exit. A familiar ploy. There was going to be no escape until he was finished, unless she went over or through him …

'Pauline', he began, 'you know how much I respect your skills and experience, right?'

She waited for the inevitable 'But'.

'But things have changed and you need to change with them', he continued, passing her the print-out of her appraisal score.

'This sort of performance just won't do'.

She sighed.

'Norm, tell me this: how am I supposed to help the guy if I don't get to know him and what makes him tick. That takes time.'

'That's the problem right there, Pauline'.

Norm lent back in his seat and smiled his patronising, faux-patient smile, pausing for dramatic effect.

'You're still labouring under the illusion that your job is to *help* these people. It's not. Let me put this in the simplest possible terms: Your job is to stop them from reoffending — at least until their good behaviour triggers our results-related payment. I know what you're thinking but it's not about profit for profit's sake; I want to invest that revenue in getting better and better at protecting communities'.

She couldn't resist: 'What? You mean communities where people don't have time for each other, don't know each other and don't help each other?'

Norm's face coloured a little, his fixed smile starting to look like a rictus grin, but he retained his composure:

'Pauline, please. You know me better than that. I value community as much as the next individual, but we are not here to **build** the community, we are here to **protect** it.'

The slow-spoken bold-print was starting to make Pauline's eyeballs itch.

'And we need to do that as time-efficiently as possible. We need to reduce costs and maximise returns. We owe it to the taxpayers. They don't want their money wasted on tea and sympathy. We're here to control and challenge behaviour that threatens communities. And we're here to make offenders pay back for their crimes. Yes, it's great if we can also improve and develop them as people, but the thing is Pauline, there's really no convincing evidence that 'help' is all that helpful … at least not in reducing offending.'

Pauline couldn't believe that Norm was putting air-quotes around 'help'.

Trying not to rise to the bait, she settled in for the duration. She determined to apply her apparently outmoded appreciative perspective to the significant challenge of understanding the genesis of Norm's distorted worldview. The sad thing — the dangerous thing — was that he genuinely seemed to believe this shit.

ANY CHANCE OF A REFILL?

Pauline wondered if she had earned the right to ask the next question, and then ploughed ahead:

'Look Joe. Let me be honest with you. I can understand why you were so pissed off with your boss; he sounds like a total dick. And I can see that the red paint made a point about him bleeding you dry over the years. I'm not saying it was justified but I get it. But — to be blunt — pissing on the reception floor? What was that all about?'

'I know', Joe replied, head in hands and eyes fixed on the bare floor-boards below, 'I'm totally mortified about that. I did send Tracey some flowers by way of apology. She's the office cleaner. Lovely woman. I hate the thought of her having to mop that up'.

Joe took a deep breath, lifted his head, looked Pauline in the eye and continued:

'Look, the simple fact was that I had drunk five or six pints winding myself up for the confrontation. Confrontation is just not my thing — nor is beer, it turns out. But, in the heat of the moment, and finding myself with a bladder fit to burst, spraying piss around like Michael Douglas in that movie *Wall Street* just seemed like a great way to mess with Steve's massive ego. Needless to say, it didn't look so clever on the CCTV the police showed me — but then none of it did'.

Pauline smiled and shook her head: 'Pretty moronic, eh? Any chance of a refill?'

While Joe re-boiled the kettle, Pauline studied their surroundings. Joe's place was not, she imagined, a deliberate effort at Scandinavian minimal-ism taken to extremes; more likely, it revealed that lack of self-care that often accompanies depression. The living room in his one-bedroom apart-ment boasted only a large beanbag, an easy chair (bottom of the range Ikea) and a small coffee table. An old TV sat on the floor in the corner. The un-curtained window looked out over the courtyard of what was a converted 1920s fire station. A gated community, sealed off from the city life outside. She'd seen much worse places, but she couldn't imagine Joe's kids being keen on sleepovers, unless they shared their dad's newfound ascetic tastes.

Joe placed a fresh cup of instant coffee in front of Pauline and resumed his place awkwardly on the beanbag, sitting cross-legged and trying not to feel like an errant child.

'Anyway', Pauline continued, enough about what happened. Let's talk about now. And let's talk about the future. We've got 17 months of this order to get through; and you have the tag and your 7–7 curfew for the next five. I suppose there are really just two or three questions: How do we get you through this without any further bother, and what do you want out of it — what do you want your future to be?

Joe felt blindsided by the last two questions. The future? What future? He hadn't been able to think clearly since the wheels came off the cart. It wasn't just that he wasn't driving the cart, it was that he hadn't stopped falling since his life crashed. There didn't seem to be any solid ground from which to take a view, just a constant tumble of words and images. Was Pauline going to help him find some solid ground?

'The first question is a lot easier to answer than the other two. I'm fine with the tag – I haven't had much of a social life since the divorce. It turned out that most of the friendships that we had kept up since we married were my wife's – sorry – ex-wife's. I have a couple of old pals, but we don't see that much of each other; the odd football match or night in the pub – at least, before all this happened. I'm totally off the drink for now – and not missing it. I have the TV and the radio'.

Joe took a sip of his tea, looked out the window and continued:

'To be honest, the days are harder than the nights. Work was such a habit that I can't get used to the sheer emptiness of the days. I miss the action and the sense of purpose much more than the money – though my ex and the kids might take a different view about that. I am looking for work, but it's not easy at my age. It's also pretty tricky explaining to your potential future boss why you assaulted your former boss. On the two occasions when I have got as far as interviews, I've seen the colour drain from their faces at that point'.

'Work isn't the only possible kind of action and purpose, though, is it?', Pauline interjected.

'No, I guess not: I still want to be a proper dad, but it's hard when that amounts to a trip to the movies and a KFC Family Bucket once a week'.

Pauline could feel herself sinking into Joe's hopelessness. The emptiness and desolation of the flat wasn't helping, nor was the sense of being locked in ... but it was giving her the germ of an idea.

'Look Joe: you're an experienced accountant with a hell of a lot of skills and resources. You're not broke – you still have some redundancy money, even after paying for the office clean-up. You said it yourself: You need some action and some purpose. You need to break out of this cell'. A smile crept across her face, and Joe raised an eyebrow in trepidation or curiosity. 'And I have an idea about how we might spring you ...'

A STRANGELY APPEALING ASSEMBLY

Joe couldn't quite get his head around this place or these people. In fact, he felt a bit dazed. Or maybe dazzled. The meeting room was bristling with energy. The people were like fireflies alight with friction; sparks looking for tinder. He wasn't sure whether to be excited or just plain terrified. Probably both.

Pauline had introduced Joe to Petra the week before, describing her as the convenor of the 'Conviction Collective'. Petra said the collective was 'part self-help group, part social movement' (though Joe thought it sounded more like a 70s folk-rock super-group). The only membership qualifications, she said, were a criminal conviction and a personal conviction, born of experience that the justice system needed to change. Most of the fireflies in the room had both kinds of conviction, but they welcomed a few 'associates' – community activists, social workers, students and academics – who could boast only the second sort.

To be honest, Joe was sold on neither self-help nor social movements (nor 70s folk-rock super-groups), but Petra wasn't the sort of person to take 'no' for an answer, and their initial conversation had piqued his curiosity. When she told him her own story – and the story of the group's genesis – it made him realise that he had been so busy trying to cope with his own spectacular and self-propelled fall from grace that he hadn't stopped to think that there were other people in his situation, also subject to the vagaries of the 'system' in which he found himself entangled.

Petra had spoken so passionately and so practically about the obstacles put in the way of re-building a life during and after punishment, and how things could and should be done better, that – for the first time since the incident – Joe felt the stirrings of interest in something beyond his personal troubles.

So, he had agreed to come to the meeting ... and now he wondered if he regretted it. He felt uncomfortable, uncertain and ill-at-ease. The incessant din of chatter and laughter was giving him a headache. It had been a while since he had been around so many people. They could certainly be described as a motley crew, but they were also a strangely appealing assembly of diverse characters, perhaps held together only by their shared convictions. A little like a church without religion, Joe thought, still figuring out its doctrine and its rituals, a fellowship connected by a common hope for change.

Petra looked across at him and smiled encouragingly. Joe felt the same unnerving sensation that he often experienced with Pauline; they both made him feel as if his thoughts were appearing as subtitles on his forehead.

A little later, as they tidied up the room, Petra asked:

'So, what do you reckon, Joe? I know that it can be a bit of a brain-melt, but if this collective is going to achieve anything, we're going to need a fund-raiser and a treasurer. You've got the skills and qualifications – and Pauline says you need a project if you're ever going to get your head out of your arse. As someone once said, 'From each according to his ability, to each according to his need'. What do you say? You up for it?'

ADMINISTERING SHOCKS AND SICKNESS

[12 months later]

Joe heard two sounds as he woke: his own low moan and the insistent, monotonous electronic bell tolling from his ankle bracelet. He fumbled for the clock – it read 08.01 – he had 59 minutes to get to the probation office for his check-in. He knew that somewhere, somehow, some algorithm had determined that this was the moment to test his commitment, to strengthen his resolve, to keep him from temptation. At least that was how Norm had explained it, but Joe saw that the bracelet-bell was a call to worship, an invitation to obey. He pressed the button to acknowledge the signal and the bell stopped.

Joe washed and dressed cautiously, taking care not to let his sock break the contact between bracelet and skin. He knew that any interruption in the signal that allowed remote biometric analysis of his pulse and sweat could constitute an infraction. He had no wish to repeat his recent experience of a weekend in the compliance cells as part of the new SaCS (Swift and Certain Sanction) approach. That had been a high price to pay for trying to use ice cubes and hypoallergenic wipes to relieve the skin irritation that the bracelet caused.

Forty minutes later, Joe was glad to find a reporting booth empty at the probation office. It looked like a cross between an arcade game, a confessional and an upright coffin. He took a deep breath and sat inside, pulling the black curtain across. The touchscreen invited him to provide his hand-print while the retinal scan double checked and confirmed his identity. When prompted, Joe put on the virtual reality headset and was met by the smiling face of 'Virpro', the virtual probation officer. She spoke in slow, soft and maternal tones:

'Good morning, Joe. Well done. You have arrived on time and drug- and alcohol-free. We have no record of adverse contact with the author- ities since your last appointment. There are 4 months and 2 weeks of your revised order remaining to be served. The conditions remain the same. Would you like me to remind you of them?'

'No, thank you', Joe replied.

'That is your choice. Do you require any support or counselling at this time?'

'No, thank you', Joe replied. He guessed he should probably show willing but couldn't get out of the booth quickly enough. He already felt suffocated.

'That is your choice. Please wait for a message from future Joe, after which you are free to go'.

This part always freaked Joe out. Virpro smiled her farewell and faded from view; in her place came an avatar of Joe, looking a few years older but well-groomed, confident, contented, suited and booted. His 'brief motivational intervention' was becoming as predictable as it was sinister:

'Hi Joe. I'm proud of you. You've done so well since that last infrac- tion. The Swift and Certain Sanction really seems to have worked for you. You're back on track, pal. And there are only a few months to go until you are a free man. Just keep at it. Keep your head down. Keep away from troublemakers'.

Future Joe paused for effect, losing his saccharine smile and replacing it with the furrowed brow of his most earnest expression. Though his intense stare met Joe's eyes, it also seemed to look right through him, somewhere into the middle distance.

'Joe: remember, you can become me, if you want it enough, if you really commit. I can be your future. Meantime, take care and look after us both'.

Outside, Joe steadied himself on the railing, taking in as much air as he could. As he walked away, he wondered what Pauline was doing now. He hadn't expected to miss her this much.

...

Upstairs, Norm looked at the three huge screens in front of him: 59's green flag caught his eye. One of Pauline's cases, he recalled. He had to admit that he kind of missed the lifers. The office was quiet without them.

Still, Norm took some pride in that fact that he was now managing 412 low-medium risk cases himself; or rather, he was maintaining and monitoring the system that was managing them. It was remarkably efficient now that it was up and running, even if it would take 25 years (with caseloads at current levels) to recoup the installation costs. In the long run, it was worth it. Now that the infrastructure existed, the possibilities of combining remote biometric monitoring with VR and AI were limitless.

That said, Norm still harboured doubts. The newly proposed GATE (Geo-Aversion Tag Enhancer) tech troubled him. These tags could respond to remote signals by releasing nausea-inducing drugs implanted in pellets under the offender's skin. In an emergency, they could issue taser-style shocks. Both measures disabled offenders who strayed beyond their permitted spaces, or showed the classic signs of over-stimulation associated with imminent risk of offending.

Norm had a lot of sympathy for the argument that GATE allowed high risk offenders to be managed safely in the community. As the marketing slogan put it, 'GATE retrains and restrains'. The pilot studies seemed promising, despite one or two admittedly very unfortunate cases. Yet, even though the offenders would have to consent to GATE and even though they signed the relevant disclaimers, he didn't much like the idea that he would be the one administering shocks and causing sickness, or even administering a system that did so. He tried to reassure himself that GATE wasn't about punishment; it was just doing what was necessary for public safety. And *he* wasn't being asked to press those buttons yet.

Norm thought it was probably best to keep his doubts to himself.

OR

REHABILITATING NORM(S)

[12 months later]

Norm heard two sounds as he woke: his own low moan and the insistent, monotonous electronic bell tolling from his alarm clock. It read 08.01 — he had 59 minutes to get ready and catch that train. Today was the day of the Justice Committee hearing on the future of supervision.

Norm hadn't slept well, though already he couldn't quite recollect the plots and sub-plots of the anxiety dreams that had plagued him in the night. Did Joe bring a tin of red paint to the hearing in one version? Did Petra accuse the parliamentarians of 'techno-fascism' in another? He was pretty sure Pauline had been late in every scenario his unconscious had so kindly visualised for him.

The old Norm would have run for cover long before now but, despite his fears, the new Norm was excited about the day ahead. There was no doubt that the past 12 months had changed him. As he looked in the mirror, tying his tie, he admitted that he liked what he was becoming better than what he had been.

His first encounter with the Conviction Collective – at Pauline's insistence – had left him unconvinced. Initially, he was sceptical about the willingness and ability of people under supervision to provide meaningful and effective peer support. But he reasoned that if the Collective was a free supplement to formal services, then why not give it a chance? To offset any risk to his personal reputation and standing in the Company, Norm made clear that it was Pauline's initiative and Pauline's responsibility.

Within weeks though, seeing the glint in her eye and the spring in her step, he decided he should attend the weekly gathering and see what was going on. At first, the answer seemed to be 'Not much'. About 12–15 people met and shared some pizza (it was never clear who paid for it, but Norm suspected Pauline). They talked together, sometimes they walked together. Someone found an old table tennis table and they played.

But, they also got organised. Ever the accountant, Joe had been instrumental in persuading them to identify, recognise and detail all the forms of 'capital' that they held. He made an inventory of their skills, resources and contacts. They started to exchange goods, services and introductions for one another – from each according to their abilities, to each according to their needs. The group grew and so did the inventory. The founding members invested more of themselves, the new members brought new assets and abilities. In sum, they advised, assisted and befriended one another.

Group members also began to share more and more of their experiences – both good and bad – of the justice system. They invited other 'expert witnesses' to plug the gaps in their understanding; criminologists, lawyers, sociologists – even a historian. Norm himself had been invited to explain the logic of the current supervision system. That had been quite a challenge and quite a grilling. Soon, the Collective had written a manifesto, naming it: 'Just Conviction, Fair Supervision'. Norm didn't agree with all its prescriptions, but he admired its clarity, its use of evidence and the force of its arguments.

The press soon took an interest. Petra turned out to be quite an operator; proving more than adept at handling everything from hostile questions from cynical political hacks to irate callers on early morning phone-ins. Surprisingly perhaps, listening to Petra and the others, people seemed to become more cautious and more curious about what court sentences did to people and about what they achieved or failed to achieve for society.

Initially, Norm's bosses had liked the positive PR that came with supporting the Collective; they thought it made them look progressive. They hadn't been so happy about 'Just Conviction, Fair Supervision' – worried about their market share, he supposed, if those proposals were ever to be implemented. That said, Norm and Joe didn't have to work too hard to convince the company that excessive supervision wasn't especially lucrative; not at least while there were stubbornly high revocation and reconviction rates.

The company also knew that re-nationalisation was back on the political agenda; it was time to look for better business opportunities elsewhere. At the very least, Joe had argued, working with the government and the courts to scale down supervision and to deliver better results might minimise losses in the meantime. And in reputational terms, it also meant that the company wasn't left carrying the can on its own.

It was now Norm's job to lead the Ministry-sanctioned local pilot of 'Just Conviction, Fair Supervision'. And the very early results of the pilot had led to the invitation to Norm, Petra, Pauline and Joe to give evidence to the committee today.

The gang of four met at the coffee stall in the train station. Even Pauline was on time. They greeted one another as old friends, collected their orders and, as was their habit, made for the front carriage. They knew they were going to be in a hurry when they arrived in the capital. They had already come a long way together in a short time, but there was a lot of work still to be done.

* * *

NOTES

1. See Mawby and Worrall (2014).

2. 'Tag' is the colloquial term in the UK for an anklet worn to allow electronic monitoring of people subject to certain kinds of 'curfew' or 'home detention' or other movement restriction.

BIBLIOGRAPHY

Abraham, M., Van Dijk, B., & Zwaan, M. (2007). *Inzicht in Toezicht: De Uitvoering van Toezicht door de Reclassering [Views on probation: Provision of supervision by the probation services]*. The Hague: WODC.

Aebi, M. F., Delgrande, N., & Marguet, Y. (2015). Have community sanctions and measures widened the net of the European criminal justice systems? *Punishment & Society, 17*(5), 575–597.

Alexander, M. (2010). *The New Jim Crow*. New York, NY: The New Press.

Allen, F. (1981). *The Decline of the Rehabilitative Ideal: Penal Policy and Social Purpose*. New Haven, CT: Yale University Press.

Allen, R., & Hough, M. (2007). Community penalties, sentencers, the media and public opinion. In L. Gelsthorpe & R. Morgan (Eds.) *Handbook on Probation* (pp. 565–601). Cullompton: Willan.

Anderson, E. (2006). The epistemology of democracy. *Episteme, 3*(1–2), 8–22.

Anderson, B. (2009) Affective atmospheres. *Emotion, Space and Society, 2*(2009), 77–81.

Anderson, S., Hinchliffe, S., Homes, A., McConville, S., Hutton, N., & Noble, S. (2015). *Evaluation of Community Payback Orders, Criminal Justice Social Work Reports and the Presumption Against Short Sentences*. Edinburgh: Scottish Government Social Research.

Anderson, T. (2013). *Popular Music in a Digital Music Economy: Problems and Practices for an Emerging Service Industry*. Abingdon: Routledge.

Barker, V. (2017). *Nordic Nationalism and Penal Order: Walling the Welfare State.* Routledge: Abingdon.

Bates, E. (2004). Glitches, bugs and hisses: The degeneration of musical recordings and the contemporary musical work. In C. Washburn and M. Derno (Eds.), *Bad Music: The Music We Love to Hate* (pp. 275–293). Abingdon: Routledge.

Bauman, Z. (1997). *Postmodernity and Its Discontents.* Cambridge: Polity Press.

Bauman, Z. (2016). *Strangers At Our Door.* Cambridge: Polity Press.

Beetham, D. (1991). *The Legitimation of Power.* London: Macmillan.

Bilton, C. (2013). Playing to the gallery: Myth, method and complexity in the creative process. In K. Thomas & J. Chan (Eds.), *Handbook of Research on Creativity* (pp. 125–137). Cheltenham: Edward Elgar.

Blomberg, T. (1987). Criminal justice reform and social control: Are we becoming a minimum security society? In J. Lowman, R. Menzies, & T. Palys (Eds.), *Transcarceration: Essays in the Sociology of Social Control.* Brookfield, VT: Gower.

Boden, M. (1992). *The Creative Mind: Myths and Mechanisms.* London: Abacus.

Boone, M. (2016). Community punishment in the Netherlands: A history of crises and incidents. In G. Robinson & F. McNeill (Eds.), *Community Punishment: European Perspectives.* London: Routledge.

Boone, M., & Maguire, N. (2017). *The Enforcement of Offender Supervision inEurope. Understanding Breach Processes.* Abingdon: Routledge.

Bottoms, A. (1980). An introduction to 'the coming crisis'. In A. Bottoms & R. Preston (Eds.), *The Coming Penal Crisis.* Edinburgh: Scottish Academic Press.

Bottoms, A. (1995). The philosophy and politics of punishment and sentencing. In C. Clarkson & R. Morgan (Eds.), *The Politics of Sentencing Reform.* Oxford: Clarendon Press.

Bradford, B., & McQueen, S. (2011). *Diversion from Prosecution to Social Work in Scotland. Scottish Centre for Crime and Justice Research Report No. 1/2011.* Glasgow: Scottish Centre for Crime and Justice Research. Retrieved from http://www.sccjr.ac.uk/wp-content/uploads/2012/10/Diversion%20from%20prosecution.pdf. Accessed on 19 January 2015.

Brandes, B., & Cheung, M. (2009). Supervision and treatment of juveniles with sexual behaviour problems. *Child Adolescent Social Work Journal*, 26, 179–196. Retrieved from https://www.researchgate.net/publication/225157702_Supervision_and_Treatment_of_Juveniles_with_Sexual_Behavior_Problemsf

Brangan, L. (2013). A framework for comparative research on supervision? *Offender Supervision in Europe*, blog-site. Retrieved from http://www.offendersupervision.eu/blog-post/a-framework-for-comparative-research-on-supervision. Accessed on 26 January 15.

Brennan, M. (2006). The rough guide to critics. Musicians discuss the role of the music press. *Popular Music*, 25(2), 221–234.

Brown, M. (2009). *The Culture of Punishment: Prison, Society, and Spectacle.* New York, NY: NYU Press.

Brown, M. (2014). Visual criminology and carceral studies: Counter-images in the carceral age. *Theoretical Criminology*, 18(2), 176–197.

Brown, M., & Carrabine, E. (2017). Introducing visual criminology. In M. Brown & E. Carrabine (Eds.), *Routledge International Handbook of Visual Criminology* (pp. 1–10). London and New York, NY: Routledge.

Buchanan, W. (1934, April). The duties of a probation officer. *Probation*, 295–296, 302.

Buchanan, W. (1936, April). Probation in Glasgow. *Probation*, 55–56, 58.

Bunker, E. (2012 [1973]). *No Beast So Fierce* (eBook ed.). Harpenden: No Exit Press.

Burnard, P. (2012). *Musical Creativities in Practice.* Oxford: Oxford University Press.

Burke, L., Collett, S., & McNeill, F. (2018). *Reimagining Rehabilitation: Beyond the Individual*. Abingdon: Routledge.

Canton, R. (2006). Penal policy transfer: A case study from Ukraine. *Howard Journal of Criminal Justice*, 45(5), 502–520.

Canton, R. (2009). Taking probation abroad. *European Journal of Probation*, 1(1), 66–78.

Canton, R. (2017). *Why Punish? An Introduction to the Philosophy of Punishment*. London: Palgrave.

Canton, R. (2018). Probation and the philosophy of punishment. *Probation Journal*, 65(3), 252–268.

Caplow, T., & Simon, J. (1999). Understanding prison policy and population trends. *Crime and Justice*, 26, 63–120. Retrieved from http://citeseerx.ist.psu.edu/viewdoc/download?doi=10.1.1.474.9556&rep=rep1&type=pdf

Carlen, P. (Ed.). (2008). *Imaginary Penalities*. Cullompton: Willan.

Carson, E. A., & Anderson, E. (2016). *Prisoners in 2015*. Washington, DC: Bureau of Justice Statistics.

Casey, L. (2008). *Engaging Communities in Fighting Crime: A Review (Casey Report)*. London: Cabinet Office.

Cavadino, M., Dignan, J., & Mair, G. (2013). *The Penal System: An Introduction* (5th ed.). London: Sage.

Christie, N. (1977). Conflicts as property. *British Journal of Criminology*, 17(1), 1–15.

Christie, N. (2004). *A Suitable Amount of Crime*. Abingdon: Routledge.

City of Glasgow. (1955). *Probation. A Brief Survey of Fifty Years of the Probation Service of the City of Glasgow 1905–1955*. Glasgow: City of Glasgow Probation Area Committee.

Clear, T., & Frost, N. (2013). *The Punishment Imperative: The Rise and Failure of Mass Incarceration in America*. New York, NY: NYU Press.

Cohen, S. (1983). Social-control talk: Telling stories about correctional change. In D. Garland & P. Young (Eds.), *The Power to Punish* (pp. 101–129). Aldershot: Gower.

Cohen, S. (1985). *Visions of Social Control: Crime, Punishment and Classification.* Cambridge: Polity Press/Blackwell.

Council of Europe. (1992). *Recommendation No. R (92) 16 of the Committee of Ministers to member states on the European rules on community sanctions and measures.* Strasbourg: Council of Europe.

Cox, A. (2011). Doing the programme or doing me? The pains of youth imprisonment. *Punishment and Society, 13*(5), 592–610.

Cox, A. (2013). New visions of social control? Young peoples' perceptions of community penalties. *Journal of Youth Studies, 16*(1), 135–150.

Cox, A. (2017). *Trapped in a Vice: The Consequences of Confinement for Young People.* Newark, NJ: Rutgers University Press.

Crewe, B. (2009). *The Prisoner Society: Power, Adaptation and Social Life in an English Prison.* Oxford: OUP, Clarendon.

Crewe, B. (2011). Depth, weight, tightness: Revisiting the pains of imprisonment. *Punishment and Society, 13*(5), 509–529.

Crewe, B., Liebling, A., & Hulley, S. (2014). Heavy-light, absent-present: Rethinking the 'weight' of imprisonment. *British Journal of Sociology, 65*(3), 387–410.

Davidson, N., Linnpaa, M., McBride, M., & Virdee, S. (Eds.). (2018). *No Problem Here: Racism in Scotland.* Edinburgh: Luath Press.

DCMS (Department for Culture, Media and Sport). (1999). *Policy Action Team 10: Report to the Social Exclusion Unit – Arts and Sport.* London: DCMS.

Deering, J. (2011). *Probation Practice and the New Penology: Practitioner Reflections.* Farnham: Ashgate.

De Giorgi, A. (2013). Punishment and political economy. In J. Simon & R. Sparks (Eds.), *The Sage Handbook of Punishment and Society.* London: Sage.

Deleuze, G. (1990). *Postscript on the Societies of Control.* OCTOBER, 59, Winter 1992. Cambridge, MA: MIT Press.

Dickinson, E. (1924). *The Complete Poems of Emily Dickinson.* Boston, MA: Little Brown.

Digard, L. (2010). When legitimacy is denied: Sex offenders' perceptions and experiences of prison recall. *Probation Journal*, 57(1), 1–19.

Digard, L. (2014). Encoding risk: Probation work and sex offenders' narrative identities. *Punishment and Society*, 16(4), 428–447.

Doherty, F. (2016). Obey all laws and be good: Probation and the meaning of recidivism. *Georgetown Law Journal*, 104(2), 291–354.

Donzelot. (1977). *La Police des Familles* (Trans. The Policing of Families). Paris: Edition de Minuit.

Dougan, J. (1999). The mistakes of yesterday, the hopes of Tomorrow: Prise, pop music and the Prisonaires. *American Music*, 17(4), 447–468.

Downes, D. (1988). *Contrasts in Tolerance*. Oxford: Clarendon Press.

Drake, D., Earle, R., & Sloan, J. (Eds.). (2015). *The Palgrave Handbook of Prison Ethnography*. Basingstoke: Palgrave.

Duff, A. (2001). *Punishment, Communication and Community*. New York, NY: Oxford University Press.

Duff, A. (2003). Probation, Punishment and Restorative Justice: Should Al Truism Be Engaged in Punishment? *The Howard Journal*, 42(1), 181–197.

Durkheim, E. (1958). The state. In E. Durkheim (Ed.), (1986), *Durkheim on Politics and the State* (pp. 45–50). Stanford, CA: Stanford University Press.

Durkheim, E. (1973). Two Laws of Penal Evolution. *Economy and Society*, 2(3), 285–308.

Durkheim, E. (1984). *The Division of Labour in Society*. Hampshire: Palgrave Macmillan.

Durnescu, I. (2011). Pains of probation: Effective practice and human rights. *International Journal of Offender Therapy and Comparative Criminology*, 55(4), 530–545.

Durnescu, I. (2015). Romania: Empty shells, emulation and Europeanization. In G. Robinson & F. McNeill (Eds.), *Community Punishment: European Perspectives* (pp. 156–172). London: Routledge.

Durnescu, I., Enengl, C., & Grafl, C. (2013). Experiencing supervision. In F. McNeill & K. Beyens (Eds.), *Offender Supervision in Europe* (pp. 19–50). Basingstoke: Palgrave.

Durnescu, I., Kennefick, L., Sucic, I., & Glavak Tkalic, R. (2018). Experiencing offender supervision in Europe: The Eurobarometer – Lessons from the pilot study. *Probation Journal, 65*(1), 7–26.

Dzur, A., Loader, I., & Sparks, R. (Eds.), (2016). *Democratic Theory and Mass Incarceration*. Oxford: Oxford University Press.

Escobar, O. (2011). *Public Dialogue and Deliberation: A Communication Perspective for Public Engagement Practitioners*. Edinburgh: Beacons for Public Engagement.

Feeley, M., & Simon, J. (1992). The new penology: Notes on the emerging strategy of corrections and its implications. *Criminology, 30*(4), 449–474.

Feeley, M., & Simon, J. (1994). Actuarial justice: The emerging new criminal law. In D. Nelken (Ed.), *The Futures of Criminology* (pp. 173–201). London: Sage.

Fitzgibbon, W., Graebsch, C., & McNeill, F. (2017). Pervasive punishment: Experiencing supervision. In E. Carrabine & M. Brown (Eds.), *The Routledge International Handbook of Visual Criminology* (pp. 305–319). London: Routledge.

Fitzgibbon, W., & Healy, D. (2017). Lives and spaces: Photovoice and offender supervision in Ireland and England. *Criminology and Criminal Justice*. Retrieved from http://journals.sagepub.com/doi/abs/10.1177/1748895817739665

Forester, J. (2009). *Dealing with Differences: Dramas of Mediating Public Disputes*. Oxford: Oxford University Press.

Foucault, M. (1977). *Discipline and Punish: The Birth of the Prison* (English translation1977). London: Allan Lane.

Fraser, N. (2007). Reframing justice in a globalizing world. In T. Lovell (Ed.), *Misrecognition, Social Inequality and Social Justice. Nancy Fraser and Pierre Bourdieu* (pp. 17–35). London and New York, NY: Routledge.

Freeman, S., & Seymour, M. (2010). "Just waiting": The nature and effect of uncertainty on young people in remand custody in Ireland. *Youth Justice*, *10*(2), 126–142.

Freiberg, A. (2001). Affective versus effective justice: Instrumentalism and emotionalism in criminal justice. *Punishment and Society*, *3*(2), 265–278.

Fricker, M. (2007). *Epistemic Injustice: Power and the Ethics of Knowing*. Oxford: Oxford University Press.

Gainey, R., & Payne, B. (2000). Understanding the experience of house arrest with electronic monitoring: An analysis of quantitative and qualitative data. *International Journal of Offender Therapy and Comparative Criminology*, *44*(1), 84–96.

Garfinkel, H. (1956). Conditions of successful degradation ceremonies. *American Journal of Sociology*, *61*(5), 420–424.

Gargarella, R. (2016). Democracy all the way down – deliberative democracy and criminal law: The case of social protests. In A. Dzur, I. Loader, & R. Sparks (Eds.), *Democratic Theory and Mass Incarceration* (pp. 298–328). Oxford: Oxford University Press.

Garland, D. (1985). *Punishment and Welfare: A History of Penal Strategies*. Aldershot: Ashgate.

Garland, D. (1990). *Punishment and Modern Society: A Study in Social Theory*. Oxford: Clarendon Press.

Garland, D. (1990). *Punishment and Modern Society*. Oxford: Clarendon Press.

Garland, D. (1996). The limits of the sovereign state: Strategies of crime control in contemporary society. *British Journal of Criminology*, *36*(4), 445–471.

Garland, D. (1997). Probation and the reconfiguration of crime control. In R. Burnett (Ed.), *The Probation Service: Responding to Change, Proceedings of the Probation Studies Unit First Colloquium* (pp. 2–10). Probation Studies Unit Report No. 3, Oxford: University of Oxford Centre for Criminological Research.

Garland, D. (2001). *The Culture of Control: Crime and Social Order in Contemporary Society*. Oxford: Oxford University Press.

Garland, D. (2010). *Peculiar Institution: America's Death Penalty in an Age of Abolition*. Oxford: Oxford University Press.

Garland, D. (2013a). Punishment and social solidarity. In J. Simon & R. Sparks (Eds.), *The Sage Handbook of Punishment and Society* (pp. 23–39). London: Sage.

Garland, D. (2013b). Penality and the penal state. *Criminology*, *51*(3), 475–517.

Garland, D., & Young, P. (Eds.). (1983). *The Power to Punish: Contemporary Penality and Social Analysis*. Aldershot: Gower.

Glaze, L. E. (2010). *Correctional Populations in the United States, 2009*. Bureau of Justice Statistics, Washington, DC: U.S. Department of Justice.

Goodman, P., Page, J., & Phelps, M. (2017). *Breaking the Pendulum: The Long Struggle Over Criminal Justice*. Oxford: Oxford University Press.

Gottschalk, M. (2013). The carceral state and the politics of punishment. In J. Simon & R. Sparks (Eds.), *The Sage Handbook of Punishment and Society* (pp. 205–241). London, NY: Sage.

Green, L. (2002). *How Popular Musicians Learn: A Way Ahead for Music Education*. Aldershot: Ashgate.

Hainge, G. (2007). Of glitch and men: The place of the human in the successful integration of failure and noise in the digital realm. *Communication Theory*, *17*(1), 26–42.

Halliday, S., Burns, N., Hutton, N., McNeill, F., & Tata, C. (2008). Shadow writing and participant observation: A study of criminal justice social work around sentencing. *Journal of Law and Society*, *35*(2), 189–213.

Hannah-Moffatt, K. (1999). Moral agent or actuarial subject: Risk and Canadian women's imprisonment. *Theoretical Criminology*, *3*(1), 71–94.

Hannah-Moffat, K. (2005). Criminogenic needs and the transformative risk subject: Hybridizations of risk/need in penality. *Punishment and Society, 7*(1), 29–51.

Happer, C., McGuinness, P., McNeill, F., & Tiripelli, G. (2018). Punishment, legitimacy and taste: The role and limits of mainstream and social media in constructing attitudes towards community sanctions. *Crime Media Culture.* Retrieved from http://journals.sagepub.com/doi/10.1177/1741659018773848

Hayes, D. (2013). Reading between the lines: English newspaper representations of community punishment. *European Journal of Probation, 5*(3), 24–40.

Hayes, D. (2015). The impact of supervision on the pains of community penalties in England and Wales: An exploratory study. *European Journal of Probation, 7*(2), 85–102.

Hayes, D. (2016). Penal impact: Towards a more intersubjective measurement of penal severity. *Oxford Journal of Legal Studies, 36*(4), 724–750.

Hayes, D. (2018). Proximity, pain and state punishment. *Punishment & Society, 20*(2), 235–254.

Hayes, D., & McNeill, F. (2017). The Pains of Oversight: Comparing the Penal Severity of Electronic Monitoring and Human Supervision. A paper presented at the European Society of Criminology Annual Conference, Cardiff, September 2017.

Herzog-Evans, M. (2015). France: Legal architecture, political posturing, 'prisonbation' and adieu social work. In G. Robinson & F. McNeill (Eds.), *Community Punishment: European Perspectives.* London: Routledge.

Hofer, S. (2006). I am they: Technological mediation, shifting conceptions of identity and techno music. *Convergence: The International Journal of Research into New Media Technologies, 12*(3), 307–324.

Honneth, A. (1995). *The Struggle for Recognition: The Moral Grammar of Social Conflicts* (Trans. Joel Anderson). Cambridge, MA: MIT Press.

Houchin, R. (2005). *Social Exclusion and Imprisonment in Scotland: A Report.* Glasgow: Glasgow Caledonian University.

Hough, M., & Park, A. (2002). How malleable are attitudes to crime and punishment? Findings from a British deliberative poll. In J. Roberts & M. Hough (Eds.), *Changing Attitudes to Punishment: Public Opinion, Crime and Justice* (pp. 163–183). Cullompton: Willan.

Hucklesby, A., Beyens, K., Boone, M., Dünkel, F., McIvor, G., & Graham, H. (2016). *Creativity and Effectiveness in the Use of Electronic Monitoring: A Case Study of Five Jurisdictions* [comparative report]. Leeds: University of Leeds and Criminal Justice Programme of the European Commission.

Hudson, B. (1996). *Understanding Justice: An Introduction to Ideas, Perspectives and Controversies in Modern Penal Theory*. Buckingham: Open University Press.

Hudson, B. (2003). *Understanding Justice*. Buckingham: Open University Press.

Hulsman, L. (1976). *Strategies to Reduce Violence in Society: Civilising the Criminal Justice System*. An Address to the Annual Meeting of the Howard League for Penal Reform (unpublished).

Hutchinson, S. (2006). Countering catastrophic criminology: Reform, punishment and the modern liberal compromise. *Punishment and Society*, *8*(4), 443–467.

Ignatieff, M. (1983). State, civil society and total institutions: A critique of recent social histories of punishment. In S. Cohen & A. Scull (Eds.), *Social Control and the State* (pp. 75–105). Oxford: Martin Robertson.

Jermyn, H. (2001). *The Arts and Social Exclusion: A Review Prepared for the Arts Council of England*. London: The Arts Council of England.

Jermyn, H. (2004). *The Art of Inclusion*. London: The Arts Council of England.

Johnson, C., Dowd, T., & Ridgeway, C. (2006). Legitimacy as a social process. *Annual Review of Sociology*, *32*, 53–78. Retrieved from https://www.annualreviews.org/doi/abs/10.1146/annurev.soc.32.061604.123101?cookieSet=1

Johnstone, G. (1996). *Medical Concepts and Penal Policy*. London: Cavendish Publishing.

Justice Department. (2001). *Criminal Justice Social Work Services: National Priorities for 2001–2002 and Onwards*. Edinburgh: Scottish Executive.

Kaeble, D., & Glaze, L. E. (2016). *Correctional Populations in the United States, 2015*. Bureau of Justice Statistics, Washington, DC: U.S. Department of Justice.

Kelly, C. (2017). Probation officers for young offenders in 1920s Scotland. *European Journal of Probation*, 9(2), 169–191.

Kilbrandon Report. (1964). *Children and Young Persons (Scotland)*. Cmnd 2306. Edinburgh: HMSO.

Kim, B., Spohn, C., & Hedberg, E. (2015). Federal sentencing as a complex collaborative process: Judges, prosecutors, judge-prosecutor dyads, and disparity in sentencing. *Criminology*, 53(4), 597–623.

King, R., & McDermott, K. (1995). *The State of Our Prisons*. Oxford: Clarendon Press.

King, S. (2013). Assisted desistance and experiences of probation supervision. *Probation Journal*, 60(2), 136–151.

Klingele, C. (2013). Rethinking the use of community supervision. *The Journal of Criminal Law and Criminology*, 103(4), 1015–1070.

Lacey, N. (2008). *The Prisoner's Dilemma: Political Economy and Punishment in Contemporary Democracies*. Cambridge: Cambridge University Press.

Lacombe, D. (2008). Consumed with sex: The treatment of sex offenders in risk society. *British Journal of Criminology*, 48(1), 55–74.

Levenson, J., & Prescott, D. (2009). Treatment experiences of civilly committed sex offenders: A consumer satisfaction survey. *Sexual Abuse: A Journal of Research and Treatment*, 21(1), 6–20.

Lilly, J., & Nellis, M. (2012). The limits of techno-utopianism: Electronic monitoring in the United States of America. In M. Nellis, K. Beyens, & D. Kaminski (Eds.), *Electronically Monitored Punishment: Critical and International Perspectives* (pp. 164–189). London: Routledge.

Lipsitz, G. (1994). *Dangerous Crossroads: Popular Music, Postmodernism and the Poetics of Place*. New York, NY: Verso.

Lipsky, M. (1980). *Street-Level Bureaucracy: Dilemmas of the Individual in Public Services*. New York, NY: Russell Sage Foundation.

Lister, R. (2007). (Mis)Recognition, social inequality and social justice: A critical social policy perspective. In T. Lovell (Ed.), *Misrecognition, Social Inequality and Social Justice. Nancy Fraser and Pierre Bourdieu* (pp. 157–176). London and New York, NY: Routledge.

Littlejohn, S., & Domenici, K. (2003). *Engaging Communication in Conflict. Systemic Practice*. Thousand Oaks, CA: Sage.

Loader, I. (2009). Ice cream and incarceration: On appetites for security and punishment. *Punishment & Society*, *11*(2), 241–257.

Loader, I. (2010). For penal moderation: Notes towards a public philosophy of punishment. *Theoretical Criminology*, *14*(3), 349–367.

Loader, I., & Sparks, R. (2010). *Public Criminology?* London: Routledge.

Loader, I., & Sparks, R. (2012). Beyond lamentation: Towards a democratic egalitarian politics of crime and justice. In T. Newburn & J. Peay (Eds.), *Policing: Politics, Culture and Control* (pp. 11–42). Oxford: Hart.

Loader, I., & Sparks, R. (forthcoming) *Reasonable Hopes: Social Theory, Critique and Reconstruction in Contemporary Criminology*. Forthcoming in an edited festschrift in honour of Professor Sir Anthony Bottoms.

Loewy, E. H. (1997). *Moral Strangers, More Acquaintance, and Moral Friends. Connectedness and its Conditions*. Albany, NY: State University of New York Press.

Lowman, J., Menzies, R., & Palys, T. (Eds.). (1987). *Transcarceration: Essays in the Sociology of Social Control*. Brookfield, VT: Gower.

Lucken, K. (1997). The Dynamics of Penal Reform. *Crime, Law and Social Change*, *26*(4), 367–384.

Maguire, M., & Raynor, P. (2006). How the resettlement of prisoners promotes desistance from crime: Or does it? *Criminology and Criminal Justice*, 6(1), 19–38.

Maguire, M., & Raynor, P. (2017). Offender management in and after prison: The end of 'end to end'? *Criminology and Criminal Justice*, 17(2), 138–157.

Maguire, N., & Carr, N. (2013). Changing shape and shifting boundaries—The media portrayal of probation in Ireland. *European Journal of Probation*, 5(3) 3–23.

Mahood, L. (1991). *Policing Gender, Class and Family in Britain, 1950–1940*. London: UCL Press.

Mair, G., & Nee, C. (1990). *Electronic Monitoring: The Trials and Their Results*. Home Office Research study 120. London: Home Office.

Mair, G., & Mills, H. (2009). *The Community Order and the Suspended Sentence Order Three Years On: The Views and Experiences of Probation Officers and Offenders*. London: Centre for Crime and Justice Studies.

Marsland, M. (1977). The decline of probation in Scotland. *Social Work Today*, 8(23), 17–18.

Martinson, R. (1974). What works? Questions and answers about prison reform. *The Public Interest*, 35, 22–54.

Maruna, S., & King, A. (2008). Selling the public on probation: Beyond the bib. *Probation Journal*, 55(4), 337–351.

Mathieson, T. (1983). The future of control systems: The case of Norway. In D. Garland & P. Young (Eds.), *The Power to Punish: Contemporary Penality and Social Analysis*. Aldershot: Gower.

Mawby, R., & Worrall, A. (2014). *Doing Probation Work: Identity in a Criminal Justice Occupation*. London: Routledge.

May, D., & Wood, P. (2010). *Ranking Correctional Punishments: Views from Offenders, Practitioners and the Public*. Durham, NC: Carolina Academic Press.

McAra, L. (1999). The politics of penality: An overview of the development of penal policy in Scotland. In P. Duff & N. Hutton (Eds.), *Criminal Justice in Scotland* (pp. 355–380). Aldershot: Ashgate/ Dartmouth.

McAra, L. (2005). Modelling penal transformation. *Punishment and Society*, 7(3), 277–302.

McAra, L. (2008). Crime, criminology and criminal justice in Scotland. *European Journal of Criminology*, 5(4), 481–504.

McBride, M. (2017). *Rethinking Sectarianism in Scotland,* [PhD Thesis]. Glasgow: University of Glasgow.

McConnell, J. (2003). *Respect, Responsibility and Rehabilitation in Modern Scotland*, Apex Lecture 1, September. Edinburgh: Scottish Executive.

McCulloch, P., & McNeill, F. (2007). Consumer society, commodification and offender management. *Criminology and Criminal Justice*, 7(3), 223–242.

McFarlane, M., & Canton, R. (2014). *Policy Transfer in Criminal Justice: Cross Cultures, Breaking Barriers.* Basingstoke: Palgrave.

McGuinness, P. (2014). *Room for Reparation? An Ethnographic Study into the Implementation of the Community Payback Order.* Unpublished University of Glasgow, [PhD thesis].

McIntyre, P. (2008). Creativity and cultural production: A study of contemporary Western popular music songwriting. *Creativity Research Journal*, 20(1), 40–52.

McIvor, G. (2010). Paying back: 30 years of unpaid work by offenders in Scotland. *European Journal of Probation*, 2(1), 41–61.

McIvor, G., & McNeill, F. (2007). Probation in Scotland: Past, present and future. In L. Gelsthorpe & R. Morgan (Eds.), *The Probation Handbook: A Policy, Practice and Research Handbook* (pp. 131–154). Cullompton: Willan.

McNeill, F. (2005). Remembering probation in Scotland. *Probation Journal*, 52(1), 23–38.

McNeill, F. (2006). A desistance paradigm for offender management. *Criminology and Criminal Justice*, 6(1), 39–62.

McNeill, F. (2009). 'Helping, holding, hurting: Recalling and reforming punishment', the 6th Annual Apex Lecture, at the Signet Library, Parliament Square, Edinburgh. Retrieved from https://pure.strath.ac.uk/portal/files/521675/strathprints026701.pdf. Accessed on 8 September 2009.

McNeill, F. (2010). *Community Payback and the New National Standards for Criminal Justice Social Work*. Briefing Paper 02/10, Glasgow: Scottish Centre for Crime and Justice Research. Retrieved from http://www.sccjr.ac.uk/documents/Briefing_Paper_2010_02_community_payback.pdf

McNeill, F. (2011). Changing lives, changing work: Social work and criminal justice. In R. Taylor, M. Hill, & McNeill, F. (Eds.), *21st Century Social Work: A Resource for Early Professional Development*. Birmingham: Venture Press.

McNeill, F. (2012). *Experiencing Supervision in Scotland*. Retrieved from http://www.offendersupervision.eu/wp-content/uploads/2012/10/Experiencing-Supervision-in-Scotland.pdf. Accessed on 4 June 2018.

McNeill, F. (2013). Community sanctions and European penology. In T. Daems, S. Snacken, & D. van zyl Smit (Eds.), *European Penology* (pp. 171–191). Oxford: Hart.

McNeill, F. (2014). Punishment as rehabilitation. In G. Bruinsma & D. Weisburd (Eds.), *Encyclopedia of Criminology and Criminal Justice* (pp. 4195–4206). New York, NY: Springer Science and Business Media.

McNeill, F. (2016). Reductionism, rehabilitation and reparation: Community punishment in Scotland. In G. Robinson & F. McNeill (Eds.), *Community Punishment: European Perspectives* (pp. 173–190). London: Routledge.

McNeill, F. (2017). *Supervisible: Experiences of Criminal Justice in Scotland*. London: The Howard League for Penal Reform. Retrieved from http://howardleague.org/publications/supervisible-experiences-of-criminal-justice-supervision-in-scotland/

McNeill, F. (2017b). Postscript: Guide, guard and glue—electronic monitoring and penal supervision. *European Journal of Probation*, 9(1), 103–107.

McNeill, F. (2018). Mass supervision, misrecognition and the Malopticon. *Punishment and Society*. Retrieved from http://journals.sagepub.com/doi/full/10.1177/1462474518755137

McNeill, F., & Beyens, K. (Eds.), (2013). *Offender Supervision in Europe*. Basingstoke: Palgrave.

McNeill, F., & Beyens, K. (2016). *Offender Supervision in Europe: COST Action IS1106 Final Report*. Retrieved from http://www.offendersupervision.eu/wp-content/uploads/2016/03/Final-Report.pdf

McNeill, F., & Dawson, M. (2014). Social solidarity, penal evolution and probation. *British Journal of Criminology*, 54(5), 892–907.

McNeill, F., & Robinson, G. (2012). Liquid legitimacy and community sanctions. In A. Crawford & A. Hucklesby (Eds.), *Legitimacy and Compliance in Criminal Justice* (pp. 116–137). Abingdon: Routledge.

McNeill, F., & Robinson, G. (2016). Explaining probation. In F. McNeill, I. Durnescu, & R. Butter (Eds.), *Probation: 12 Essential Questions* (pp. 245–262). Basingstoke: Palgrave.

McNeill, F., & Whyte, B. (2007). *Reducing Re-offending: Social Work and Community Justice in Scotland*. Cullompton: Willan.

McNeill, F., Burns, N., Halliday, S., Hutton, N., & Tata, C. (2009). Risk, responsibility and reconfiguration: Penal adaptation and misadaptation. *Punishment and Society*, 11(4), 419–442.

McNeill, F., Raynor, P., & Trotter, C. (Eds.). (2010). *Offender Supervision: New Directions in Theory, Research and Practice*. Cullompton: Willan.

McWilliams, W. (1983). The Mission to the English Police Courts 1876–1936. *The Howard Journal*, 22(1-3), 129–147.

McWilliams, W. (1985). The Mission transformed: Professionalisation of probation between the wars. *The Howard Journal of Criminal Justice*, 24(4), 257–274.

McWilliams, W. (1986). The English probation system and the diagnostic ideal. *The Howard Journal of Criminal Justice*, 25(4), 241–260.

McWilliams, W. (1987). Probation, pragmatism and policy. *The Howard Journal of Criminal Justice*, 26(2), 97–121.

Melossi, D. (1998). *The Sociology of Punishment: Socio-Structural Perspectives*. Aldershot: Dartmouth.

Michigan Department of Corrections. (2011). *Biannual Report*. Lansing, MI: Field Operations Administration, Office of Community Alternatives.

Miller, R. (2014). Devolving the carceral state: Race, prisoner reentry, and the micro politics of urban poverty management. *Punishment and Society*, 16(3), 305–335.

Miller, R., & Stuart, F. (2017). Carceral citizenship: Race, rights and responsibility in the age of mass supervision. *Theoretical Criminology*, 21(4), 532–548.

Moore, G. (1978). Crisis in Scotland. *Howard Journal*, 17(1), 32–40.

Moore, G., & Whyte, B. (1998). *Moore and Wood's Social Work and Criminal Law in Scotland* (3rd ed.). Edinburgh: Mercat Press.

Morgan and Thapar Björkert. (2006). "I'd rather you'd lay me on the floor and start kicking me": Understanding symbolic violence in everyday life. *Women's Studies International Forum*, 29(5), 441–452.

Morgenstern, C. (2016). "Der Resozialisierungsgrundsatz" – Social reintegration as the dominant narrative for community punishment in Germany? In G. Robinson & F. McNeill (Eds.), *Community Punishment: European Perspectives* (pp. 72–94). London: Routledge.

Morgenstern, C., & Larrauri, E. (2013). European norms, policy and practice. In F. McNeill & K. Beyens (Eds.), *Offender Supervision in Europe* (pp. 125–154). Basingstoke: Palgrave.

Morison Report. (1962). *Report of the Departmental Committee on the Probation Service*. Cmnd 1650. London: Her Majesty's Stationery Office.

Morris, N. (1974). *The Future of Imprisonment*. London: University of Chicago Press.

Morrison, K. (2015). The management of community justice services in Scotland: Policy-making and the dynamics of central and local control. In M. Wasik & S. Santatzoglou (Eds.), *The Management of Change in Criminal Justice: Who Knows Best* (pp. 152–169). Basingstoke: Palgrave.

Morton Report. (1928). *Committee on Protection and Training.* Edinburgh: HMSO.

Motorhead. (1979). *On Parole.* Beverly Hills, CA: United Artists.

Munro, M., & McNeill, F. (2010). Fines, community sanctions and measures. In H. Croall & G. Mooney (Eds.), *Criminal Justice in Scotland* (pp. 216–237). Cullompton: Willan.

Murphy, J. (1988). Mercy and legal justice. In J. G. Murphy & J. Hampton (Eds.), *Forgiveness and Mercy* (pp. 162–186). Cambridge: Cambridge University Press.

Mutz, D. C. (2006). *Hearing the Other Side: Deliberative versus Participatory Democracy.* Cambridge: Cambridge University Press.

Nellis, M. (2009). Surveillance and confinement: Explaining and understanding the experience of electronically monitored curfews. *European Journal of Probation, 1*(1), 41–65.

Nellis, M. (2010). Electronic monitoring: Towards integration in offender management? In F. McNeill, P. Raynor, & C. Trotter (Eds.), *Offender Supervision: New Directions in Theory, Research and Practice* (pp. 509–533). London: Routledge.

Nellis, M. (2018). Electronically monitored offenders as "coercive connectivity": Commerce and penality in surveillance capitalism. In T. Daems & T. Vander Beken (Eds.), *Privatizing Punishment in Europe?* (pp. 124–142). Abingdon: Routledge.

Nellis, M., Beyens, K., & Kaminski, D. (Eds.). (2012). *Electronically Monitored Punishment: International and Critical Perspectives.* London: Routledge.

Nelson, S. (1977). Why Scotland's after-care is lagging. *Community Care, 14*(12), 87.

O'Malley, P. (2009). *The Currency of Justice: Fines and Damages in Consumer Societies.* Abingdon: Routledge Cavendish.

Padfield, N. (2012). Recalling conditionally released prisoners in England and Wales. *European Journal of Probation*, 4(1), 34–45.

Page, J. (2013). Punishment and the penal field. In J. Simon & R. Sparks (Eds.), *The Sage Handbook of Punishment and Society* (pp. 152–166). London: Sage.

Palibroda, B., Krieg, B., Murdock, L., & Havelock, J. (2009). *A Practical Guide to Photovoice: Sharing Pictures, Telling Stories and Changing Communities*. Winnipeg: The Prairie Women Health's Centre of Excellence.

Pauwels, L. (2017). Key methods of visual criminology: An overview of different approaches and their affordances. In M. Brown & E. Carrabine (Eds.), *Routledge International Handbook of Visual Criminology* (pp. 62–73). London: Routledge.

Payne, B., & Gainey, R. (1998). A qualitative assessment of the pains experienced on electronic monitoring. *International Journal of Offender Therapy and Comparative Criminology*, 42(2), 149–163.

Payne, B., & Gainey, R. (2004). The electronic monitoring of offenders released from jail or prison: Safety, control, and comparisons of the incarceration experience. *The Prison Journal*, 84(4), 413–435.

Pease, K. (1980). The future of the community treatment of offenders in Britain. In A. E. Bottoms & R. H. Preston (Eds.), *The Coming Penal Crisis* (pp. 137–151). Edinburgh: Scottish Academic Press.

Pedelty, M. (2012). *Ecomusicology: Rock, folk, and the Environment*. Philadelphia, PA: Temple University Press.

Petersilia, J., & Deschenes, E. (1994). What punishes? Inmates rank the severity of prison vs. intermediate sanctions. *Federal Probation*, 58(1), 3–8.

Pfaff, J. (2014). Escaping from the standard story: Why the conventional wisdom on prison growth is wrong, and where we can go from here. *Federal Sentencing Reporter*, 26(4), 265–270.

Phelps, M. (2013a). *The Paradox of Probation: Understanding the Expansion of an 'Alternative' to Incarceration During the Prison Boom* [PhD thesis]. Princeton University, Ann Arbor: ProQuest/UMI.

Phelps, M. (2013b). The Paradox of Probation: Community supervision in the age of mass incarceration. *Law and Policy, 35*(1–2), 55–80.

Phelps, M. (2017a). Discourses of mass probation: From managing risk to ending human warehousing in Michigan. *British Journal of Criminology, 58*(5), 1107–1126.

Phelps, M. (2017b). Mass probation: Toward a more robust theory of state variation in punishment. *Punishment and Society, 19*(1), 53–73.

Phelps, M. (2018). Mass probation and inequality: Race, class, and gender disparities in supervision and revocation. In J. T. Ulmer & M. S. Bradley (Eds.), *Handbook on Punishment Decisions: Locations of Disparity* (pp. 43–63). New York, NY: Routledge.

Pratt, J., Brown, D., Brown, W., Hallsworth, S., & Morrison, W. (2005). *The New Punitiveness: Trends, Theories, Perspectives.* Cullompton: Willan.

Pratt, R. (1990). *Rhythm and Resistance: Explorations in the Political Uses of Popular Music.* New York, NY: Praeger.

Ratner, R. (1987). Mandatory supervision and the political economy. In J. Lowman, R. Menzies, & T. Palys (Eds.), *Transcarceration: Essays in the Sociology of Social Control* (pp. 291–308). Gower: Aldershot.

Raynor, R., & Robinson, G. (2009). *Rehabilitation, Crime and Justice.* Basingstoke: Palgrave.

Rengifo, A., & Stemen, D. (2010). The impact of drug treatment on recidivism: Do mandatory programs make a difference? Evidence from Kansas's Senate Bill 123. *Crime and Delinquency, 57*(6), 1–21.

Rimmer, M., Higham, B., & Brown, T. (2014). Whatever Happened to Community Music? AHRC Research Network Project Report. Retrieved from https://ueaeprints.uea.ac.uk/47880/1/Whatever_Happened_to_Community_Music_AHRC_CM_Research_Network_Report_final_.pdf

Roberts, J. (2004). *The Virtual Prison: Community Custody and the Evolution of Imprisonment.* Cambridge: Cambridge University Press.

Robinson, G. (2002). Exploring risk management in the probation service: Contemporary developments in England and Wales. *Punishment and Society*, *4*(1), 5–25.

Robinson, G. (2008). Late-modern rehabilitation: The evolution of a penal strategy. *Punishment and Society*, *10*(4), 429–445.

Robinson, G. (2016). The Cinderella Complex: Punishment, society and community sanctions. *Punishment and Society*, *18*(1), 95–112.

Robinson, G., & McNeill, F. (2004). Purposes matters: The ends of probation. In G. Mair (Ed.), *What Matters in Probation Work* (pp. 277–304). Cullompton: Willan.

Robinson, G., & McNeill, F. (Eds.), (2015). *Community Punishment: European Perspectives*. London: Routledge.

Robinson, G., McNeill, F., & Maruna, S. (2013). Punishment *in* society: The improbable persistence of community sanctions. In J. Simon & R. Sparks (Eds.), *The Sage Handbook of Punishment and Society* (pp. 321–340). London: Sage.

Rose, N. (2000). Government and control. *The British Journal of Criminology*, *40*(2), 321–339.

Rotman, E. (1989). Statement: Minimum rules for Non-institutional treatment. In International Penal and Penitentiary Foundation (Ed.), *The Elaboration of Standard Minimum Rules for Non-Institutional Treatment (Proceedings of the Sixth International Colloquium of the IPPF Poitiers/ France 3–6 October 1987)* (pp. 169–172). Bonn: International Penal and Penitentiary Foundation.

Rubin, A., & Phelps, M. (2017). Fracturing the penal state: State actors and the role of conflict in penal change. *Theoretical Criminology*, *21*(4), 422–440.

Ruggerio, V. (2012). How public is public criminology? *Crime Media Culture*, *8*(2), 151–160.

Rusche, G., & Kirchheimer, O. (1939[2003]). *Punishment and Social Structure*. New Brunswick, NY: Transaction.

Sangild, T. (2004). Glitch – The beauty of malfunction. In C. Washburn & M. Derno (Eds.), *Bad Music: The Music We Love to Hate* (pp. 257–274). Abingdon: Routledge.

Schept, J. (2014). (Un)seeing like a prison: Counter-visual ethnography of the carceral state. *Theoretical Criminology, 18*(2), 198–223.

Schept, J. (2017). Sunk capital, sinking prisons, stinking landfills: Landscape, ideology and the carceral state in central Appalachia. In M. Brown & E. Carrabine (Eds.), *Routledge International Handbook of Visual Criminology* (pp. 495–513). London: Routledge.

Scott, J. (2017). Defeating the muse: Advanced songwriting pedagogy and creative block. In G. D. Smith, Z. Moir, M. Brennan, S. Rambarran, & P. Kirkman (Eds.), *The Routledge Research Companion to Popular Music Education* (pp. 190–202). Abingdon: Routledge.

Scottish Government. (2010). *National Outcomes and Standards for Social Work Services in the Criminal Justice System.* Edinburgh: Scottish Government.

Scottish Government. (2014). *Scottish Social Attitudes Survey 2014: Public Attitudes to Sectarianism in Scotland.* Edinburgh: The Scottish Government.

Scottish Government. (2015). *Examination of the Evidence on Sectarianism in Scotland: 2015 Update.* Edinburgh: Scottish Government.

Scottish Prisons Commission. (2008). *Scotland's Choice.* Edinburgh: Scottish Prisons Commission.

Scottish Labour. (2003). *Scottish Labour Manifesto 2003: On Your Side.* Glasgow: Scottish Labour Party.

Scottish Office. (1947). *The Probation Service in Scotland. Its Objects and Its Organisation.* Edinburgh: HMSO.

Scottish Office. (1955). *The Probation Service in Scotland.* Edinburgh: HMSO.

Scottish Office. (1961). *The Probation Service in Scotland.* Edinburgh: HMSO.

Scottish Office. (1998). *Community Sentencing: The Tough Option: Review of Criminal Justice Social Work Services.* Edinburgh: Scottish Office Home Department.

Scottish Prisons Commission. (2008). *Scotland's Choice*. Edinburgh: Scottish Prisons Commission.

Scull, A. (1977). *Decarceration: Community Treatment and the Deviant – A Radical View*. Englewood Cliffs, NJ: Prentice Hall.

Scull, A. (1983). Community corrections: Panacea, progress or pretence? In D. Garland & P. Young (Eds.), *The Power to Punish: Contemporary Penality and Social Analysis*. Aldershot: Gower.

Shammas, V. (2014). The pains of freedom: Assessing the ambiguity of Scandinavian penal exceptionalism on Norway's Prison Island. *Punishment and Society*, *16*(1), 104–123.

Shapland, J., Bottoms, A., & Muir, G. (2012). Perceptions of the criminal justice system among young adult would-be desisters. In F. Losel, A. Bottoms, & D. Farrington (Eds.), *Young Adult Offenders: Lost in Transition?* (pp. 128–145). Abingdon: Routledge.

Shuker, R. (1994). *Understanding Popular Music*. London: Routledge.

Simon, J. (1993). *Poor Discipline: Parole and the Social Control of the Underclass 1890–1990*. Chicago, IL: University of Chicago Press.

Sirianni, C. (1984). Justice and the division of labour: A reconsideration of Durkheim's *A Division of Labour in Society*. *Sociological Review*, *32*(3), 449–470.

Skeem, J. L., & Manchak, S.(2010). Back to the future: From Klockars' model of effective supervision to evidence-based practice in probation. *Journal of Offender Rehabilitation*, *47*(3), 220–247.

Small, C. (1998). *Musicking: The Meanings of Performing and Listening*. Middletown: Wesleyan University Press.

Smart, A. (1969). Mercy. In H. B. Acton (Ed.), *The Philosophy of Punishment* (pp. 212–227). London: Macmillan/St Martin's Press.

Snacken, S. (2010). Resisting punitiveness in Europe? *Theoretical Criminology*, *14*(3), 273–292.

Social Exclusion Unit. (2002). *Reducing Reoffending by Ex-Prisoners*. London: Office of the Deputy Prime Minister.

Social Work Services Group. (1991a). *National Objectives and Standards for Social Work Services in the Criminal Justice System.* Edinburgh: Social Work Services Group.

Social Work Services Group. (1991b). *Social Work Supervision: Towards Effective Policy and Practice – A Supplement to the National Objectives and Standards for Social Work Services in the Criminal Justice System.* Edinburgh: Social Work Services Group.

Solomon, E., & Silverstri, A. (2008). *Community Sentences Digest* (2nd ed.). London: Centre for Crime and Justice Studies.

Snacken, S., & McNeill, F. (2012). Scientific recommendations. In D. Flore et al. (Eds.), *Probation Measures and Alternative Sanctions in the European Union* (pp. 561–571). Cambridge: Intersentia.

Sparks, R., & McNeill, F. (2009). *Incarceration, Social Control andHuman Rights.* Research Paper (Final Draft) for the International Council onHuman Rights Policy Project on Social Control and Human Rights. Geneva: International Council on Human Rights Policy. Retrieved from http://www.ichrp.org/files/papers/175/punishment_and_incarceration_sparks_and_mcneill.pdf

Stuntz, W. (2011). *The Collapse of American Criminal Justice.* Cambridge, MA: Belknap Press of Harvard University Press.

Suchman, M. (1995). Managing legitimacy: Strategic and institutional approaches. *Academy of Management Review, 20*(3), 571–610.

Sucic, I., Ricijas, N., & Glavak Tkalic, R. (2014). Informed consent as a requirement for probation work with (in)voluntary clients. *European Journal of Probation, 6*(3), 260–277.

Tannen, D. (1999). *The Argument Culture. Changing the Way We Argue.* London: Virago Press.

Tee Grizzley. (2017). *First Day Out.* New York City, NY: 300 Entertainment.

Thompson, E. P. (1977). *The Making of the English Working Class.* London: Penguin Books.

Travis, J., Western, B., & Redburn, S. (2014). *The Growth of Incarceration in the United States.* Washington, DC: National Academy of Sciences.

Turner, E. (2016). Beyond 'facts' and 'values': Rethinking some recent debates about the public role of criminology. *British Journal of Criminology*, 53(1), 149–166.

Vanhaelemeesch, D. (2015). *De beleving van het elektronisch toezicht in vergelijking met de gevangenisstraf.* Den Haag, Nederlands: Boom Criminologie. Retrieved from http://www.cep-probation.org/the-pains-and-gains-of-electronic-monitoring/. Accessed on August 10, 2017.

van Zyl Smit, D. (1993). Legal standards and the limits of community sanctions. *European Journal of Crime, Criminal Law and Criminal Justice*, 1(4), 309–331.

van Zyl Smit, D., & Snacken, S. (2009). *Principles of European Prison Law and Policy.* Oxford: Oxford University Press.

van Zyl Smit, D. Snacken, S., & Hayes, D. (2015). "One cannot legislate kindness": Ambiguities in European legal instruments on non-custodial sanctions. *Punishment and Society*, 17(1), 3–26.

Vanstone, M. (2004). Mission control: The origins of a humanitarian service. *Probation Journal*, 51(1), 34–47.

Wacquant, L. (2001). Deadly symbiosis: When ghetto and prison meet and mesh. *Punishment and Society*, 3(1), 95–133.

Wacquant, L. (2009). *Punishing the Poor: The Neoliberal Governance of Insecurity.* Durham, NC: Duke University Press.

Wacquant, L. (2011). From 'public criminology' to the reflexive sociology of criminological production and consumption. A review of public criminology? by Ian Loader and Richard Sparks (London: Routledge, 2010). *British Journal of Criminology*, 51(2), 438–448.

Walker, N. (1991). *Why Punish?* Oxford: Oxford University Press.

Walker and Beaumont's. (1981). *Probation Work: Critical Theory and Socialist Practice.* Chichester: Wiley-Blackwell.

Wakefield, S., & Uggen, C. (2010). Incarceration and stratification. *Annual Review of Sociology*, *36*, 387–406. Retrieved from https://www.annualreviews.org/doi/10.1146/annurev.soc.012809.102551

Wang, C., & Burris, M. A. (1997). Photovoice: Concept, methodology, and use for participatory needs assessment. *Health Education & Behavior*, *24*(3), 369–387.

Ward, T., & Maruna, S. (2007). *Rehabilitation: Beyond the Risk Paradigm*. London: Routledge.

Weaver, B., & McNeill, F. (2010). Public protection in Scotland. In A. Williams & M. Nash (Eds.), *The Handbook of Public Protection* (pp. 272–294). Cullompton: Willan.

Weisberg, R., & Petersilia, J. (2010). The dangers of pyrrhic victories against mass incarceration. *Daedalus*, *139*, 124–133. Retrieved from https://law.stanford.edu/wp-content/uploads/sites/default/files/publication/260016/doc/slspublic/WeisbergPetersilia%20FINAL_1.pdf

Werth, R. (2011). I do what I'm told, sort of: Reformed subjects, unruly citizens, and parole. *Theoretical Criminology*, *16*(3), 329–346.

Werth, R. (2013). The construction and stewardship of responsible yet precarious subjects: Punitive ideology, rehabilitation, and 'tough love' among parole personnel. *Punishment and Society*, *15*(3), 219–246.

Werth, R. (2016). Breaking the rules the right way: Resisting parole logics and asserting autonomy in the USA. In R. Armstrong & I. Durnescu (Eds.), *Parole and Beyond: International Experiences of Life after Prison* (pp. 141–170). Basingstoke: Palgrave.

Western, B. (2006). *Punishment and Inequality in America*. New York, NY: Russell Sage Foundation.

Wicke, P. (1990). *Rock Music: Culture, Aesthetics and Sociology*. Cambridge: Cambridge University Press.

Wiltshire, S. (2010). *Offender Demographics and Sentencing Patterns in Scotland and the UK*. Edinburgh: The Scottish Parliament Public Petitions Committee.

Wodahl, E., Ogle, R., & Heck, C. (2011). Revocation trends: A threat to the legitimacy of community-based corrections. *The Prison Journal, 91*(2), 207–226.

Worrall, A., Carr, N., & Robinson, G. (2017). Opening a window on probation cultures: A photographic imagination. In E. Carrabine & M. Brown (Eds.), *The Routledge International Handbook of Visual Criminology* (pp. 268–279). London: Routledge.

Worrall, A., & Hoy, C. (2005). *Punishment in the Community: Managing Offenders, Making Choices* (2nd ed.). Cullompton: Willan.

Young, I. M. (2001). *Inclusion and Democracy*. Oxford: Oxford University Press.

Young, P. (1976). A sociological analysis of the early history of probation. *British Journal of Law and Society, 3*(1), 44–58.

Zedner, L. (2002). Dangers of dystopias in penal theory. *Oxford Journal of Legal Studies, 22*(2), 341–366.

INDEX

Abbott, L., 126, 129
Aggregation, notion of, 12
Althusser, L., 29
Ambulant or mobile
    punishment, 5

Beaumont, 31
Brangan, L., 37
Burke, L., 144

Carlen, P., 144–145, 168
Christie, N., 70
Clemency, 8
Cognitive legitimacy of
    supervision, 81–82
Cohen, S., 70
    fishing net analogy, 23
    Visions of Social Control,
    23
Cohen, Stanley, 5
Community-based sentence, 3
Community corrections, 5
    sanctions and measures,
    6
Community Payback Orders
    (CPOs) in Scotland,
    61–64, 82–83, 96,
    109, 117, 119–120,
    163
Community Rehabilitation
    Companies (CRCs),
    144

Community sanctions and
    measures (CSM),
    81–82
European statistics on,
    46–47
in Scotland, 82, 84
Community warehousing, 12
Confederation of European
    Probation (CEP), 46
Control, 36
Correctional supervision, 3
COST Action (IS1106) on
    Offender Supervision,
    15, 108–109, 117,
    147, 168
Counter-visual criminology,
    14, 146–148, 156
Counter-visualising
    supervision, 146–149
Cox, A., 115
Crewe, B., 113–114
Criminal justice supervision,
    3
Custodial sentence, 3

Depoliticisation of crime
    and penal policy,
    149–150
Deviance-control system, 5,
    23
Dickinson, E., 155
Donzelot, 30

Drug treatment and testing
    orders (DTTOs), 83
Durkheim, E., 31, 78
    evolution of punishment,
        24–28
    form or style of
        punishment, 26
    probation in UK, 28
    relationships between
        culture and political
        power, 26
    social processes of
        punishment, 25–26
    social solidarity, 25
    *Two Laws of Penal
        Evolution*, 26
Durnescu, I., 110
Dzur, A., 152

Economic arrangements in
    society, 29–30
Electronic monitoring,
    160–164
    as 'coercive connectivity',
        162–163
    deprivations of liberty and
        autonomy, 165–166
    in European jurisdictions,
        163–164
    gains and limitations of,
        166–167
    severity of, 164–167
Ethnographies of penal
    supervision, 113–117
Eurobarometer on
    Experiencing
    Supervision (EES), 110
European Prison Rules and
    European Rules for
    Probation and for
    'Community Sanctions
    and Measures', 46

European statistics on
    community sanctions
    and measures, 46
    prison and probation rates
        (1990–2010), 46–47
Experiencing supervision,
    109–112
    audio representations of,
        122–130
    visual representations of,
        117–122

Fishing net analogy, 23
Focused supervision, 173
Foucault, M., 31, 78
    disciplinary mechanisms in
        late-modern societies,
        21–22
    Discipline and Punish,
        21–22
    notion of disciplinary
        power, 21–24
    rise and proliferation of
        surveillance
        technologies, 24

Gains of supervision,
    166–167
Gargarella, R., 154–155
Garland, D., 30, 32–33, 35,
    37
    welfarist criminology, 33
Glasgow Probation Area
    Committee, 85
Goodman, P., 38–39, 138
Gramsci, A., 29

Hannah-Moffatt, K., 79
Hayes, D., 110–111, 166
Hegemony, 29
Hiddleston, V., 87–89
Houchin, R., 60

Hudson, B., 169
Humanistic materialism, 30
Hutchinson, S., 79

Ideal-type criminologists, 149
Imaginary penalties, 168
Internal autonomy, 36

Juvenile probation in UK, 30

Kelly, C., 85–87
Kilbrandon Report, 90
King, S., 111

Lacombe, D., 115
Legitimation of supervision
    cognitive, 81–82
    Kilbrandon reforms,
        90–91
    moral, 81
    pragmatic, 81
    in Scotland, 81–82, 84,
        90–93
    Social Work (Scotland)
        Act 1968, 90
Loader, I., 149–153

MacAskill, K., 99
Mahood, L., 30
Managerial adaptation of
    supervision, 80
Maruna, S., 78
Marx, K., 31
    defence of capital, 28–29
    perspectives on
        punishment and
        supervision, 28–31
    probation's development, 31
Mass incarceration, 44
Mass supervision, 11–14, 44,
    150
    Scotland, 57–70

USA, 48–57
    See also Supervision
Mathieson, T., 5
McAra, L., 94
McWilliams, B., 30
Mechanical solidarity, 25
Mill, M., 44–45, 173–174
Miller, R., 115
Moral legitimation of
    supervision, 81
Morton, Sir G., 85
    Report, 86
Murray, J. B., 86

Nellis, M., 162

Offender supervision, 83
Organic solidarity, 26

Page, J., 38–39
Parole, 3, 7, 14, 22, 24, 27,
    113, 116, 124, 130,
    141, 162, 165, 167,
    173
    parole and non-parole
        licences, 64, 68–69,
        84
    US parole population,
        48–49, 56–57, 64, 66
Penal changes, 138
    Durkheim's account of
        penal evolution,
        24–28
    Foucault's notion of
        disciplinary power,
        21–24
    indices of, 32–33
    institutional dynamics of
        penal states and
        systems, 35–37
    late modern, 31–35
    Marxist perspectives, 28–31

role of capitalist system of
economic production,
29
in UK and USA, 35
uses of slavery and
servitude, 29
Penal character of
contemporary
imprisonment, in
England and Wales,
113–114
Penal fields, 20, 35–39,
78–79, 138–139
Penal imaginaries, 144–145,
147, 155, 157, 187
Penal power, modes of, 36
Penal reductionism, 85, 95,
99, 101–102,
139–141, 143
Penal state, 35–37
dimensions of, 36
Penal welfarism, 33, 78
Phelps, M., 38–39, 49–55,
68, 71, 108,
138–139, 143, 164,
173
Picturing Probation project, 4
Power resources, 36
Pragmatic legitimation of
supervision, 81
Prison-based sex offender
programme, 115
Probation, practice of, 3, 19,
31
in England, 110–111
role of charity, 31
Probation legitimacy
paradox, 79–82
Probation officer, 19
Probation of Offenders Act
1907, 19
Probation overcrowding, 12

'P's–parsimony,
proportionality
and productiveness
in supervision,
169–172
Public criminology,
149–156, 174
Punishment, 139
Durkheim's account of
penal evolution,
24–28
Foucault's notion of
disciplinary power,
21–24
late modern penal changes,
31–35
Marxist perspectives,
28–31
Punitive adaptation of
supervision, 80, 110

Re-entry organisations, 116
Rehabilitating supervision,
172–176
Rehabilitation, 22, 24, 34,
51–52, 80, 84, 91,
94–99, 101,
110–111, 114–116,
139–140, 143,
161–162, 165, 169,
183, 188
Rehabilitative adaption of
supervision, 14, 80,
110
Reparative adaption of
supervision, 80–81
Repressive state apparatus,
30
Restriction of liberty orders
(RLOs), 83
Robinson, G., 6, 78–81
Ruggiero, V., 151–152

Scotland, 78
    average length of
        community payback
        order, 66
    community sanctions in,
        82, 84, 102
    community sentences in, 66
    constitutional change and
        penal reform, 97
    constitutional position and
        supervision, 93–97
    Criminal Justice and
        Licensing Act 2010,
        82, 98
    criminal justice in, 93–97
    Criminal Justice (Scotland)
        Act 1949, 89
    'currently supervised'
        statutory throughcare
        cases, 64
    custodial sentences in, 99
    dissolution of probation
        services, 91–93
    distribution of Community
        Payback Orders
        (CPOs) in, 61–64,
        82–83, 96, 109, 163
    ethnicity of prison
        population in, 58
    Glasgow police-probation
        arrangement, 86–87
    imprisonment rate for men
        in, 60
    institutionalisation of
        'social work with
        offenders', 89–100
    legitimation of social work
        supervision, 90–93
    Management of Offenders
        Act 2005, 95
    mass supervision in,
        57–70

monetary penalties, 68
notion of Community
    Payback, 98
penal reductionism, 85,
    139–143
penal welfarism, 78
post-release supervision
    rates in, 67–69
Prisoners and Criminal
    Proceeding Act 1993,
    83–84, 93
Prisoners (Control of
    Release) Act 2015,
    84
prison population and
    imprisonment rate, 65
probation disposals, 90
The Probation Service in
    Scotland: Its Objects
    and its Organisation,
    89–90
provision of prisoner
    aftercare and
    probation services, 82,
    85–89
Reducing Reoffending
    Programme, 99
religious sectarianism in,
    58–59
'R's–reparation,
    rehabilitation,
    restriction and
    reintegration, 98–99
scale of supervision and
    imprisonment in,
    65–70
Scotland's Choice, 96, 98
Scottish Children's
    Hearings system, 90
Scottish research on
    experiencing
    supervision, 111–112

social concentration of
deprivation and
supervision, 62
Social Work (Scotland)
Act 1968, 89
socio-economic
distribution of
punishment in,
57–64
standard terms of parole
and non-parole
licences, 84
The Tough Option, 93
use of probation with
juveniles, 89
Scottish Index of Multiple
Deprivation, 60
Scottish Social Attitudes
Survey, 58
Scull, A., 5
Severity of supervision,
164–167
Shapland, J., 111
Simon, J., 24
Social insecurity, 34
Social work supervision, 84
Song development from
supervision
authenticity, 188–190
'depth,' 'weight,'
'tightness' and
'suspension', 192
perspectives, 190–192
purpose, 186–188
sound, 192–194
Sparks, R., 149–153
State autonomy, 36
Story development from
supervision
Administering Shocks and
Sickness, 158–160,
204–206

Any Chance of a Refill?',
105–107, 200–202
beginnings, 180–181
characters and contexts,
181–183
17 Minutes and 14
Seconds Wasted,
41–43, 197–199
Rehabilitating Norm(s),
174–176, 206–208
Screen-Weary Eyes,
17–19, 196–197
settings and plotlines,
183–184
A Strangely Appealing
Assembly, 135–137,
203–204
substance and style,
184–186
Waiting Room, 1–2,
181–182, 195–196
We're Not Here To Build
The Community,
We're Here To Protect
It, 75–77
Supervisible project, 4,
122–123, 131, 145,
182
Supervision
conjunctural approach,
32–33
creative representations of,
147
experiencing, 109–112
invisibility as punishment,
167–169
managerial adaptation of,
80
neglect of, 7
penal character of, 108
professionalisation of,
31

'P's—parsimony, proportionality and productiveness in, 169–172

punitive adaptation of, 80

rehabilitative adaption of, 80

reparative adaption of, 80–81

See also Song development from supervision; Story development from supervision

Supervisory sanctions and measures, 7–8, 10, 49, 55, 62, 68, 80–81, 102, 110

reparative adaption of, 80–81

Woodward case, 9

Surveillance technologies, 24

Suspended Sentence Order (SSO), 9, 13

Techno-corrections in mass supervision, 160–164

Thompson, E. P., 30

Transcarceration, 6

Turner, E., 151–153

Unger, R., 153–154

Unjustified moral superiority, 151–152

Unlawful wounding, 8

USA, 139

carceral citizenship, 55

character of mass incarceration in, 54

distinction between jails and prisons, 72

estimated correctional population, 48–49

expansions of probation and imprisonment, 52–54

forms of community-based supervision, 49

index crimes, 49–50

mass supervision in, 48–57

probation supervision rates, disparities in, 51–52, 54–56

racialised character of mass incarceration, 54–56, 60

regime of 'incapacitative control', 52–53

sentencing and probation reform efforts, 51–52, 173

socio-economic distribution of supervision, 54–57

supervision and imprisonment rates, 49, 65–67

Vanstone, M., 30–31

'Visible' supervision, 13–14

Wacquant, L., 34–35, 37, 150

Walker, N., 31

Weaver, B., 88

Weber, M., 31

Welfarist criminology, 33

Werth, R., 116

Young, P., 31

Printed in the United States
By Bookmasters